THE FIGHT GAME IN SCOTLAND

THE FIGHT GAME IN SCOTLAND

Brian Donald

MAINSTREAM PUBLISHING

First published in Great Britain in 1988 by
MAINSTREAM PUBLISHING COMPANY (EDINBURGH) LTD
7 Albany Street
Edinburgh EH1 3UG

British Library Cataloguing in Publication Data

Donald, Brian
The fight game in Scotland : an historical
scrapbook, 1892 – 1988
1. Scotland, Boxing, to 1987
796.8′3′09411

ISBN 1 – 85158 – 143 – X
ISBN 1 – 85158 – 144 – 8 Pbk

Typeset in 11 on 12pt. Baskerville, by Action Typesetting Ltd., Gloucester.
Printed in Great Britain by Billings & Sons, Worcester.

CONTENTS

DEDICATION

This book is respectfully dedicated to my father, William Donald who introduced me to the noble art via the Sparta Boxing Club, Edinburgh circa March 1951.

ACKNOWLEDGEMENT

A book such as this obviously depends on the cooperation of private individuals and organisations giving generously of their time and knowledge, consequently, I would like to record my sincere thanks to the following: Joe Aitchison; Bobby Boland; Dick Currie; The Right Hon. Lady Colquhoun of Luss; Barry Hugman, Hugman Enterprises; Century Hutchinson; Mr Endell Laird Executive editor of the *Sunday Mail*; Mrs Kay Elder; Peter Keenan; Cathie Keenan; John "Cowboy" McCormack; Len Mullen; "Dunky" Jowett; Terry Lawless; Walter McGowan MBE; Bobby Neil; Eugene Henderson; George Smith; "Tiny" Clephane; Jim Manderson, Dundee; Robert Hale & Son; Elm Tree Books/Hamish Hamilton; Pat Garrow (for information on Charlie Cotter); Ron Olver (for various tidbits of helpful information). Special thanks also to staff at the Scottish National Library, Edinburgh, and the Mitchell Library, Glasgow.

I am also grateful to the following for their permission to reproduce copyright material: Harry Mullan and *Boxing News*; the *Daily Record*; D.C. Thomson, Dundee; The *Edinburgh Evening News*. Special thanks to the *Daily Record* and *Sunday Mail* for permission to reproduce photographic material and extract from Benny Lynch comic strip. Thanks also to *Boxing News* for permission to reproduce the cover photograph.

Further thanks are due to Mrs Margaret Smith, Markinch, and Miss Donna McLeod, Glenrothes, who both shared the typing of the manuscript.

Last but not least sincere gratitude to my wife Iris Donald who acted as a research assistant (unpaid) and general factotum.

FOREWORD

This is not a chronological history of professional or amateur boxing in Scotland. It is a thematic treatment of a subject that in the past has been seen very much as an afterthought in much larger books on boxing such as Fleischer and Andre's *Pictorial History of Boxing.*

There are of course good reasons for this. Scotland is after all a small (but never insignificant) segment of the entire global village. Less than a dozen Scots have held world boxing championship titles and it is natural that foreign writers, especially those from the USA, should concentrate only on those Scots who have distinguished themselves in the international arena.

However, ignorance of Scottish boxing history becomes more pronounced the closer to Caledonia's shores that one comes. Numerous boxing yearbooks, annuals, anthologies and articles printed and written in England continue to perpetuate errors such as the one concerning the proper venue for the Ted "Kid" Lewis v. Tommy Milligan scrap in November 1924. Consult any of the printed forms that have been published south of the border and you will be wrongly informed that this scrap took place in the Waverley Market, Edinburgh – in fact it took place one mile away in Annandale Street's Industrial Hall.

One of my favourite radio broadcasters is the highly professional Mr Benny Green, yet even he, when he ventured into writing a boxing book in 1978, managed to turn Lanarkshire's Tommy Milligan into a Cockney! "The world champion Mickey Walker had come to London to give a spectacular beating to the LOCAL challenger, Tommy Milligan . . ."; Milligan was in fact born in Edinburgh but lived almost all his life in the Wishaw area of Lanarkshire.

Many of these problems stem from too heavy a reliance on secondary sources such as press cuttings. Wherever possible I have used primary sources either by personally interviewing the people involved or their relatives if they are deceased.

This process led me into many interesting experiences. I partook of tea and biscuits with "Tiny" Clephane in his neat council flat and had the same fare served to me by Lady Colquhoun in "Ross-Dhu," ancestral home of Sir Ian Colquhoun of Luss. A faulty carburettor and a too imperfect knowledge of Glasgow's one-way traffic system made my journey to Joe Aitchison's Rutherglen bungalow more perilous than I had ever anticipated. The hassle was worth it though – as I hope those who read the chapter on the Bridgeton boxing bard will agree.

Nevertheless, I have inevitably had to use secondary sources although I shall not offer them as an excuse for any errors of fact that I may have inadvertently written into this book. The opinions, errors, judgements contained herein are uniquely my own (except where I am quoting directly a third party). I accept in advance full responsibility for them.

Finally, perhaps the most profound ignorance about Scottish boxing exists within Scotland itself. The fact that Nat Dresner and Hugh Roddin (to name but two) almost invariably prompt the response, "Who?" – even amongst Scots who are quite knowledgeable about the hardest game – is one of the principal reasons why this book was written.

I can only hope that the pleasure of those who read this book exceeds the great pleasure I had in writing it.

Brian Donald
Kirkcaldy
January, 1988

INTRODUCTION

Scotland and Boxing – The Glasgow Myth Exploded

On Monday, 5 December 1887 the *Edinburgh Evening News* reported:

> A prize fight took place in a field near Glasgow on Saturday morning between two young men named Orman and Gallacher, the former belonging to Edinburgh and the latter to Glasgow. The fight was the best of three rounds for £5-a-side. In the first round matters stood pretty equal between the two, but in the second round Orman had the best of it, shutting up one of his opponent's eyes. In the third round Gallacher received a thorough thrashing leaving the ring with his eyes both closed and his face very much cut.
>
> Orman who then retired to dress was surrounded and severely handled by a gang of Glasgow roughs who were present. He received a blow with a stick on the head and was knocked down and kicked . . . It was afterwards ascertained that his left arm was broken from a kick and a deep cut made in his head . . . .

The extract is firm proof that boxing rivalry between Edinburgh and Glasgow is deeply rooted in pugilistic history. Yet if Edinburgh emerged triumphant from that early bareknuckle encounter "Auld Reekie" has most certainly lost the public relations war from a historical viewpoint. Thousands of fans north and south of the border and indeed throughout the world believe without question that Glasgow is – and ALWAYS has been Scotland's first city of fisticuffs.

This is a myth. It simply cannot be squared with the historical facts.

The first Scots to win an Olympic boxing medal and a Lonsdale belt respectively were east coast men. Despite attempts by the Glasgow-dominated Olympic Selection Committee to exclude him Hugh Roddin of Musselburgh won Scotland's first ever Olympic boxing medal at the 1908 London games. James "Tancy" Lee of Leith became Scotland's first ever Lonsdale belt winner, defeating Jimmy Wilde at the London NSC in January 1915.

In truth, with regard to the question of Scottish boxing "firsts" Glasgow comes a poor second to her eastern neighbour. The first British and European lightweight title fight held north of the border was the battle between James Hall and Johnny Brown. This was promoted by Scotland's greatest ever promoter – Nat Dresner of Leith. Dresner also staged in Edinburgh the first ever title fight for the British and European welterweight crown held in Scotland. This was the struggle between Ted "Kid Lewis" and Tommy Milligan in November 1924.

Similarly, Scotland's first ever British and European middleweight title contest, between Tommy Milligan and Alex Ireland, took place in Scotland's capital city between Tommy Milligan and Alex Ireland, took place in Scotland's capital city under Dresner's promotion. The Milligan v. Lewis bout was also the first professional boxing contest filmed for cinema viewing in Scotland.

Again, when Aberdeen boxing promoter David Smith secured the Phil Scott v. George Cook fight for Scotland – the first and last British Empire heavyweight title fight to be staged there – he was faced with choosing a venue. Smith had no emotional ties with either Edinburgh or Glasgow, being a son of the northern granite city, yet he did not hesitate to choose the Industrial Hall in Edinburgh's Annandale Street for this prime bout. His reason? Like all Scots in the 1920s he regarded Edinburgh as the Mecca of Scottish boxing and the Industrial Hall in Annandale Street was without any serious rival during this period as Caledonia's Madison Square Garden.

In contrast, Glasgow-based national champions such as Jim Higgins – winner of a bantamweight Lonsdale belt in record time – and flyweight Elky Clark had to travel over the border to do their championship fighting because no Glasgow promoter in the 1920s was big enough to stage their fights.

The place of Edinburgh as Scotland's fight capital was recognised by such internationally renowned American fighters as Augie Ratner – conqueror of Harry Greb. Ratner figured in the first top-class contest involving an American and a Scotsman – the September 1923 conflict between Ratner and Hamilton's Johnny Brown in Edinburgh. The £500-a-side purse paid to both contestants was a Scottish record for the time.

But it was not only fighters who recognised Edinburgh as Scotland's First City of boxing. Ted Broadribb, who was shrewder than most when it came to identifying the real centres of boxing power, was employed throughout the early 1920s as a referee at Edinburgh-based Nat Dresner's promotions.

Since the inception of the noble art the aristocracy have always had a part to play in the sport and Scotland was no exception to this rule. In this connection the two greatest noble exponents of boxing in Scotland were without doubt the Marquis of Clydesdale and Sir Iain Colquhoun of Luss.

The Marquis was heir to the Dukedom of Hamilton. Hamilton is about a half hour drive from Glasgow. Sir Iain's home at Luss is a similar distance from the west of Scotland's premier city. Yet both these aristocratic gentlemen firmly based their boxing activities in Edinburgh throughout the Twenties.

In November 1924 the Marquis of Clydesdale fought a "trial" to decide whether he should become a professional middleweight boxer. His opponent was Eddie Eagan, 1920 Olympic champion and a future chairman of the New York State Athletic Commission. The chosen venue was Charlie Cotter's gym at 84 Leith Street in the heart of Edinburgh. Nor was this any mere aristocratic whim. Charles Cotter of Edinburgh was recognised as Scotland's premier trainer of fighters between 1895 and his retirement in the 1930s.

It was also to Cotter's gym that the young west of Scotland aristocrat Sir Iain Colquhoun was taken by his father to learn to box. Sir Iain learned well because he became British Army Champion at welterweight in 1913.

But it was a pillow fight this time! One of the items in the sports programme which marked the concluding day of the young Marquis of Douglas and Clydesdale's majority celebrations at Hamilton. The Marquis was a kenspeckle figure at all major Edinburgh boxing shows where he acted as Dresner's timekeeper.

Sir Iain was also especially ambitious to make his mark in boxing as his subsequent career proves. By 1946 he had become chairman of the Scottish Area Council of the BBBC. Yet he chose to devote the bulk of the Twenties to acting as an MC at all Dresner's major Edinburgh promotions. Conversely, the Marquis of Clydesdale was official timekeeper at all the big Edinburgh shows in this period.

It is inconceivable that had equal or better opportunities existed in the west at this time they would have made the trek eastwards as often as they did.

In the actual staging of world title fights Glasgow would seem to be in a class of its own. All world title fights promoted in Scotland have taken place there. Yet this statement requires heavy qualification. The Jackie Patterson v. Joe Curran world title scrap in 1946 was exclusively promoted by a Dundonian, Mr George Grant.

Nor have promoters always had their faith rewarded by west of Scotland fans. Despite there being no live TV in 1946 and being blessed with beautiful weather for his promotion, Mr Grant could only attract 15,000 spectators into Hampden Park. Similarly, the Watt v. Howard Davis fight (although handicapped by a freak cloudburst) was a disappointment in terms of attendance for the promoters. An exception was of course the Benny Lynch v. Peter Kane world title fight held in Glasgow's Shawfield Stadium. This attracted 40,000 people – a Scottish record that has yet to be equalled.

However, before then the Scottish record was established at the Frank Moody v. Tommy Milligan fight held on 7 August 1928 when 32,000 spectators packed into the Carntyne Stadium. Carntyne Stadium is situated in Glasgow's east end but the show was exclusively promoted by the Edinburgh-based Nat Dresner syndicate!

This underscores the main thrust of our argument – that Glasgow's supremacy in boxing matters north of the border is far from being the clear cut fact supposed by those who adhere to the myth.

Even when it comes to officiating at world title fights Edinburgh scores heavily over her western rival. No Glasgow referee has ever officiated at a world heavyweight title fight. In contrast, George Smith of Edinburgh handled the Muhammad Ali v. Henry Cooper tussle in 1966.

Again, no Glasgow based third man can compete with Edinburgh's own Eugene Henderson. Two of the key world title fights held in Britain in the immediate post-war period were Freddie Mills v. Gus Lesnevich and Sugar Ray Robinson v. Randolph Turpin. Both were handled by Mr Henderson.

In fairness it must be stated that throughout its history boxing in Glasgow has suffered from a handicap not imposed at anytime upon the sport in Edinburgh. A handicap based on the fact that if the common people of Glasgow were boxing-mad the city's powers-that-be did not share their passion.

In December 1898 the Glasgow *Daily Record* reported that plans to hold the Scottish Amateur Boxing Championships in the city had been scrapped and the tournament removed to Edinburgh. The reason? Glasgow city magistrates had flatly rejected the staging of any boxing tournament within the city's limits.

The period of the "Red Clydesiders" scare in 1919–1922 caused Glasgow's magistrates similarly to veto any boxing show likely to attract large numbers of working class men together – especially if it had violent implications. This fact was openly debated in the newspapers of the time, and, ironically, it was the city fathers of Glasgow who prevented Benny Lynch from winning his world title from Jackie Brown before "his ain folk". The *Edinburgh Evening Dispatch* of Wednesday, 20 February 1935 reported that Glasgow magistrates had refused an application from Lynch's manager, George Dingley, to stage the forthcoming world title bout with Brown in the Kelvin Hall. The fight was eventually staged in Bellevue, Manchester.

The support given by Glasgow District Council and ex-Lord Provost David

Johnny King the British bantam champion, down for a short count in the fight with Jim O'Neil, of Cambuslang, in the Music Hall, George Street, Edinburgh. King won in the seventh round, when O'Neil's seconds signalled that their man had had enough.

Hodge to the Watt v. Pitalua world title fight in Glasgow in 1979 was not only crucial for its success – it marked a considerable advance in municipal attitudes to boxing within Glasgow. Yet the spirit of 1898 and 1935 is far from dead in Glasgow's corridors of power. Mr Michael Kelly, a very recent Lord Provost of the city, wrote an article condemning professional boxing in the *Daily Record* some two years ago.

Edinburgh's civic leaders have always taken a very different stance. Throughout the 1920s a permanent ringside fixture at all of the city's major fights was Police Judge Harvey. He even acted as an assistant timekeeper and MC – activities that would have been unthinkable to the Glaswegians who vetoed the Lynch v. Brown fight in 1935.

Yet the end of the 1920s did see a significant movement of power westwards within the Scottish professional game. In January 1929 Sir Iain Colquhoun of Luss gave a dinner party in Glasgow's St Enoch Hotel "to promote the better advancement of Scottish boxing". In attendance were the Earl of Lonsdale and the Marquis of Clydesdale and all living Scottish Lonsdale belt holders and former amateur champions.

Although this marked the beginning of a process that has seen Glasgow finally emerge as the centre of the Scottish fight game Edinburgh more than held her own throughout the 1930s. In November 1933 boxing's weekly trade paper *Boxing* reported that Glasgow's boxing promoters were attracting widespread criticism due to their policy of pairing English boxers in Glasgow's city halls to the exclusion of the home-grown variety. *Boxing* openly scoffed at the reason for this – "that Scottish opposition to southern lads would not provide sufficient incentive to a crowd to attend in the multitudes that gladden a promoter's heart".

In Edinburgh throughout the Thirties promoters such as Paddy McGreechan at the Edinburgh National Sporting Club and Harold Bownas at the Music Hall thoroughly vindicated *Boxing* newspaper's judgement. Both these Edinburgh-based promoters were amply rewarded for staging such Anglo-Scottish battles as Jack London v. Alex Bell; Johnny McGrory v. Dave Crowley, and Manchester's bantam champ Johnny King v. Jim O'Neil. The bouts were watched by capacity crowds.

Even in boxing politics in the 1930s Edinburgh did not play second fiddle to Glasgow. One of the most momentous decisions affecting the future of all Scottish boxers was taken at an Edinburgh meeting of the Scottish Area Council of the BBBC held on 6 February 1933 under the chairmanship of "Auld Reekie's" own Charles Wood. On the motion of the legendary George Aitchison of Dalmarnock (a Glaswegian who had been a major ticket agent for Nat Dresner throughout Edinburgh's days of boxing supremacy in the 1920s) all boxers would in future be allowed legal/third party representation at any disciplinary hearing, a basic right previously denied them. This motion formed the basis of all the board's contemporary discipline procedures which are a model of fairness.

In conclusion, the question naturally arises as to the truth of the commonly made assertion that Glasgow has always been Scotland's premier fight town. The answer must be that for the first 50 years of this century there is absolutely no truth in this concept.

From the 1950s onwards a different picture emerges. Between 1958 and April 1984 no professional boxing contest took place in Edinburgh. During the same period Glasgow could boast of featuring such international boxing stars as Sugar Ray Robinson, Sonny Ray, Von Clay and Willie Pastrano. Therefore, it is only in the last 30 years or so that the concept of Glasgow's boxing supremacy in Scotland has become accurate.

JOHN L. SULLIVAN and Scotland – the Trip that Never Was

John Lawrence Sullivan (1858 – 1918) is generally recognised as playing the same role in boxing as Al Jolson in cinema history. Just as Jolson's training and performances were rooted in the soon-to-be obsolete vaudeville theatre, so Sullivan's fistic roots lay in the crudities of the London Prize Ring Rules governing the bare knuckle era from whence he came.

Yet both these very different troubadors were heralds of a new era which was zooming rather than looming on the horizon of their respective ages. Jolson ushered in with his *Jazz Singer* movie the multi-million dollar recording contract and the musical biopic; Sullivan made world heavyweight title fights the staple diet of cosmic communication that they have become today. When he crossed gloved hands with fellow Irish-American James J. Corbett in the Olympic Sporting Club in New Orleans in 1892 every blow was being echoed world-wide on the keys of the numerous telegraph operators who surrounded the ring.

Sullivan also instituted another tradition amongst heavyweight kings. A tradition that has become as hallowed as that of our own monarch's annual progress to the Derby or some far flung outpost of the Commonwealth – the Grand Tour of Europe. Jack Johnson (whom Sullivan detested as he detested all negroes) did it, visiting Paris and Berlin; Muhammad Ali was carried in 1977 through Newcastle-on-Tyne like the Emperor Hadrian of old. With the exception of Johnson, who suffered at the hands of the prevailing ethos of racialism of his time, all were accorded rapturous welcomes.

Sullivan, despite his racial bigotry, had a great deal in common with Muhammad Ali. Both were invincible for long periods of their respective careers. Both were as famous with their mouths as their fists. In other respects they were vastly different. Sullivan was a prodigious guzzler of anything alcoholic. So much so that had any of the beer brand names that now decorate the centre of all-American world title rings been in existence in his day it is a fair bet he might have fallen to his knees – not from an opponent's blow – but just to acquaint himself with their names!

At this point one may ask what a bombastic, boozy, Irish-American pugilist is doing in a book about Scottish boxing? The answer resides in the fact that Sullivan was as much a champion liar as he was a boxer, particularly when it came to Scotland. Indeed if Sullivan's punches in the ring had contained the same degree of accuracy as his statements in relation to Scotland he would have spent his career with a permanent black eye or swollen mouth. It is also doubtful if he would have even attained championship status.

That Sullivan visited England cannot be doubted. He arrived in Liverpool on the Cunard liner *Cephalonia* on 6 November 1887.

Heavyweight champions tend to carry in their wake an entourage which resembles the supporting cast of a Cecil B. De Mille biblical epic. Not only was Sullivan not an exception to this custom, he may be said to have established it. In his wake followed his newly acquired manager Harry S. Philips, his trainer and sparring partner Jack Ashton, his secretary and personal servant John Barnett, Edward Holske his press agent, Arthur Brisbane of the *New York Sun*, and last but certainly not least in the champion's eyes – the great love of his life, Ann Livingstone.

He received the kind of rapturous acclaim on landing that modern Liverpudlians tend to reserve for their football teams. There was however one group among the welcoming hordes who were so resolutely impassive that the Irish-American champion may have at first thought they were relatives of his most hated English rival – Charlie Mitchell of Birmingham. They were in fact members of HM Customs and Excise. They had come to charge duty of £120 on the magnificent diamond-studded championship belt presented to him by an adoring American public a few months previously. Sullivan, in high dudgeon, refused point blank to pay it – so the belt languished unseen in a bonded warehouse throughout the tour.

Nevertheless, this bureaucratic hiccup could not dampen his triumphal progress southwards towards London. At Crewe mobs stormed Sullivan's carriage, even sitting on the roof from where they were removed with the greatest difficulty. At London's Euston Station a scene direct from a modern pop idol's average day was enacted when a crowd of enthusiastic fans piled into a cab containing Sullivan simply to touch the great man. The cab springs failed, disgorging hero and hailers on to the street.

However, HM Customs were not the only Englishmen intent on spoiling the party as far as "The Boston Strong Boy" was concerned. Sullivan's *bête noir*, Charlie Mitchell, decided to get in on the act.

Mitchell had been described by Sullivan as "a bombastic sprinter" – a reference to the fact that the Birmingham man anticipated Muhammad Ali by some 90 years by dint of "psyching out" his opponents verbally then using his speed and boxing skill to avoid their punches, tactics which infuriated a slugger like Sullivan.

The three weeks which followed Sullivan's arrival in London were met by cheers and jeers. Cheers from the vast crowds that greeted the American champion whenever he appeared publicly. Jeers from Charlie Mitchell who was taunting his way into a lucrative fight contract with Sullivan.

Consequently, sick to the teeth with Mitchell's calling into question everything from his ancestry to his fistic prowess, Sullivan signed a contract to meet the Englishman for a purse of £500 plus the championship of the world. This deal was struck on Tuesday, 29 November 1887.

It is at this point that Sullivan and his latter-day biographer, the late Nat Fleischer, stray from the firm land of hard fact to the quicksands of fantasy masquerading as fact.

Nat Fleischer is justly revered as one of boxing's great historians – the man who founded single-handed the highly influential *Ring* magazine that most modern boxing fans await with the same eagerness as their monthly pay cheque. However, as the recent sad case of Lord Hugh Trevor-Roper (Lord Dacre) and the totally phoney Hitler diaries proves, even the most respected figures can be gulled. In Fleischer's case being an unabashed acolyte of "The Boston Strong Boy" caused him to rewrite uncritically in his 1952 biography *John L. Sullivan* (Robert Hale, London) many of the latter's claims. These claims do not stand up under closer examination.

Paraphrasing Sullivan's own autobiography Fleischer wrote: "With the Mitchell matter taken care of, the Champion set out on an exhibition tour of the British Isles . . . Birmingham, Liverpool, Manchester, Newcastle-upon-Tyne, Leicester, Nottingham, Derby, Sheffield, Preston, Oldham and lesser boxing centres in England greeted him ecstatically. Next, having crossed to the land of his parents' birth, he was given a hero's welcome by the enraptured Irish – Waterford, Dublin, Cork, Limerick and Belfast fell at his feet. Even Scotland, home of a dour and traditionally silent and restrained people, gave him a rousing welcome – Glasgow, Dundee, Aberdeen and Edinburgh screamed themselves hoarse." From Edinburgh the Boston fighter claimed to have gone south to Cardiff in Wales. The truth of the Welsh leg of the journey cannot be disputed, for a Cardiff newspaper of the day concluded that Sullivan's visit to the Welsh capital had created a bigger stir than that of the Prime Minister.

But the so-called "Scottish Tour" must be adjudged a hoax.

Fleischer claims that Sullivan started his UK tour immediately after signing the contract with Mitchell. At the earliest this would have been on the next day, Wednesday, 30 November. According to Fleischer he was back in London's Pelican Club by Monday, 8 December 1887. So his Grand Tour of Great Britain as described above must have only taken eight days!

Improbable? – No! – Impossible.

Consultation of old newspapers reveals that the period between 30 November, when the tour of the UK began, and 7 December when it terminated, was marked by severe bad weather. Frost alternated with storms up to 10 December. This would have certainly have caused delays in the Irish leg of the tour, given that access in and out of Ireland could have only have been by ferry steamer across the choppy Irish Sea.

From Ireland Sullivan is supposed to have entered Scotland, yet this was a Scotland racked by severe storms, according to the *Fife Free Press* newspaper for December 1887. Storms that would have interrupted and delayed Sullivan's journey throughout the country. Modern readers should also consider that in November/December 1887 the Forth Railway Bridge that now so majestically links Fife with the Lothians was but a trilogy of skeletal spans awaiting completion. This made rail journeys to and from Aberdeen in the 1880s a long haul. Yet the implications of Sullivan's claims are that he travelled by rail, presumably Stranraer to Glasgow, Dundee, Aberdeen and Edinburgh in stormy conditions –

stopping at each to receive homage – all in the space of at most two days!

Intrigued further by the improbability of this assault by train on the world's land speed record I went to the National Library of Scotland's newspaper archive. There I examined all the extant newspapers published in 1887. None save one carried any reports of anything remotely to do with pugilism. The exception was the *Edinburgh Evening News* for 5 December 1887 which reported a bare-knuckle battle at Glasgow the details of which can be found elsewhere in this volume.

But no Sullivan.

It is inconceivable that someone of Sullivan's stature would have been ignored by the Scottish press, especially when one section of it had already taken the trouble to report a bare-knuckle battle in a field outside Glasgow between two men whose names are at best a footnote in boxing history.

Sullivan was a man of ferocious egotism, a man who regarded modesty as a kind of halitosis to be avoided at all times. In this connection it is significant that he does not mention the name of one single important person or building in any of the places in Scotland he claimed to have visited.

His biographer and latter-day torch bearer Nat Fleischer also betrays a surprising naïvety about the nature of the Scots people in this passage when he calls them "a dour and traditionally silent and restrained people" – former Jim Watt opponents from the USA such as Sean O'Grady and Howard Davis might not agree with this assessment in the light of their experiences in the Kelvin Hall and Ibrox Stadium!

There is another reason which makes it almost certain that Sullivan toured Scotland in imagination only. He was scheduled to give an exhibition before the Prince of Wales – the future King Edward VII – by 9 December in London. To Sullivan, the supreme egotist, anything less than his best on such an occasion would have been sacrilege. Consequently, anything which would have endangered his ring fitness – such as an arduous tour at the breakneck speed with which he would have had to have zoomed around Scotland – would have simply been regarded as not on.

In truth, Sullivan's Scottish safari is pure Baron Munchausen. He did however make the acquaintanceship of some natives of Caledonia. His meeting with the Prince of Wales on 9 December 1887 at St James Barracks was arranged by Captain Clifford Drummond of the Scots Guards. Sullivan breakfasted with Captain Drummond and his brother officers. Also in attendance was Lord Randolph Churchill – father of Sir Winston – whose "playing of the orange card" in Irish politics was to torpedo the first Irish Home Rule Bill calculated to give Sullivan's Irish compatriots freedom over their own affairs, an irony that seems to have gone unremarked at the time.

Fleischer reports in some detail what was eaten by Sullivan and his Scottish companions and also gives – unwittingly – a further clue as to why the Irish-American's Scottish trip was pure fantasy. "Conversation," Fleischer writes, "centred naturally on the glorious history of the prize ring, and many toasts were drunk to heroes living and dead." Not too many by Sullivan one hopes as he was due to appear an hour later in the Fencing Club to give his sparring exhibition for HRH the Prince of Wales.

Be that as it may, the main point here is that there is a thundering silence in both Fleischer's and Sullivan's accounts of this meeting about the one topic of conversation any Scotsman – including Scots Guards officers – would almost certainly have hiked to the top of the agenda, namely the American Champion's impressions of their homeland. Most American visitors even today find themselves being universally canvassed for their impressions of Scotland from day one of their arrival. Sullivan too would opine on almost anything at the drop of a whisky glass. That he failed manifestly to comment even on Caledonia's most famous type of spirit is stretching credulity beyond breaking point.

Had he done what he claimed in this respect a good dozen of Scotland's most famous distilleries would now boast "John L. Sullivan drank here" brass plates and the publicity departments of the ones he did visit would have long ago had his scowling face in "ads" aimed at the important American drinks market. That none ever has is further eloquent testimony to the fiction that was "John L.'s" Scottish trip. A John L. Sullivan who progressed through Old Caledonia without sipping a "dram" is as credible as Mr Yasser Arafat at a "Bar Mitzvah" ceremony.

Perhaps we are being too harsh on the famed Irish-American. Fleischer does recount that Sullivan once confessed when talking of his schooldays that "I was always on the lookout to avoid geography when it was geography day". Such modesty is most unusual coming from "John L.". The arrogant boast and the whopping lie were more his style.

Whatever his modern apologists may say Sullivan's Scottish safari is as much a part of mythology as Jason's epic excursion with the Argonauts in search of the Golden Fleece. The wool has been pulled over our eyes long enough. It is time to shear away falsehood with truth. This chapter has been a modest attempt in that direction.

POSTSCRIPT

Further proof that John L. Sullivan's alleged visit to Scotland was a product of his fevered imagination comes appropriately enough via his nemesis – James J. Corbett.

Between May 28 and May 31 1894 Corbett appeared on stage in the melodrama "Gentleman Jack" at the Royal Lyceum Theatre.

The drama critic of the *Edinburgh Evening News* assessed Corbett's performance as an actor thus in the newspaper's edition of Tuesday May 29... "The kind of play in which such a worthy as Mr John L. Sulivan first posed as the virtuous man was a *novelty* in Edinburgh until 'Gentleman Jack' was staged last night but the price for the *new* thing constituted a large tax on public patience..."

HUGH RODDIN Of Musselburgh
Scotland's First Boxing Olympian

In boxing terms few would dispute that Dick McTaggart, the blond, Dundee southpaw, was the most famous Scot to win Olympic honours. Arguably, McTaggart was the best amateur boxer ever produced by Scotland. By winning a gold medal at the 1956 Melbourne Olympics he accomplished a feat that not even Ken Buchanan was able to emulate as an amateur.

One distinction the Dundonian portsider could not claim however, was that of being Scotland's first boxing Olympian. That particular honour belongs to Hugh Roddin of Musselburgh.

"Hughie", as he was universally known, was born of Irish-Catholic parents in the Newbigging district of "The Honest Toun". Baptised in the town's "Our Lady of Loretto" church and raised as a devout son of the Catholic faith, there were the usual family aspirations towards the priesthood for a much cherished son – aspirations which vanished for ever once "Hughie" came into contact with the fight game through the legendary Charles "Charlie" Cotter.

From 1895 when he established his Edinburgh Amateur Gymnastic Society based at his gym at 84 Leith Street, until the advent of Nat Dresner in 1922, Charlie Cotter dominated Scottish boxing.

Cotter was a man of many parts. He had acted as timekeeper at one of the last bare-knuckle contests held in Scotland – at Roslin – on the outskirts of Edinburgh. In direct contrast to his participation in this blatantly unlawful activity Cotter was also a renowned physical trainer of the ultra-respectable Scottish aristocracy and upper middle classes. Advocates, aristocrats and city merchants could be found submitting themselves to a rigorous programme of conditioning under Cotter's tutelage at his "Eleven O'Clock Club" at 84 Leith Street. The club was thus described because that was the appointed hour of the evening that they came together.

In addition, Charlie Cotter was boxing coach at Edinburgh University, another bastion of upper middle class respectability. The *Edinburgh Evening Dispatch* carried an advertisement which publicised Cotter's services and assured clients that if the great man was not available they would still be in the hands of his assistant who was "a Sandow medallist". (Eugene Sandow was the Edwardian equivalent of Charles Atlas – offering the same postal body building courses that the latter has become famous for.)

Hugh Roddin had therefore entrusted his fistic future to a man of impeccable fighting pedigree. It is hardly surprising then that the Musselburgh man rapidly

Left: *Jim Driscoll. Some say one of the greatest stylists ever – and adviser to Hugh Roddin.*

Below: *Hugh Roddin. First Scottish olympic boxing medallist and terror of New York's pro' bantams.*

annexed two Scottish Eastern District featherweight titles soon after coming under Cotter's wing.

But even better was to follow in season 1907–08. In April 1908 the Scottish Amateur Boxing Championships were held in the "Grand" Theatre, Glasgow before a capacity crowd of 2,000 spectators. A record entry of 66 boxers kept the crowd entertained from two in the afternoon until late that evening.

Ample testimony to Charlie Cotter's ability to teach the finer points of pugilism came from the boxing correspondent of the *Evening Dispatch*. Writing in the edition for 6 April 1908, he stated: "Some very good boxing was witnessed in the preliminary rounds and the Edinburgh men acquitted themselves well. They as a whole were the better boxers, too many of the western men placing reliance on their right."

Hugh Roddin had an easy passage to the finals, thanks to his boxing skill allied to great natural strength and a terrific right-hand wallop – a wallop that forced his semi-final opponent Jimmy Strain of Partick to throw in the towel in the second round. Strain had looked like winning in the first thanks to some first-rate left jabbing. But in the second Roddin started to cross his deadly right over the Glaswegian's straight left. To this he added some hefty left hooks to the body, punches which prompted Strain's capitulation.

If the Partick fighter's surrender was unexpected it was small beer when contrasted with the element of surprise in the final. Roddin's foe was another Partick boxer called Harry Young. He was a powerful slugger who had poleaxed Millar of the Scottish National Club in the first round; Norton, also of the Scottish National, had been overpowered in a similar fashion.

Now Young seemed poised to inflict similar mayhem on his more skilled opponent from Musselburgh. The consensus of ringside opinion was that this would be a battle of right crosses; whoever landed first would triumph.

Few could have visualised the bout ending in 30 seconds. But end it did when Roddin's right fist sent his much fancied opponent crashing to the canvas after a little preliminary sparring. Roddin was now Scottish Amateur featherweight champion, with the Olympic Games beckoning in London later that year.

Two facts must have raised young Roddin's hopes of representing his country in the fourth Olympic Games in London. The first was his sensational championship victory over Young, the second that, unlike today, Scottish boxers were chosen for Olympic duty by their own national association – although they fought under the Great Britain banner.

However, not for the last time was a boxer to discover that administrative politics could provide a bigger challenge to his fistic ambitions than any opponent inside the ropes. When the ruling body – The Scottish Gymnastic Association – announced their original Olympic choices there was an uproar. Only three boxers – McGurk, Wallace and Norton – were chosen. To add insult to injury they were all from one club – The National, in Glasgow.

The eastern clubs protested so vehemently that the Glasgow faction appeared to have caved in when they agreed to add two names to the Olympic squad – Hugh Roddin and Patrick "Paddy" Fee.

Paddy Fee was Roddin's clubmate and a fellow protégé of Charlie Cotter. Later generations would somewhat unfairly remember Fee as "Tancy Lee's brother-in-law", yet he deserves to be remembered for his own amateur boxing achievements. The present writer can remember Paddy Fee as a very fit septagenarian boxing instructor with the now defunct "Tweedie" Boys' Club in the Grassmarket district of Edinburgh in 1955.

Fee was Scottish featherweight champion in 1904 and lightweight champion in 1907. This pedigree alone was not considered sufficiently impressive for the Scottish selectors. Having agreed to select him in principle they then declared that Fee must meet his own expenses if he wished to box for his country! Charlie Cotter declared his club would sponsor Paddy Fee. This must be one of the few cases in Olympic history when an amateur boxer had to pay for the privilege of representing his country!

As a reigning champion "Hughie" Roddin was spared this indignity only to be offered another. Roddin was asked to box a "trial" in Charlie Cotter's gym at 84 Leith Street.

As though to express his contempt for the rigmarole to which he was being subjected the Musselburgh man chose an opponent two stones heavier than himself. Among the assembled crowd was a sports reporter from the *Edinburgh Evening News* who declared: "He (Roddin) boxed against an opponent nearly two stones heavier than himself and acquitted himself so admirably as to call forth the praise of the many good judges present, one of whom declared it was the finest exhibition he had witnessed in the town for years."

The same journalist went on to outline the qualities that were to bring Scotland its very first Olympic boxing medal: "Roddin, in addition to a grand reach, knows effectively how to bring the right into execution." So it was to prove in London.

Posterity has not recorded what Hugh Roddin's emotions were on witnessing the exit, in rapid succession, of the more favoured trio of Glasgow boxers from the Olympic boxing ring at London's Northampton Institute in Clerkenwell. One thing is certain. He clearly justified the faith placed in him by his mentor Charlie Cotter. The latter acted as chief second to Roddin throughout the Olympics. The same right cross that had wrecked Young earlier in Glasgow now smote the Welsh champion to the canvas inside a round.

An interested spectator at ringside was the English featherweight champion, Tommy Ringer. The effect of the Musselburgh man's devastating punching power was such that Ringer refused point blank to dispute with Roddin the Olympic bronze medal final for beaten semi-finalists!

The strangest aspect of the whole affair is that Ringer's decision to put discretion before valour did not seem logical given that he had beaten Roddin's eventual conqueror, Charles Morris, earlier that year!

It is also interesting to note that the eventual winner of the Olympic featherweight medal was Richard Gunn. Gunn was a three-time ABA titlist (in 1894 – 95 – 96) and being 38 years and 242 days old was the oldest man ever to win an Olympic boxing title. A record that still stands.

The Olympic Committee however had a problem to resolve. Could a medal be awarded to Roddin without his actually fighting for it? After due consideration they decided the award should be made to the Musselburgh boy as he could not be reasonably penalised for the actions of an opponent. It was no more than

"Hughie" deserved given the earlier difficulties that he had to overcome.

For the majority of young working-class men in 1908 long hours of monotonous toil for low pay was the harsh daily reality. Little wonder then that within a year of his Olympic triumph Hugh Roddin had turned professional, marking his professional debut by beating Harry Thomas in Leith Drill Hall.

His next bout was to be in somewhat more exalted company for on Saturday, 6 November 1909, he appeared at the Waverley Market on the same bill as "Peerless" Jim Driscoll, the reigning world featherweight champion. The late James Butler, one of Britain's most respected boxing experts stated that Driscoll, or "The Welsh Maestro" as he was known, was the finest boxer he had ever seen.

The show was a charity affair on behalf of the Scottish Lifeboat Fund. Charlie Cotter had been one of the organisers, hence Roddin's appearance against the Londoner Charlie Brittle in an exhibition bout. Brittle was the star of the London Polytechnic Club but he was no match for Roddin who by common consent outshone his English foe, so much so that Driscoll complimented the young Scotsman on his showing, having watched him prior to his own contest against his arch-rival, the English featherweight champion, George Moore of Barking. At the time this Driscoll-Moore bout was considered as a dress-rehearsal for the real thing (though they never did meet for the world title) but from Hugh Roddin's point of view the main benefits were that he was able to study at first hand two premier examples of first-class professional featherweight boxing. He saw the standard he would have to match if he too wanted to be a world beater.

What had provoked Driscoll's particular enthusiasm was the systematic way that Roddin had employed his long reach and wrecking ball-like right hand against Brittle. Yet within a month of this massive boost to his ego the Musselburgh man was to taste the bitterness of defeat.

The event took place on 7 December 1909 at the Scottish National Athletic Club in the Bridgeton district of Glasgow. Roddin's opponent was Private Evans of Edinburgh. Evans was considerably heavier and stronger than his foe from "The Honest Toun". He was also more experienced. Handicapped by a cut eye received in the sixth round Roddin fought "in the gamest fashion" – according to an eyewitness – for another six rounds before the referee adjudged the injury too severe to continue.

Defeat is always traumatic and it normally has two major effects on any promising boxer. It tests to the utmost his ability to overcome adversity and continue. (The virtual hibernation of Gerry Cooney subsequent to his defeat by Larry Holmes is a case in point.) It also causes many of them to reflect deeply on their future strategy within the hardest game.

Roddin passed the first test. His subsequent career proved that. His next move in response to defeat was less predictable. He decided to drop down a rung to bantamweight (8 stone 6 pounds). The benefits of this course of action were twofold. The famed right hand and the long reach would be doubly effective. Fighting against "natural" bantams Roddin would also have advantages of height. Most bantams tend to be diminutive in stature. Conversely featherweights are normally

Charlie Cotter. The doyen of Scottish boxing trainers in the first thirty years of this century.

fairly tall. (Three of the greatest featherweights of this century – Sandy Saddler, Eusebio Pedroza and Barry McGuigan averaged 5 feet 9 inches in height.)

Once this decision had been implemented the man from the "Honest Toun" decided to forsake the shores of the Firth of Forth for those of the United States.

Hugh Roddin set sail for New York in February 1911. His choice of the "Big Apple" was not as surprising as it might at first appear. In the 1890s one of the top boxing spots in New York had been "The Scottish-American Athletic Club". Again, when Hugh Roddin fought his great American rival Johnny Lore in the Sharkey Club in May 1911 there were an estimated 500 Scots emigrants there to cheer him on to a ten rounds points victory.

The tour had started in sensational fashion in April 1911 when the famed right fist despatched Mickey Finegan into dreamland in the fourth round. This kayo took place at the Fairmount Club.

There was further evidence of the enhanced punching power resulting from the transformation to bantamweight when Young Devlin was kayoed in similar fashion at the Arcanium Club in July of the same year. The remarkable thing about this victory was that it took place at two o'clock in the morning. (Close circuit TV fights beamed from the USA at unearthy hours are now commonplace but fights at such times were unusual earlier this century.) "Hughie Boy", as his American fans called him, was roused by some of his most ardent Yankee admirers and persuaded to fight. By 3.30 a.m. he had resumed his slumbers after kayoing his Irish-American foe.

Perhaps the greatest testimony to "Hughie's" increased hitting power occurred in October 1911. On this occasion he knocked out Patsy Donovan at the Congress Club in Brooklyn with a terrific uppercut in the seventh round. This blow produced a mixed bag of fortune for the Musselburgh boxer. It lifted Donovan clean off his feet and dumped him unconscious on the canvas. It also broke the forefinger of Hugh Roddin's prized right mitt, forcing him to lay off for four months.

This could have been a disaster for the Scotsman but for his innate frugality and his scorn for the more popular forms of dissipation that have ruined many boxers throughout the ages. During his forced holiday further evidence of his enormous popularity with the New York fistic fraternity emerged. He was made a life member of the "Acme" boxing club and presented with a gold watch and chain bought by funds raised on his behalf by club members.

Of the 23 victories notched up in New York between April 1911 and November 1912 it is his 18 points victories that reflect greatest credit on this Scottish battler. This might seem a strange statement given the timeless fascination of the KO to boxing fans.

Strange indeed, until one recalls that until 1920 boxing in New York was governed by the Frawley Law, a moralistic measure designed to stamp out gambling. This was to be achieved by the simple expedient of making it illegal for any kind of decision to be rendered by any referee or judges.

Again, boxing could only be legal if carried out in licensed clubs, such as the "Acme" which had taken Hugh Roddin under their wing so that he could box legally. Just as a decade later, Americans would go to elaborate lengths to frustrate laws designed to stop them drinking booze so New-Yorkers by-passed Frawley by consulting newspapers. Thus journalists rather than referees became the final judges of contests and gambling continued as before.

This arrangement may have been fine for gamblers from the "Big Apple" but it presented foreign boxers with a particularly difficult problem – how to overcome the ultra-patriotic prejudices of American sportswriters? Prejudices that were apt to take an especially virulent turn when a "Limey" was in the opposing corner to a native son of Uncle Sam's.

This factor was referred to by Hugh Roddin himself when he returned to Musselburgh to spend the Christmas of 1912 with his family. He continued to train at Charlie Cotter's gym and it was there that he granted an interview to a sportswriter from the *Evening Dispatch*.

Roddin made clear his reservations about the Frawley Law. "I can tell you a Scottish boxer has to fight very hard for a win or even a draw in New York . . . a case in point was when I fought young Leroy in November of this year. I had a very easy journey and I was sick hitting him . . . Judge my surprise then when next day some papers came out with the statement that I had "a shade on him" . . . I thought it very funny." This underscores the great credit due to the Scots fighter in remaining unbeaten throughout his stay in New York.

The interview also yielded further reasons as to why the man from the "Honest Toun" was so respected by hard-bitten American fight fans. During his second scrap with arch-rival Johnny Lore he suffered a broken nose – which inhibited his breathing – yet he continued fighting and gained a draw! The injury was so bad that he continued to have breathing problems until an operation was carried out which removed the bones from his nose.

There were also other disappointments to be endured in New York, primarily his failure to land a fight with the reigning Scottish bantamweight champion, his arch-rival Alex Lafferty of Airdrie.

Alex Lafferty had enjoyed as distinguished a career in New York as his Musselburgh counterpart. Throughout 1912 Lafferty had fought and won seven bouts in the "Big Apple". He had met Roddin there socially but spurned all and every offer to continue their acquaintanceship in the ring with his title at stake.

Had Lafferty accepted the challenge it would have been the only occasion that a Scottish title was decided in the USA. It was not to be.

There was certainly more than a shade of personal "needle" in their rivalry, rivalry that was rooted in the close relationship that existed between Roddin's mentor, Charlie Cotter and James "Tancy" Lee of Leith.

On 18 April 1911 Alex Lafferty had met Lee for the Scottish bantamweight title at the Olympia Ice Rink in Edinburgh's Annandale Street. With Cotter as his chief second Lee had started in spectacular fashion by dropping the Airdrie fighter to the canvas. Lee then proceeded to outsmart and outbox the Lanarkshire fighter to such an extent that by the ninth round he had Lafferty in deep trouble. But from the tenth round onwards, despite Cotter's promptings, Lee's stamina began to falter. From then on Lafferty began to gain the upper hand until a hard left jab to the stomach in the 13th round spelt curtains for the exhausted Leith man.

From that time on Cotter encouraged Roddin to regard himself as the agent of his revenge. Hence the Musselburgh boxer's relentless pursuit of his Lanarkshire rival. Yet they were fated never to meet in the ring. Lafferty spent most of the year of 1913 touring Wales, England and Ireland. The first six months of 1914 were spent in New York. In August of that year a far greater conflict between nations broke out, a conflict that literally and metaphorically killed Roddin's chances of fighting Lafferty for the title. One of the many casualties of Ludendorff's Spring offensive in 1918 was Sergeant Alex Lafferty of the Royal Engineers.

Roddin's professional boxing career did not survive the Great War either. Yet if he won no professional titles Hugh Roddin deserves to be remembered – not only as Scotland's first boxing Olympic medallist but also as the scourge of American bantamweights at a time when "Limey" fighters were openly mocked for their lack of guts.

Nobody ever had reason to lay that charge on Musselburgh's finest fighting son.

HUGH RODDIN'S AMERICAN RECORD

April 1911: Knocked out Mickey Finegan in four rounds at Fairmount AC, New York.

May 1911: Beat Johnny Lore on points in a ten round contest at Sharkey AC, New York.

May 1911: Beat Knock-out Smith on points over ten rounds at Sharkey AC.

June 1911: Beat Johnny Lore on points over ten rounds at Sharkey AC.

July 1911: Beat Darky Griffin, a coloured boxer, on points over ten rounds at Sharkey AC.

July 1911: Knocked out Young Devlin at the Arcanium Club, Brooklyn, in five rounds.

August 1911: Beat Charlie Grime on points over six rounds at the Hollywood Club, Yonkers.

September 1911: Drew with Johnny Lore in a ten rounds contest at Sharkey AC.

September 1911: Beat Patsy White on points over ten rounds at the Carlyle AC, Brooklyn.

October 1911: Beat Young Gitney, another coloured boxer, on points over ten rounds at Sharkey AC.

October 1911: Knocked out Patsy Donovan in seven rounds at the Congress AC, Brooklyn.

February 1912: Beat Young Packey McFarland on points over ten rounds at the Irving AC, Brooklyn.

March 1912: Beat Frankie Pass on points over ten rounds at the Gowanus AC, Brooklyn.

May 1912: Drew with Frankie Pass in ten rounds at the Gowanus AC.

July 1912: Knocked out Bob Zieman, of Chicago, in the sixth round of ten-round contest at the Royal AC, Brooklyn.

August 1912: Knocked out Sailor Kane in seven rounds at the Royal AC.

August 1912: Beat Willie Chandler on points over ten rounds at the Royal AC.

September 1912: Beat Larry Lundy on points over ten rounds at the Royal AC.

September 1912: Beat Irish Mahone on points over ten rounds at the Queensborough AC, Long Island City.

October 1912: Beat Mike Malin on points over ten rounds at East New York AC, Brooklyn

October 1912: Beat Young Packey McFarland on points over ten rounds at East New York AC, Brooklyn.

October 1912: Beat George McGregor on points over ten rounds at Brooklyn Beach AC, Brooklyn.

November 1912: Beat Young LeRoy on points over ten rounds at National AC.

November 1912: Beat Eddie Cook on points over ten rounds at East New York AC.

Fought 25 **Won 23** **Drew 2**

NAT DRESNER of Leith
Scotland's Forgotten Boxing Pioneer

As already mentioned in the introduction to this book, one of the most deeply embedded myths in Scotland's sporting and cultural history concerns Glasgow's being the traditional capital of Scottish professional boxing. It is not difficult to ascertain why this myth has gained such ready and uncritical acceptance, particularly amongst modern Scots. With the exception of Ken Buchanan, every Scottish holder of a world boxing title has hailed from Glasgow and environs. Furthermore, supporters of the Benny Lynch cult have nurtured this myth of Glasgow's traditional pre-eminence as the Mecca of Scottish fisticuffs by creating a ready market for the abundance of plays, novels, biographies and radio programmes cataloguing the rise and fall of the wee man from the Gorbals.

Yet 65 years ago any sports-minded Scotsman if asked to name the epicentre of Scottish professional boxing would have unhesitatingly nominated Edinburgh. Any claims for Glasgow would have provoked looks of ill-concealed incredulity towards the author of such a statement. The primary reason was that between 1921 and 1929 Edinburgh was not only Scotland's civic capital but the country's boxing capital as well. This was entirely due to one man, a Jewish pawnbroker from Leith named "Nat" Dresner. He alone put professional boxing in Scotland well and truly on the map from the unlikely setting of his father's pawnshop at 21 Market Street, Leith.

Nathaniel "Nat" Dresner was born in Leith in 1882 into a comfortable middle-class Jewish family. His father, Philip Dresner, was a noted Baltic boot importer and pawnbroker in the port. Philip Dresner prospered in both lines and in 1906 was elected as councillor for the Third Ward of the old Leith Town Council. He later became a Leith Burgh Magistrate, a position he held until his retiral from public life in 1915.

"Nat" showed no desire to emulate his father's civic achievements, preferring instead to become a theatrical manager and impresario. So successful was he in this field that he soon acquired a substantial financial interest in the Kings Theatre. He later became a director of the Theatre Royal whose demise due to a fire occurred in 1946. The experience gained in theatre management was invaluable when he entered the world of boxing because two hallmarks of all Nat Dresner boxing promotions were a flair for spectacular showmanship and a minute attention to detail.

The young pawnbroker-cum-impresario gained his entry into boxing through two men, Tancy Lee and Fred Lumley. James "Tancy" Lee is chiefly

George McKenzie
Nephew of Tancy Lee. He died ironically in the same year (1941) as his illustrious uncle.

Alex Ireland
Dresner gave him his opportunity to shine as a professional.

remembered as conqueror of Jimmy Wilde, former world flyweight champion and one of Wales' greatest fighters. A fellow Leither, Dresner accompanied him to London to see his fight with the great Welshman. Fred Lumley was the owner of what was then Edinburgh's most famous sports shop, Lumley's, and was a noted sports organiser.

Dresner and Lumley collaborated in staging a two-night amateur boxing tournament in aid of the Heart of Midlothian FC War Memorial Fund. Success in this venture whetted Dresner's appetite for an even greater challenge – to establish big-time professional boxing in Edinburgh and then throughout Scotland.

That he was a pioneer in this respect cannot be doubted. The *Edinburgh Evening News* of Friday, 14 January 1922 declared: "It is now many moons since we had a professional boxing show in Edinburgh." Again, a journalist writing in the same newspaper on Saturday, 4 March 1922 observed: "Since the war, with the exception of one or two bright patches, the boxing fare served up in Edinburgh has been rather mediocre in quality."

All that was to change utterly thanks to Nat Dresner. Within three months of the *Evening News* lamenting the quality of Edinburgh's professional boxing fare Dresner had become the manager of three outstanding local fighters and had staged his first "sell-out" show in the Waverley Market in July 1922. The fighters were Alex Ireland and George McKenzie of Leith, both future champions – Ireland at British and European level, McKenzie at Scottish and British level – and Dave Gordon of Newtongrange.

Victorious Scottish amateur boxers in 1920. Alec Ireland front left and George McKenzie extreme right would go on to British pro' titles.

The *Evening News* observed that Dresner's decision to hold a boxing show in July was "something of an experiment". Yet it was a shrewdly calculated risk by the aspiring young Leith promoter, for he knew that Alex Ireland and Dave Gordon had been famous in their amateur days for the bitterness of their rivalry. This was reflected in the packed seats at the Waverley Market where supporters of both boxers were greatly in evidence.

To describe Nat Dresner's subsequent progress as meteoric would be an understatement. Four months after his initial July triumph, Dresner had the distinction of promoting the first professional boxing tournament in Scotland to be graced by a member of the Royal Family. On 18 November 1922 Prince George was a ringside spectator at the Waverley Market tournament headed by George McKenzie of Leith who beat Fred Bullions of London by stoppage. The prince was enjoying a spot of shore leave from his Royal Navy ship which was berthed at Port Edgar.

This "Royal" show is also of interest in that Dresner had originally contracted the legendary battling Siki – who defeated Georges Carpentier for his world light-heavyweight crown – to appear as his bill-topper. A suspension for misbehaviour by the French Boxing Federation eventually frustrated the appearance in Edinburgh of this fearsomely eccentric Senegalese who had once terrified New Yorkers by marching down the sidewalks of Fifth Avenue with a lion secured only by a dog's collar and lead! Yet this move fully illustrates the two great hallmarks of Nat Dresner's promotional style – a showman's flair for publicity and the shrewd recognition that professional boxing at the highest level could only be sustained by top quality bouts.

Mick McAdam. One of the "Lanarkshire School" who did so much to help Dresner gain promotional eminence.

Sir Iain Colquhoun, Bart., DSO., Master of Ceremonies. First World War hero – army boxing champion and M.C. at most major Dresner promotions. He became chairman of the BBBC Scottish Area Council.

Another ingredient of his success was his flair for organisation. Someone who had first-hand experience of this was George Smith the boy from Leith who rose rapidly through the ranks of British boxing's third men to referee Muhammad Ali v. Henry Cooper in 1966 for the world's heavyweight championship. Smith recalls: "I was a programme seller at all Dresner's major promotions (in the Drill Hall, Forrest Road, the Industrial Hall, Annandale Street, and Waverley Market). We were all immaculately dressed by the promoter in white wollen jumpers with "Nat Dresner" inscribed back and front in bold green letters. Everything was meticulously planned. He was a shrewd customer."

Dresner was indeed shrewd, as any ambitious boxing promoter who wishes to succeed must be. There is evidence of this in his first major championship promotion, the bout between Seaman James Hall of Peebles and Johnny Brown of Hamilton for the British and European lightweight title. Hall, the reigning champion, easily outboxed his west of Scotland opponent over 20 rounds.

The date of this promotion – 2 January 1923 – coincided with the Powderhall

Dave Gordon
Never fulfilled his amateur promise but was another local boy encouraged by Dresner.

THISTLE THAT PROVED TOO MUCH FOR LEWIS.

Sprint Championships when many people from all over Britain congregated in Edinburgh. Dresner reasoned rightly that a top-class boxing match would prove an ideal and lucrative après race entertainment and so it proved. Twelve thousand people crowded into the Industrial Hall, Annandale Street (now Lothian Region Transport's Bus Depot).

The success of this promotion was crucial to Dresner and is indicative of his strategy in establishing "big-time" professional boxing in Scotland. The Hall v. Brown contest was not only the first British and European fight staged in Scotland but it also broke the monopolistic stranglehold of the London-based National Sporting Club on all British boxing titles. In this connection it is highly significant that the only west of Scotland fighters to win British titles in the 1920s – Jim Higgins and Elky Clark – had to travel to London to do so. That fact emphasises the lack of any west of Scotland boxing promoter of Nat Dresner's stature to challenge the London monopoly.

There is also substantial evidence that the Leith-based promoter sought to consolidate his success by widening the social appeal of professional boxing to as broad a social spectrum as possible. The famous contemporary cartoonist, Baillie Tom Curr, celebrated the Hall v. Brown contest with a cartoon in the *Evening News*

Nat Dresner
The undisputed father of big time boxing in Scotland.

where he observed that "women and the cloth (clergymen) were well represented".

The presence of women in large numbers was a direct result of Dresner's practice of reserving a portion of ringside seats for the exclusive use of the fair sex at all his shows. This practice may be favourably contrasted with the rigidly anti-feminine stance of the London National Sporting Club which excluded women throughout its lifetime.

Again, as the son of a working pawnbroker, Nat Dresner could not avoid being aware of the increasing army of the unemployed which was as depressing a feature of the 1920s as it is today. They were not excluded. A large advertisement in the *Evening News* advised the jobless that they would be admitted to his shows at greatly reduced prices on production of their "dole" cards.

At the opposite end of the social scale the aristocracy have always been attracted

Bob Donati
Donati's main distinction in a mediocre pro' career was appearing in the first big-time boxing show in Dundee in December 1922 – promoted by Dresner.

to pugilism and Nat Dresner was only too happy to accommodate two scions of Scottish noble families within his organisation. Thus the Marquis of Clydesdale – who himself would capture the headlines by flying over Mount Everest – was regularly employed as a time-keeper at ringside. The Marquis was no mean boxer himself; he was a Scottish middleweight amateur champion of some note.

However, the most important contribution by a son of the nobility to Dresner Promotions came from Sir Iain Colquhoun of Luss. Sir Iain was the master of ceremonies at all Dresner's major title fights and he clearly regarded this role as a stepping stone to the greater things he hoped to achieve in the world of professional boxing. By 1946 he was chairman of the Scottish Area Council of the British Board of Boxing Control and a leading organisational light in Scotland's first post-war world boxing championship contest – Jackie Paterson v. Joe Curran – at Hampden Park, Glasgow.

The involvement by Sir Iain in Dresner's boxing activities also accentuates the Leith promoter's total dominance of Scottish boxing during the 1920s for one can be sure that an ambitious west of Scotland based aristocrat would not have travelled to the east had equal or better opportunities obtained in the Glasgow area.

Dresner's dominance was also widely acknowledged in the west of Scotland by the two most important groups of people in any successful boxing promoter's story – the fans and the boxers.

The fans' acknowledgement of the Leith man's position as Scottish Boxing Supremo can be gleaned from a newspaper advertisement of Friday, 16 February 1923, where readers were advised that "special one day excursion trains will run from Glasgow, Hamilton, Motherwell and Bellshill". This was to Dresner's show on that day in the Waverley Market, a show that featured boxers from "The Hamilton School" managed by Paddy McGreechan.

"The Hamilton School" – principally Tommy Milligan, Johnny Brown and Jim Higgins – were the most talented boxers in Scotland at this time and Dresner enjoyed a virtual monopoly of their services until 1927. This emphasises once again the lack of opportunity for top-class professional boxers in Glasgow and district throughout the 1920s.

The undoubted star of "The Hamilton School" was Tommy Milligan who went on to lose gallantly a world middleweight title bid against the legendary American, Mickey Walker, "The Toy Bulldog" at Olympia, London, in 1927. Indeed, Milligan's contest with another boxing legend, Ted "Kid" Lewis, in November 1924 at Annandale Street was in many ways the zenith of the Leith promoter's career.

This fight provided an insight into Dresner's possession of another quality essential to success in boxing promotion – opportunism. The Ted "Kid" Lewis (born Gershom Mendlehoff) who ensconced himself with his trainer in the plushness of Edinburgh's Caledonian Hotel prior to his fight with Milligan was already a well-established boxing legend. A former world welterweight champion who fought the American Jack Britton no less than 15 times – five of these for the world title – Lewis had also won British and European honours at middleweight.

Normally such a fistic star would have cost a small fortune to entice north of the border but Dresner was aware that only a short time before this his co-religionist Lewis had been publicly examined for bankruptcy in London amidst a splash of newspaper publicity. After that sordid episode the opulence of the "Caley" at the west end of Princes Street must have provided welcome relief for the indigent English boxer.

One thing is certain, no boxing match staged in Edinburgh (and few in Scotland) has ever provided such fantastic scenes as those that accompanied the Milligan v. Lewis scrap that November day in 1924. Twenty thousand people jammed into the Industrial Hall to see Milligan annexe his English rival's British and European titles.

But far greater drama took place outside the hall in Annandale Street. Two thousand spectators had to have their 2s 10d (14 pence) admission money refunded because they could not see. The police had to make a baton charge outside the hall against a crowd composed almost entirely of west of Scotland fans whose late arriving trains ensured that they were unable to gain entry. Their response was to attempt to batter down the turnstiles, thus forcing the police to restore order with their truncheons.

The fight in the ring also had the distinction of being the first boxing contest in Scotland to be filmed for exhibition to cinema audiences. Another notable Dresner first.

Just how popular Nat Dresner made "big-time" professional boxing can be gauged from the table:

Date	*Contest*	*Title(s)*	*Venue*	*Attendance*	*Distinction*
2 Jan 1923	Seaman Hall (Peebles) v. Johnny Brown (Hamilton)	British & European lightweight titles	Industrial Hall Annandale Street	12,000	1st British & European title fight held in Scotland
25 Sept 1923	Augie Ratner (USA) v. Johnny Brown (Hamilton)	First international contest between world class American and Scottish fighters staged in Scotland	Drill Hall Forrest Rd. Edinburgh	2,000 Many locked out	£500-a-side highest prize money paid in Scotland up to that time
26 Nov 1924	Ted 'Kid' Lewis v. Tommy Milligan	British & European welterweight championship	Industrial Hall Annandale Street	20,000 Many locked out	Scottish crowd record up to that time
12 April 1927	Johnny Hill (Strathmiglo) v. Jim Hanna (Belfast)	Non-title bout	Waverley Market	3,000	Hill's Edinburgh debut
14 March 1928	Tommy Milligan v. Alex Ireland	Middleweight championship of Gt Britain & Europe	Waverley Market	10,000 Thousands locked out	First & last time a British & European middleweight title fight was decided in Edinburgh
22 Sept 1927	Alex Ireland v. Tom Berry (London)	Non-title bout	Waverley Market	7,000 1,000 turned away at door	Special trains ran from north of England and north & west of Scotland

Perhaps the most remarkable statistic included in the table concerns the bout between Alex Ireland and Tom Berry of London. Here was a non-title bout between an English veteran and a Leith boy who had not yet acquired "star" status. Yet three special trains ran from the north of England and more came from north and west Scotland – powerful testimony indeed to the ultimate success of Dresner's aspirations to become Scotland's first nationally renowned boxing promoter.

However success was bought at a heavy price in terms of the Leith man's health. Increasing problems with his heart precluded him from taking any part in the

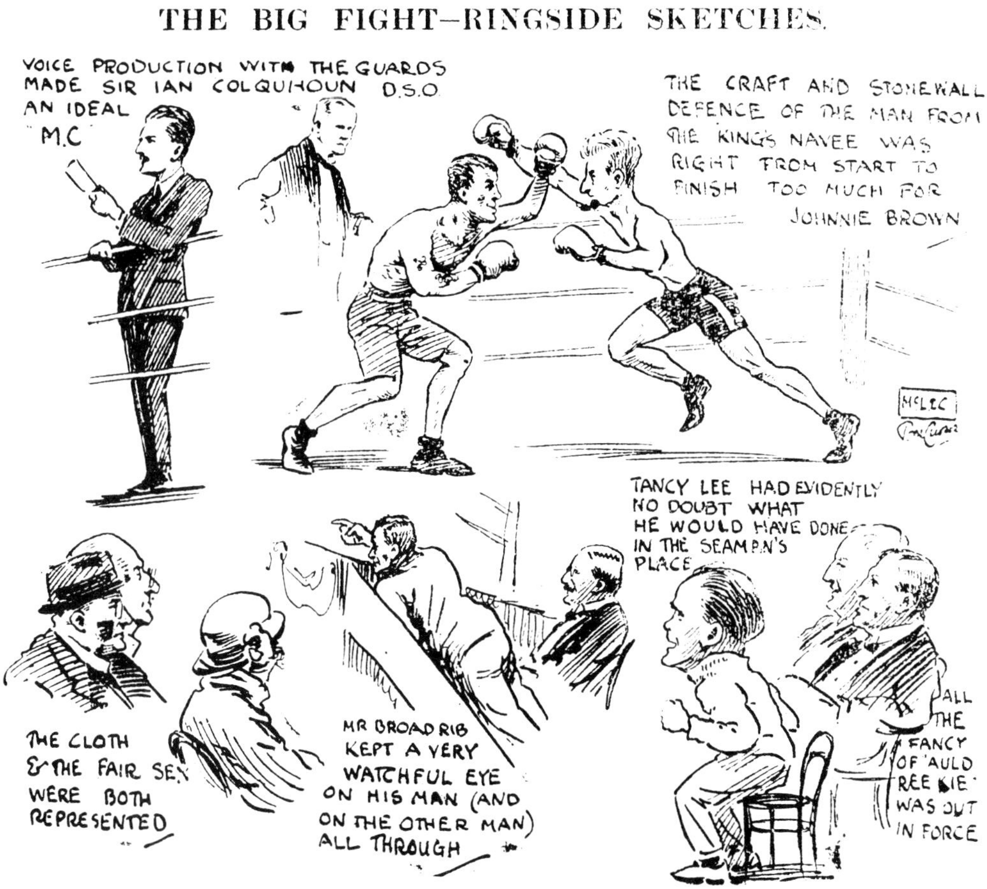

Celebrating the first big-time title fight ever promoted in Scotland.

negotiations for Tommy Milligan's world title fight with Mickey Walker. The only mention of Edinburgh as a possible venue for what would have been its first world title contest occurred when a syndicate based in Newcastle-upon-Tyne, led by former Canadian world heavyweight champion Tommy Burns, briefly considered Scotland's capital.

Between January 1928 and 14 March 1928 when he managed a token appearance at the Milligan v. Ireland fight Dresner was unable to leave the family home at 4 James Place, Leith.

Nat Dresner died at seven o'clock in the morning of Saturday, 31 March 1928. He was just 46 and unmarried.

A few hours later on this day eleven blue-clad Scotsmen would win immortality as the "Wembley Wizards" by thrashing England 5 – 1 in London. As one Scottish sporting legend perished so another was born. Yet posterity has been much kinder to the footballers than it has to Nat Dresner.

On 7 August 1928, a syndicate bearing the magic "Nat Dresner" name attracted 35,000 spectators to Carntyne Greyhound Racing Stadium in Glasgow. There the assembled fans saw Welshman Frank Moody despatch old Dresner favourite Tommy Milligan in 1 minute 45 seconds of the first round.

The contest was highly symbolic on two counts. It marked the beginning of the inexorable shift westwards of power in Scottish professional boxing – where it has resided ever since – and the nemesis of a boxer who had been central to Dresner's promotional success.

As late as April 1930 the syndicate bearing the Dresner name could still attract 5,000 people into the Waverley Market to witness Aberdonian Steve McCall annex Alex Ireland's Scottish middleweight title on points. But this was the swan song of Edinburgh's dominance as Scotland's boxing capital. The guiding spirit of that supremacy was gone and further proof of the westward march of boxing power was furnished by a meeting held in the St Enoch Hotel, Glasgow in 1930, organised by Sir Iain Colquhoun of Luss "to arrange the better organisation of boxing in Scotland".

Other promoters such as Harold Bownas attempted to fill the vacuum created by Dresner's death but the fact remains that since the Leith pawnbroker's demise Edinburgh has not played host to an internationally important professional boxing tournament.

Nat Dresner, Leith's promoter and boxing pioneer extraordinaire, deserves a place in Scotland's boxing pantheon beside Lynch, Paterson, Watt and Buchanan. An infinitely greater place than posterity has thus far accorded him.

The Day an Italian Alp Slipped Into Waverley Station

One may rightly ask what the black-shirted followers of Italian dictator Benito Mussolini had in common with the benificiaries of the famous Victorian philanthropist Dr Thomas Guthrie? Or what, on a chilly November Thursday in 1929, prompted this incongruous coalition to share a platform in Edinburgh's Waverley Station with Mr J. W. Fraser, manager of the Marine Gardens Ballroom and a vast crowd of other capital citizens, a crowd that included the cream of Scottish fistic talent.

The answer was a giant Italian peasant from Sequals, a village just north of Venice. No ordinary peasant to be sure. The presence of the Italian Consul at the head of the large crowd guaranteed that. The gentleman eagerly awaited by dignitary and ordinary person alike was called Primo Carnera and his profession was boxing.

What made him so different from conventional prize fighters who almost never received such auspicious welcomes as this to Edinburgh can be summarized in one word – size. This fact can be gauged from the nicknames appended to the keenly anticipated visitor to "Auld Reekie" – "The Ambling Alp", "Satchel Feet", "The 20th Century Colossus". Carnera justified these titles. In addition to scaling 6 feet 5¾ inches, he weighed a massive 19 stones 4 pounds of finely tuned muscle.

What tended to emphasise the Italian's mammoth proportions was the diminutive stature of his mentor and manager, the Parisian promoter Leon See. See was only five feet tall. He had discovered Carnera in a French circus.

Again, there were other reasons to justify the size and excitement of the crowd who watched the arrival of the London express train bearing the celebrated visitor. The conduct of the crowd reminded the *Evening News* journalist sent to cover the event of the return of the Heart of Midlothian with the Scottish Cup in 1906. For this was an equally historic occasion in Edinburgh's history. It marked the very first visit to Edinburgh of a boxer who would subsequently win boxing's greatest prize – the world's heavyweight championship. No other holder of this much coveted crown had ever previously visited the city and none – Carnera apart – has since.

When the train ground to a halt Carnera emerged from his carriage and no doubt pleased the Italian Consul and his blackshirted Scottish brethren by giving the Fascist salute. (Ironically, allied troops liberating Italy would later find Carnera serving as a sniper with the anti-Fascist resistance!) Yet he and the tiny Leon See must have been surprised at the eerie hush that settled on the crowd. A silence that prompted the *Evening News* reporter present to describe the scene in terms that a modern reader would readily identify with the opening sequence of a "spaghetti" western movie. When stunned townsfolk nervously try to assess the threatening stranger who has suddenly appeared in their community.

There is little doubt the assembled citizens of Edinburgh were at first dumbfounded by this Italian Gulliver in their midst. The spell was broken by the pipe band of Dr Guthrie's Industrial School whose rousing march tune provoked the crowd into rapturous cheering.

After exchanging a few words with the Italian Consul, Carnera and See joined the Marine Ballroom manager, Mr J. W. Fraser. Indeed it was the owner of the popular Portobello Ballroom, Mr Frederick Graham-Yool who was responsible for enticing the Italian giant north of the border – for a hefty sum of money.

Thus Carnera fell in behind Dr Guthrie's school pipers who led him on his way to the Caledonian Hotel at the opposite end of Princes Street – a truly memorable cavalcade in a street that has witnessed many.

There was to be scant time for "The Ambling Alp" to admire the slightly larger mass of Edinburgh Castle Rock from the window of his Caledonian Hotel bedroom. He departed that afternoon to the "Scottish" stadium in Glasgow where he was scheduled to box exhibitions with, among others, Bobby Sheilds, heavyweight champion of Scotland.

In the meantime the Marine Gardens management put the finishing touches to their preparations for Carnera's appearance there on Saturday, 9 November 1929. They were clearly determined not to allow the local climate to jeopardise their substantial investment for they erected not one but two rings. The first was situated in the open air of the football ground adjoining the Ballroom. The second on the dance floor of this famous Mecca of the light fantastic.

However, despite assembling a galaxy of local fistic "stars" – men such as former British and European welter and middleweight champion Tommy Milligan, former British lightheavyweight champion Tom Berry and "Tancy" Lee to spar with the massive Italian (who wore 20 ounce "pillow" gloves) the shows were neither a fistic nor a financial success. In both Edinburgh and Glasgow the fans clearly preferred their combats to be real rather than of the simulated variety, a view that was endorsed by the local press. A correspondent of the *Edinburgh Evening Dispatch* of Friday, 8 November 1929 described Carnera's performance as a "nicely staged burlesque".

Posterity has not recorded how Carnera reacted to this subsequent lack of enthusiasm displayed towards him by the Scottish public. Whatever he felt, it was but tame discomfort to what was to happen to him in the USA a short time later. The story of how little Leon See was deposed by New York mobster Owney Madden who undertook to "manage" Carnera is well known. Suffice to say that despite winning and losing the world heavyweight title and engaging in lucrative battles with Joe Louis and others, Carnera found himself abandoned, alone, paralysed and broke in a New York hospital by 1939. He even had to return to Italy on a cattle boat.

Yet there was to be a fairy-tale ending for this essentially gentle giant. His salvation was "all-in" wresting in whose burlesque atmosphere he found his true niche in life, a fact he revealed to assembled pressmen at a press conference in Portobello Town Hall during his second visit to Edinburgh in 1960. This profession was so lucrative that it permitted him a lifestyle that enabled him to pay for a university education for his son in America. His son still practises dentistry in Chicago.

Nevertheless, no matter how much he was "ripped off" by American gangsters, one thing even they could never deprive Primo Carnera of was the unique distinction of being the first – this century – world heavyweight boxing champion to visit "Auld Reekie".

POSTSCRIPT

Since first researching and writing this chapter further research reveals that the first modern heavyweight champion to visit Edinburgh was James J. Corbett in the 1890s where he appeared on the stage of the Royal Lyceum Theatre.

The Bronx Boy
Who Infected Forrest Road with Fight Fever

Due to its closeness to the University, the Royal Infirmary and George Heriot's School, Forrest Road has always had a part to play in the unfolding drama of Edinburgh's history, albeit usually a supporting role. Yet 65 years ago this familiar thoroughfare was the focal point in an event assuring it of a unique place in Scottish sporting history. This in turn was due to the popularity of Forrest Road Drill Hall as one of Edinburgh's premier boxing arenas between 1920 – 1939.

In September 1923 this territorial army depot carved an immortal niche in sporting history when it hosted the very first Scottish professional boxing match to feature a world-rated American, the Great Bronx Battler from New York – Augie Ratner. His Scottish opponent was the equally renowned Johnny Brown of Hamilton.

In the 1920s Augie Ratner was as famous in America as, say, Marvin Hagler is today. Indeed when he arrived in Edinburgh and took up residence in the Caledonian Hotel he had scored a victory over the legendary Harry Greb some time previously. Harry Greb is today universally acknowledged as one of the greatest world middleweight champions who ever lived.

One may well ask what it was that enticed this boy from the Bronx away from the glamour of Madison Square Garden to the somewhat more mundane environment of an Edinburgh Territorial Army drill hall? The answer, not surprisingly, was money – plus a desire on the part of Edinburgh's leading boxing promoter, Nat Dresner, to establish "Auld Reekie" in the first rank of international boxing centres. The £500-a-side paid by the Leith pawnbroker-cum-boxing-impresario was a Scottish record purse at the time.

Yet like all understudies who became "stars" overnight there was an element of accident in the elevation of Forrest Road Drill Hall to historical stardom. Due to the extreme novelty of the occasion the shrewd Dresner accurately visualised a certain sell-out. But for once he was beaten to the punch for his first choice of venue – The Waverley Market – by a circus and carnival company. The consequences were to have far reaching effects not only for the promoter's bank balance but also for the Edinburgh City Police and the residents of Forrest Road and environs.

Apart from the record purse money there were other indicators of just how prestigious the contest was regarded at the time. Most unusually for a bout with nothing but prestige at stake, it was fought over the full championship distance of 20 rounds.

Again when Ratner trained at Hampton Court, London (he had been warned

Typical Dresner publicity for this major international contest.

Mr Jack Smith, Manchester, one of the three referees who officiated during the evening.

against the inclement Scottish weather!) he did so under the supervision of Jack Goodwin the Cockney boxing trainer who was a veritable combination of Terry Lawless and Angelo Dundee. Goodwin only associated with the fistic élite – fighters who were champions or potential champions. His services were much sought after and it is a sure hallmark of Ratner's international status that Goodwin readily agreed to condition the Bronx Boy for his coming battle with Johnny Brown. Goodwin's view was equally shared by the Edinburgh press. "Ringsider", the boxing correspondent of the *Edinburgh Evening Dispatch*, writing on Saturday, 22 September 1923, declared ". . . I have a great admiration for the American . . . he is one of the best middleweights in the world".

But what of Ratner's Scottish opponent – Johnny Brown?

The Lanarkshire man had already played a major part in Scottish boxing history in 1922 when he had fought Seaman James Hall of Peebles in the Industrial Hall, Annandale Street. Promoted also by Dresner, this fight had the distinction of being the first British and European lightweight title fight held in Scotland. On that occasion the Hamilton man had been a lightweight (9 stones 6 pounds). However, due to an almost uncanny capacity to shed and gain weight he came against Ratner at the middleweight poundage of 11 stones.

OUR CARTOONIST'S IMPRESSIONS OF THE BIG FIGHT.

Edinburgh's citizens have always demonstrated an unerring instinct for what constitutes a historical occasion and this ability was much in evidence on the evening of Wednesday, 25 September 1923, when pandemonium reigned in Forrest Road and neighbouring Bristo Place and George IV Bridge. Thousands of disappointed fans milled around these streets jostling with the police who tried to keep them away from the already overflowing Drill Hall. Some irreverent spirits had to be chased from Greyfriars Cemetery as they explored possible entry from that quarter.

Just as great was the excitement displayed by the 2,000 fans fortunate enough

Ratner doing ground work, with Jack Goodwin, his trainer, looking on. Ratner went on to serve with distinction in the US invasion of Algeria in World War Two. Goodwin collapsed and died in a boxer's corner in 1933.

to gain admission, a fact commented on by the *Evening News* reporter present who also remarked on the calmness of Ratner despite him taking a fair amount of ribbing from the crowd due to his somewhat unusual dressing gown.

With regard to the actual contest Johnny Brown covered himself in glory despite dire predictions to the contrary, the direst of all coming from Johnny Brown's own compatriots. "Ringsider" of the *Edinburgh Evening Dispatch* forecast: "Ratner should 'do' Brown good". This was a view shared by the Englishman Fred Archer who had been one of Ratner's sparring partners and who had actually fought Brown before. Archer predicted a knockout for the American against his Scottish opponent.

From the first bell Brown adopted his usual "American" style of non-stop aggression. Ratner fought in the "British" fashion of clever boxing behind a straight left jab, slipping and blocking many punches. It is a tribute to Jack Goodwin's conditioning that Ratner appeared the stronger of the two during the final three rounds despite absorbing the bulk of the punishment exchanged in the previous 17 rounds.

The result in favour of Brown seemed a foregone conclusion to all present except the man who counted most – the London referee, Ed Humphreys. His decision of a draw caused an uproar and was roundly condemned by press and fans alike. Perhaps the only truly contented souls that September evening were the owners of the pubs in the area who were called upon to play host to the many denied access to the Forrest Road Drill Hall.

Since that memorable night almost all of the American fistic fraternity who have visited Scotland – Joe Louis, Sugar Ray Robinson, Howard Davis, Sean O'Grady – have beaten a path to Glasgow and the west of Scotland. In view of this it is easy to lose sight of the fact that the lucrative trail these illustrious boxers followed was first signposted by a tough kid from the Bronx in what is now a quiet cul-de-sac in Edinburgh's Forrest Road.

POSTSCRIPT

There are some who will dispute my claim that Augie Ratner was the first top-class American to fight under Marquis of Queensberry rules in Scotland. Those who wish to argue thus will cite the case of the "Dixie Kid" – born Aaron L. Brown – whom Nat Fleischer rated as his fifth best welterweight of all time.

The "Dixie Kid" fought Dan Flynn in Glasgow in 1912. Flynn was as noted a cyclist as he was a boxer and he went on to found a highly successful "bookie's" business in his native city.

Flynn outpointed the Dixie Kid over 12 rounds but it is difficult to take this contest seriously for reasons supplied by the noted ring historian, Denzil Batchelor. In his book *Big Fight* (1955), Batchelor states, "The Dixie Kid sometimes lost fights on purpose". In other words he went into the tank more often than Esther Williams – often betting on his opponent to win.

No such doubts can be applied to the *bona fides* of the Ratner v. Brown contest. It is my contention that "tainted" fights – no matter what the motivations of the principals – should be discounted when computing boxing records and statistics.

The Battle of Annandale Street, 1924

Any pedestrian entering Annandale Street from Leith Walk and strolling north towards Bellevue can scarcely avoid noticing, on their left, a large red-brick building topped with glass domes. The walls of this imposing structure are decorated with ornamental stonework, an adornment that seems at odds with the building's present function as a bus garage.

Yet 63 years ago when the building was universally known as "The Industrial Hall" the roars were not from revving bus engines but from human voices – the voices of 20,000 boxing fans shaking the iron roof girders. Outside, the din would be swollen by the shouts of disappointed fans, who struggled with baton wielding policemen as they tried to force entry to the hall. The date of this tumult was Wednesday, 26 November 1924.

The root cause of the historic rumpus was the staging of the first British and European welterweight title fight to be held in Scotland. As fist and foot clashed with truncheon on the pavement, champion and challenger battled in the ring. The champion was Ted "Kid" Lewis of London and his challenger Tommy Milligan from Hamilton.

Whilst everyone anticipated violence in the roped square few could have foreseen the forces of law and order and the bitterly disappointed fans engaging in the ugly scenes that were enacted on the pavements outside the hall. Yet the real culprits were not just the mob of Lanarkshire fans who rioted. Nor could anyone fault the police for trying to maintain public order. The real villain of the piece was the London Midland Scottish Railway Company. It had undertaken to transport thousands of fans from Milligan's home territory of Lanarkshire by special excursion train to Edinburgh for the fight. These "special" trains were uniformly late, therefore fuelling the frustrations and anxieties of the west of Scotland fans and resulting in many of the travelling fans who had tickets finding themselves excluded in favour of local customers who had paid cash at the turnstiles.

The solid mass of Edinburgh city policemen became a convenient focal point for the pent-up frustrations of the street crowd. Consequently, some of the wilder fans decided to storm one of the turnstiles. Not surprisingly this barrier collapsed under their cumulative weight, forcing the intervention of the police wielding their batons.

An eyewitness to this turmoil was a young Leith programme seller called George Smith. Forty years later this young man would make boxing history himself, for in 1966 George Smith became the first Scotsman to referee a world heavyweight

Tommy Milligan finished his preparation for his big fight with Kid Lewis with some road work. He is seen with his trainer, T. Murphy.

Kid Lewis (left), and Tommy Milligan (right), exchanging greetings in the Industrial Hall, the venue of the contest, which they visited together on the previous night. In the centre is the promoter, Nat Dresner.

championship fight when he was in charge of Henry Cooper v. Muhammad Ali in London. Mr Smith recalls: "The crowd kept pushing and pushing forward until the barrier collapsed, allowing some of them to spill into the hall."

Perhaps the most tragic irony of the whole episode was that many of those who had gained admission legally could see little of the ring action, a fact clearly testified to by the reporter from the *Evening News* who was present. He commented: "Inside it was difficult to distinguish anything . . . the atmosphere was impregnated with a fog that was partly tobacco smoke . . . in part autumn mist that had stolen in . . . ." The judgement of this anonymous journalist was subsequently vindicated. Promoter Nat Dresner made full cash refunds to a thousand patrons from the most rearward and cheapest seats who were unable to see the action.

One may well ask why a boxing match provoked such civil commotion in the comparatively douce atmosphere of Edinburgh in 1924? But this was no ordinary boxing contest. No fight that featured a living legend such as Ted "Kid" Lewis could be deemed "ordinary".

Born Gershom Mendlehoff in London's East End, Lewis is chiefly remembered

NSP PROMOTION

INDUSTRIAL HALL
EDINBURGH

WEDNESDAY
26th Nov. 1924
at 7 p.m.

FOR £250 A-SIDE
AND THE WELTER-WEIGHT CHAMPIONSHIP OF GREAT BRITAIN AND EUROPE

TED (Kid) LEWIS
v.
TOMMY MILLIGAN

AND OTHER CONTESTS.

Ringside Seats, numbered and reserved, **20/-**, **15/-**, and **7/6**. Unreserved, **5/9**. Floor Area, **2/4**.

Box Office Waverley Market (10 on Gallery); Lumley's, Ltd., Leith Street and Dalziel, 40 Tolbooth Wynd, Leith.

Intending Patrons please note all **10/6** *Seats are booked out.*

BOOK EARLY.

This was the first time these titles were disputed in Scotland.

for the record number of battles – 17 in all *some of which* were for the world welterweight title – he had with the Irish-American Jack Britton for the world welterweight championship. Lewis was also the first fighter in the world to wear a gumshield, now accepted as a commonplace by fighters and fans alike. Again, the "Kid" figured in the very first boxing contest broadcast in Britain – by Station "2LO" in May 1922.

However, it is most unlikely that making history would have served as much of an incentive for this experienced East End battler to come north. Lewis had more

Milligan leads with the left.

One of the numerous clinches.

Lewis plays for the body.

And glad to "hang on" at the finish.

pressing financial reasons for abetting Dresner in breaching the London-based National Sporting Club's monopoly on national boxing titles.

The evening before his Annandale Street bout Lewis settled himself into the plushness of the Caledonian Hotel. Three weeks earlier he had been in the somewhat less agreeable environment of the Central London Bankruptcy Court. Clearly he saw his northern safari as a means of restoring his flagging financial status.

What of his Scottish challenger, Tommy Milligan? There can be no doubt that this was the most important fight the Lanarkshire boy had engaged in thus far in a career that would ultimately lead to a world title fight in 1927, for the American Mickey Walker's world middleweight title at the Olympia Stadium, London.

Tommy Milligan was the undoubted star of the "Hamilton" school of professional boxers. Managed by Paddy McGreechan and trained by Tommy Murphy, the "Hamilton School" as a breeding ground of champions had no equal in Scotland in the 1920s. McGreechan had an "understanding" with Nat Dresner which meant that whilst the Leith promoter successfully breached the London monopoly on titles, he exercised his own on the cream of Scottish fistic talent.

The question naturally arises as to whether the actual contest justified the commotion it provoked? Most Scottish boxing fans would have answered a resounding "yes!".

Inside the stadium the *Evening News* correspondent was able to perceive enough through the murky atmosphere to notice that Lewis looked drawn at the welterweight limit of 10 stones 7 pounds. This was an acutely accurate judgment for unknown to the assembled thousands Lewis had spent the bulk of that morning in the turkish baths at Portobello indoor pool in Bellfield Street.

Once action commenced in the ring Milligan was the agressor throughout. No better testimony to the Scotsman's superiority exists than the fact that the referee, Joe Palmer, persistently rebuked Lewis for holding his younger rival. Only in the 17th round did Lewis briefly threaten when he caught Milligan flush on the jaw with a right-hand punch. However, by the final round there was only one winner and new champion – Tommy Milligan.

On reflection the battle of Annandale Street was probably one of the few sporting occasions in Edinburgh's history when the drama outside the venue threatened to surpass that being enacted within. Television is often blamed for inducing street violence yet it is fair to reflect that the existence of televised boxing in 1924 would have almost certainly spared Edinburgh city police from becoming embroiled in a riot. That is speculation.

What is certain is that few who were there would soon forget their visit to the Industrial Hall, Annandale Street, that historic Wednesday of 26 November 1924.

A Referee Remembers
Eugene Henderson Looks Back

For a man in his 82nd year Eugene Henderson has lost little of his alertness and his capacity to express himself in a forthright manner, as I discovered on a visit to his Edinburgh home. During the interview Mr Henderson expressed his gratitude for having led a full and happy life – a life that saw him referee world title fights such as Peter Kane v. Jackie Jurich, Freddie Mills v. Gus Lesnevich and Randolph Turpin v. Sugar Ray Robinson.

He originally became a refereee purely by chance. He was hired to MC a small boxing show in Bathgate, but when the appointed official did not appear, Eugene Henderson took over. It was the start of nearly 40 illustrious years as one of Britain's top third men.

B.D.: If I start with the first Mills v. Lesnevich fight on 14 May 1946 – you stopped the fight with only four seconds of the tenth round to go. Why were the BBBC stewards unwilling to accept your explanation of events at the hearing?

E.H.: I can answer that in one word – "betting". Now, I am going to tell you something I have never revealed to anyone else. During the actual hearing I compelled some of the stewards to admit that they had wagered on the outcome of the fight – eventually five out of the eight who interviewed me admitted this to me. I didn't say anything about this at the time because I knew some of the press would have used it against boxing – I didn't want to hurt boxing, then or now. I felt some of them were upset at me for that reason. I had to have their complete confidence or nothing. Strangely enough, six months later Freddie Mills phoned me out of the blue from the North British Hotel in Edinburgh.

B.D. What did he want?

E.H.: He had been sent north by the BBBC stewards to tell me my licence was there if I wanted to re-apply.

B.D.: Were you surprised at this?

E.H.: Yes, it was a total surprise. But I missed boxing and eventually I went back.

B.D.: You came to know Freddie Mills well?

E.H.: Yes – both in and out of the ring.

B.D.: Did Freddie Mills suicide surprise you?

E.H.: Why do you use the word "suicide"? Freddie Mills was killed. He was the biggest hearted man I ever saw in a ring. He never killed himself – he would never do that.

B.D.: Now, turning to your early life, did you once nearly KO the Queen Mother?

E.H.: Ah yes! That was a complete accident. My father was a clock and watchmaker. We had a contract to maintain the 25 clocks in Carberry Towers, the home of Lord Elphinstone. As a laddie it was my task to wind all the clocks. This meant carrying a step ladder from room to room. I was marching backwards out of a room – I turned and gave what I thought was a balustrade a terrific skelp.

B.D.: Was it the Queen Mother?

E.H.: Yes, or the Duchess of York as she was then. I didn't hear her – she had carpet slippers which, combined with the rich carpeting, had totally muffled her footsteps. She was knocked flat.

B.D.: How did she react?

E.H.: She could not have been more gracious. She blamed herself for the whole incident – a most charming lady.

B.D.: Is it true that "Tancy" Lee (*conqueror of Jimmy Wilde*) introduced you to boxing?

E.H.: Yes and no. By the time "Tancy" enrolled me in the Leith Victoria Boxing Club, I had in fact sparred dozens of rounds with big public schoolboys from Loretto Public School in Musselburgh – my father was part-time boxing coach at the school and a great friend of Tancy's.

B.D.: Did Tancy teach you a lot?

E.H.: "Tancy" and I had many gruelling sparring sessions. The thing about "Tancy" was the amazing suppleness of his upper body – he could feint you into making a mistake or roll with a punch by clever little movements of his upper body. But as a teacher? Tancy could do it himself but not explain why very well.

B.D.: Did your winning the Scottish Eastern District lightweight title with four first round KOs have anything to do with being invited to help Scottish "pro" middleweight champion Tommy Milligan?

E.H.: Yes, my father knew Paddy McGreechan, Milligan's manager, and I was invited to help Tommy prepare for his scrap with Ted Moore.

B.D.: How would you compare Milligan with Len Harvey or Randolph Turpin?

E.H.: Oh, I think Milligan was a better boxer than either of them, but then again, he was too docile for his own good.

B.D.: What do you mean "docile"?

E.H.: He lacked the "devil" that Turpin had sometimes.

B.D.: People used to say the same about Bombardier Billy Wells.

E.H.: Milligan was like that. His temperament let him down sometimes.

B.D.: Do you really think he could have beaten Mickey Walker in their 1927 title fight?

E.H.: Yes. Milligan was caught by a "lucky punch" in the first round but he wasn't properly warmed up. I could see Mickey had been well prepared in his dressing-room and that was the main difference.

B.D.: What was your greatest amateur achievement?

E.H.: That's easy. In November 1926 I won Scottish Eastern District titles at welterweight, lightweight and heavyweight. I lost the middleweight title to the man I knocked out in the light heavies!

B.D.: How did you, a welter, beat a heavyweight?

E.H.: I knocked him out with an uppercut. He was three stones heavier than me.

B.D.: Do you still have the medals?

E.H.: No. My father pointed out that medals would be easily lost and being a watchmaker he suggested I write to the Scottish ABA and request that my father make a nine-carat gold watch of equivalent value. Surprisingly, they agreed. (*E.H. showed me the watch. It is a beautiful timepiece.*)

B.D.: When you first refereed Benny Lynch against Freddie Tennant of Dundee you weren't impressed by Lynch – why?

E.H.: Lynch was an egotist then. He thought himself better than he was at that stage of his career.

B.D.: When did you first become impressed by him?

E.H.: When he fought the Welshman (*Johnny Griffiths*) he produced a punch as though it was second nature – a punch I had taken months to perfect with Johnny Hill. He knocked the Welshman out.

B.D.: How would you compare Lynch with Barry McGuigan?

E.H.: McGuigan worries me by his lack of defence – he doesn't have Lynch's defence. Lynch was a better all-round ring craftsman.

B.D.: Whom would you pick between Marvin Hagler and Sugar Ray Robinson?

E.H.: A few months ago I would have said Robinson, but recently I saw Hagler on television (*Hagler v. Mugabi*). Hagler really impressed me. He had a tough time for the first four rounds but then he made the other fellow fight his kind of fight. That is what it is all about – making the other fellow do what you want. Yes, Hagler impressed me.

B.D.: You refereed Farr and Don Cockell – who was the better heavyweight?

E.H.: No doubt about it – Tommy Farr, in his prime, any day. Cockell was strong and courageous but he lacked Farr's cunning. I used to watch Farr closely – he was always a move ahead of the other chap. Cockell came forward, forward the whole time – but Farr in his prime was wilier, much craftier.

B.D.: What do you remember most about the first Robinson v. Turpin fight you refereed?

E.H.: The gentlemanly way Robinson took defeat. I went to his dressing-room and he was very gracious in defeat.

B.D.: Yet, in his autobiography, *Sugar Ray*, Robinson claimed Turpin won by using "roughouse tactics" on him?

E.H.: That amazes me! I was not aware of that. I still have the scorecard of the fight somewhere and there are no cautions marked on it.

B.D.: Which clearly disproves Robinson's claim of "roughouse tactics"?

E.H.: It was a clean, open fight. I am really surprised at Robinson's saying that!

B.D.: You saw all the great old-time referees – Sam Russell, Moss de Yong, Barrington Dalby. Which did you regard as best?

E.H.: Sam Russell. No question about it. Do you know I twice travelled to Manchester at my own expense just to see Sam work? I paid no attention to the boxers in the ring – just Sam.

B.D.: What did Sam teach you?

E.H.: That a referee's most important tool is his voice. Sam used his voice so powerfully in the ring – I can remember ringside spectators jumping when Sam barked a command at the boxers.

B.D.: Did you copy this?

E.H.: Yes indeed. I very rarely had a bloody mark on my shirt because I never went near boxers unless absolutely required. I simply barked my commands and that was enough – they knew who was boss.

B.D.: Finally, you refereed the Dundee boxers Freddie and Norman Tennant. What do you recall about them?

E.H.: I handled Norman Tennant against Vic Herman in 1951. Both Tennants were very aggressive – good boxers.

B.D.: Eugene Henderson, thank you.

The Missing Link
Scotland and Heavyweight Boxing

Ever since that great patron of heavyweight boxing the Duke of Cumberland butchered the brawny pride of Highland manhood at the Battle of Culloden in 1746 Scotland's association with heavyweight boxing has generally been an unhappy one. (The Duke of Cumberland, incidentally, was an avid bare-knuckle boxing fan, being chief financial backer of heavyweight Jack Broughton, the man who did more than any other to establish the noble art in 18th century Britain. His brutalities were not confined to Highland clansmen: when Broughton lost to Jack Slack in 1750 – being half-blinded in the process – the duke dropped him as though he was a bundle of tartan cloth and abandoned him.)

Indeed, when one examines any one of the multitude of books on great world heavyweight boxers the mention of a Scotsman is as rare as a toast to the aforementioned duke at a Highland ceilidh. In world boxing terms one has to go back one hundred years to discover a Scotsman who briefly covered himself in glory in a tussle with a world heavyweight champion.

In December 1886 a gigantic Scottish emigrant to Colorado called Duncan McDonald stunned the world and the reigning champion John L. Sullivan by taking the latter to a draw over four rounds. Lest cynics jeer at the distance involved it should be remembered that this was prime time Sullivan – a champion who had been chopping down contenders like a berserk lumberjack at the rate of one and sometimes two a month in every state of the Union. Even Nat Fleischer, whose admiration for Sullivan was akin to that of a native of Govan for Glasgow Rangers FC, admitted: "The champion (Sullivan) doesn't mention it (the scrap with McDonald) in *Life and Reminiscences.* But not because he didn't remember him. Quite the contrary. He could never get Duncan McDonald out of his mind. He was the first man – the first of only three men in his whole career – who ever got a draw against him . . .".

Yet there have been precious few such moments of distinction amongst Scottish professional heavyweights since. True, great world heavyweight champions Jack Dempsey and Max Baer proudly laid claim to some Scottish ancestry but Dempsey also had Cherokee Indian and Irish blood in his veins and Baer had German ancestry – all good martial strains – but it would take a genetics expert (which I am not) to work out if the Scottish genes were more in evidence in the ring than the others, so Scots boxing fans can derive scant comfort from this direction in connection with heavyweight boxing.

The Duke of Cumberland may have butchered the bodies of his Scottish

Highland foes but he most certainly did not curb their descendants' taste for battle – as many have discovered throughout the world since – in places as far apart as El Alamein and Mount Tumbledown. Yet this love for a ritualised punch-up has never been translated into world-class ring success at 13 stones or more. Why? There are in my opinion several reasons.

Firstly, the descendants of the wild charges at Prestonpans and Culloden tended to go into the armed forces or the police, normally for long engagements – given the unemployment and uncertainties of civilian life in the 19th and early 20th century, the longer the engagement the better. Neither of these organisations – the police or armed forces – would have countenanced a moonlighting professional fighter in its ranks.

Had there been a nascent Scottish heavyweight star of world potential in the armed forces between 1910 – 1948 then that proud old ex-Scots Guardsman Sir Iain Colquhoun of Luss (who became chairman of the Scottish Area Council of the BBBC) would almost certainly have bought him out as Irishman Jack Doyle was bought out of the Irish Guards to pursue a pro' heavyweight career. That this never happened speaks for itself.

Secondly, another area of Scotland famed for the brawniness of its manhood is the Border Country – Selkirk, Roxburgh, Peebleshire and Berwickshire. As early as 1919 a newspaper correspondent in the *Edinburgh Evening Dispatch* was deploring the total lack of even amateur boxing in the Border Country. But Borderers have been addicted to the tough rugby code – a game whose violence arguably surpasses that of the boxing ring in intensity if not duration. Attempts to promote professional boxing in Hawick in 1951 came to naught. Handling rather than hooking won the day.

Thirdly, professional boxing in Scotland has always been principally urban-based. This, paradoxically, was to prove a handicap with regard to heavyweight boxers in Scotland. Writing in 1936 – around the time Benny Lynch was world flyweight champion – the future world famous Scottish nutritional expert, Lord John Boyd Orr, declared that investigations in Glasgow had revealed that middle-class children in the city were as a rule five-and-a-half inches taller and 13 pounds heavier than their working-class counterparts. This he ascribed to diet.

The implications of this are clear. The kind of young men from an urban environment who may have been the potential Jack Dempseys of their era were the kind of young men who attended schools such as Allan Glens and Kelvinside Academy, where boxing – if it were practised at all – was seen as being no more than a character-building rehearsal for the hard knocks of "rugger" field and boardroom.

Heavyweights of working class origin there surely were. Boxers such as Dan McGoldrick of Airdrie who was heavyweight champion of Scotland in 1908. Yet so desperate was the shortage of other heavyweights in Scotland at the time, that when George Aitchison of the Scottish National Club in Bridgeton arranged for McGoldrick to defend his title an Englishman had to be imported northwards. This was Fred Higgins of London who has the distinction of being the first and only Sassenach to fight for the Scottish heavyweight title. The contest was over the full championship distance of 20 rounds and Scottish blushes were spared by McGoldrick's victory. McGoldrick, though, like so many Scottish heavyweights, made no impact beyond his native shores.

By 1912 the "White Hope" mania that had started in the USA reached Scotland. This phenomenon arose when Jack Johnson, the Texan negro, became the first negro world heavyweight champion in 1908. Johnson openly showed his contempt for the white racism of the day, thus attracting virulent hatred in return and a world-wide search for some white fighter to re-establish the imagined supremacy of the white race.

Nor was this racism a purely American disease. Hugh Roddin of Musselburgh (whom readers will have encountered in a seperate chapter of this book) told the *Edinburgh Evening Dispatch* reporter who interviewed him in 1912: "The one thing I don't like about over there (America) is that I sometimes have to share a dressing-room with niggers – they do smell so". He also made other comments that would have landed him in serious trouble with the Race Relations Board of today.

Such then was the spirit that informed the great Scottish search for a "White Hope" which was centered on Edinburgh in 1912.

Joe Aitchison, the doyen of Scottish boxing trainers whose father George was asked to assist in training the vast army of "White Hopefuls" recounts the following: "From the mass of would-be fighters there emerged one who seemed to have it all – height, build, the lot. He also disposed of some of the other 'contenders', although most of them had probably never laced a glove on before. Anyway, my father who did know a good deal about the game was asked to spar with this would-be heavyweight champion whom the organisers were clearly sold on . . . My father boxed his ears off for the first minute of the first round when suddenly the big heavyweight raised his arms in token of surrender and proclaimed: 'Ah cannae go oan. Ma tooth is sair – I'm awa' tae the dentist,' whereupon he tore off the gloves and marched out of the ring never to be seen again.

This farcical episode guaranteed two things. Scottish heavyweight boxing could return to its normal torpor and Jack Johnson would never hear the skirl of bagpipes at ringside.

It was after World War One – in 1919 – that there emerged the first real heavyweight this century to cut any ice at world level who had strong Scottish fistic connections. He was, ironically, an Englishman called Philip Suffling – better known as Phil Scott, and somewhat unkindly by the Americans as "Faintin'" Phil Scott due to his weakness against body blows.

Born in London in 1900 Scott made his professional debut as a heavyweight whilst serving as a soon-to-be-demobbed Royal Marine stationed at picturesque South Queensferry below the Forth Rail Bridge. His debut, a winning one on points, was achieved at Edinburgh's Synod Hall. His opponent was Scotland's own but soon-to-be-forgotten Piper Taylor.

Scott recalled with affection – to a journalist of the *Edinburgh Evening Dispatch*

in January 1926 – his days as a Royal Marine at the Port Edgar Naval Base near Edinburgh. He was in Scotland's capital city to contest the British Empire heavyweight championship – the first and last time it was disputed north of the border – but his opponent was not of Caledonian hue. It is a sad comment on the state of Scottish heavyweight boxing as it stood at the time that his opponent was an Australian, George Cook.

The fight itself was an extremely poor affair, a kind of pugilistic version of the Battle of Sheriffmuir in 1715 where Highlander and Redcoat huffed and puffed to no great effect then went home for their tea having achieved little. It was the referee who ended the communal misery of the paying customers in Edinburgh's Industrial Hall when he disqualified Cook in the 17th round of a 20 round contest.

The resulting sourness of this performance clung to Scott's career like an indelible yoghurt stain. It was his undistinguished exit against Jack Sharkey in a 1930 world title eliminator in America, though, that fuelled the fires of the horizontal British heavyweight myth that has burned ever since.

To be fair to Scott, he did beat some good class men such as the Argentinian Vittorio Campolo and "Gypsy" Daniels – the latter knocked out future world heavyweight king Max Schmeling inside a round – but the bad nights always seemed to be more memorable than the good ones before he retired in 1931.

Around this time Scotland did have a native born heavyweight – Glasgow's Bobby Shields. Shields did fight top notchers such as Larry Gains but without any distinction attaching to his record.

In November 1929 Shields hit the headlines when he agreed to meet future world heavyweight champion Primo Carnera in a three round exhibition at the Grove Stadium in Glasgow. The *Edinburgh Evening News* of the day described the result of this match as being, "more burlesque than boxing."

Shields was certainly a brave individual with a very respectable amateur record but his deficiencies as a potential world-class heavyweight were cruelly exposed in a serious boxing match with former Scottish middleweight champion Steve McCall of Aberdeen – whom he outweighed by three stones. Shields only obtained a win by foul. *Boxing,* the trade newspaper, reported on 25 January 1933, "The Champion (Shields) was slow and awkward and at the time the referee, Tommy Milligan, disqualified McCall, Steve was well ahead on points and looked an assured winner".

But as Bobby Shields was beginning a slow fade from the Scottish fistic scene another star was preparing to rise in the east. Alex Bell of Leith.

If amateur records were a cast-iron guarantee for professional boxing success then Alex Bell would surely have been Scotland's first world heavyweight champion. Bell won no less than EIGHT Scottish Amateur Boxing titles – three at heavyweight between 1930 – 1934. He possessed an excellent left jab, a fair right-hand punch and good speed coupled to a good tactical brain.

Bell did not lack influential backing. He was featured at the Edinburgh National Sporting Club by promoter Pat McGreechan – the same "Paddy" McGreechan who had steered Tommy Milligan to a world middleweight title shot in 1927. When Bell fought he was sometimes seconded by Nat Sellar, one of Britain's top seconds and cornermen. Again Bell was sent at one point to the camp of Empire heavyweight kingpin Larry Gaines at Leicester to get top sparring facilities and coaching from Gaines' handlers.

Bell's sponsors even provided him with good class opposition from across the Atlantic in the shape of American heavyweight Bobby Diamond. If time has eroded some of the sparkle from this American fistic gem a re-examination of his record should restore a great deal of the lost lustre.

Bobby Diamond, whose mother hailed from Glasgow and who used boxing to finance his legal studies at an American university, gave world champions Marcel Thil and Vince Dundee tough scraps. He also fought world lightheavyweight champion John Henry Lewis. In 100 contests he had never been knocked out and had only lost on points. Not surprisingly he know too much for the Leith heavyweight who nevertheless confounded many by going the full ten round distance.

Yet Bell's pro' career was plagued by inconsistency. Against the creditable performance of the Diamond contest must be set a fiasco of the epic proportions of the Frank Bruno v. Chuck Gardner farce in Monte Carlo in 1987.

The *Edinburgh Evening Dispatch* of 14 March 1935 referred to Bell's foe Albert Dybel as a "promising Englishman". It is clear this description was not based on having watched Dybel perform but rather on the latter's claim to have beaten future British heavyweight champion Jack London. Based on his performance it is probable that the only victory Dybel could have had over London was at quoits – although given his physical condition against Bell even that is a dubious proposition.

This "match" was pure farce. A right-hand punch from Bell flattened Dybel in 2 minutes 50 seconds of the first round, dislocating his jaw. It was not the Englishman's sorely afflicted mandible that first gave the *Evening Dispatch* scribe covering the bout cause for concern. He wrote; "It was a contest that should never have taken place and it will do neither Bell nor the game any good. Dybel entered the ring with a corporation that no regular boxer ever carried and during the short life of the bout he served only as a punch bag for the Leith man".

Discontent with the proceedings was not confined to the press. Canny Leithers never like to be "conned" and there was an angry demonstration by the crowd in the Edinburgh National Sporting Club. Many demanded the return of their money from promoter Paddy McGreechan.

However, it would be wrong to conclude that Alex Bell did not have his moments of glory as a professional as well. He did. One such occasion occured in the Caledonian Stadium in Glasgow when he outpointed the giant Bert Ikin of Stoke-on-Trent over 12 rounds. Ikin had considerable advantages in height, reach and weight over his Scottish foe and even managed to cause his nose and mouth to bleed freely from a left hook in the third round, but over the piece it was the Leith boxer's crisper hitting and superior ringcraft that won the day.

Nevertheless, the *Evening Dispatch*'s boxing correspondent commented further on Bell's performance against Ikin thus: ". . . on his display against Ikin, all that Bell requires in his work is a little more 'devil'. He was content to take punches, which, with a little more action in his work, he would never have been troubled".

Any hopes raised by the Ikin performance were to prove premature and no boxer exposed the Leith heavyweight's shortcomings more than England's Jack London.

John Harper of West Hartlepool so admired writer Jack London that on becoming a professional boxer he adopted his name. Jack London is also the senior part of a unique duo in British heavyweight boxing history. Both he and his son Brian London held, 20 years apart, the British and Empire heavyweight titles. When London stepped out of the second rank of British heavyweights he nearly always lost but he equally had too much class for Alex Bell.

In their first two contests the West Hartlepool scrapper was clearly the master but Bell was obviously not convinced for he accepted with alacrity an offer from Paddy McGreechan to meet his old English foe at the Edinburgh National Sporting Club in 1935. Those who expressed a view that Bell's courage was greatly in excess of his powers of judgment were proved correct. Despite dropping London with a peach of a right cross to the chin in round four Bell was in the eyes of an eyewitness, "battered from pillar to post". This same eyewitness summed up the contest thus: "London was far too strong for the young Scot. He was crafty at close quarters, and made good use of his weight in the clinches to tire Bell out, and his heavyweight counter to the heart soon made a livid patch about Bell's ribs".

The end when it came in was as unsatisfactory as it was surprising given the earlier pattern of the fight. In the ninth round London let go a mighty swing to the body which strayed below the borderline, felling Bell who collapsed in agony to the canvas. London was immediately disqualified.

The opinion of the *Evening Dispatch* journalist present was almost like the tolling of a requiem for Bell's career: "To ask the Leith boxer to face men of London's calibre is almost folly. London is a good class British heavyweight and much too strong for Bell".

Another boxer who ensured that Alex Bell's celebrity as amateur would never be matched in the professional ranks was his fellow-Leither Manuel "Kid" Abrew, a coloured heavyweight of whom much was also expected.

Now a boxing-hating Buddhist domiciled in the English Home Counties, Abrew then stood out from his Scottish contemporaries such as Bell by the dark colour of his skin and for a time by the promise he held out to those Scots who still dreamed of a native-born heavyweight world beater.

Yet if Abrew was good enough to beat Bell as he did in September 1935 he too was plagued with that inconsistency that had hampered his Leith contemporary's progress. The highlight of Abrew's ring career was probably his meeting at Shawfield Stadium, Glasgow, on 15 September 1937, against British Empire and European lightheavyweight and heavies king Len Harvey of England – although no titles were at stake on this occasion.

From Harvey's point of view Glasgow promoter Alex Creamer's offer to appear in the Shawfield ring was a lucrative way to dispense with ten months' ring rust – he had last fought for the world's lightheavyweight title at Wembly on November of the previous year against John Henry Lewis of the USA. For Abrew here was a heaven-sent opportunity to crash the world ratings by gaining a clear cut victory over a man who was not only a former British heavyweight champion but respected on both sides of the Atlantic as a world-class fighter. Twenty thousand eager fans crowded into Shawfield eager to proclaim Abrew as the Messiah who would liberate Scottish heavyweight boxing from nearly 60 years in the wilderness.

The Scotsman was six years younger than his English rival and a stone heavier but these advantages were to prove insufficient antidotes to Harvey's superior boxing skills and cool courage.

Throughout the contest Abrew charged Harvey with the same rare and desperate courage that had impaled the Highland clansmen on Redcoat bayonets at Culloden, for it was short arm punching at close quarters – hooks and uppercuts which battered Abrew into submission forcing referee Charlie Thomas to rescue him in round 14.

With the advent of World War Two in 1939 boxing quite rightly took a back seat to the serious business of fighting for national survival and then ultimate victory. From the ashes of the immediate post-war world rose two Scottish professional heavyweights – Jock Porter and Ken Shaw from Dundee.

Porter's name only occurs today when it is connected with Yorkshireman Bruce Woodcock who was British and Empire heavyweight champion between 1945 – 1950. The Yorkshireman beat Porter inside the distance in 1945 when he was on a rising tide that would take him to a fight with Lee Savold on 6 June 1950 for a version of the world heavyweight title, which was only recognised in Britain as such.

It is a sure barometer of the Scots heavyweight's lack of class at world level that Woodcock, having halted Porter comfortably in 1945, would himself be stopped inside the distance by an ageing American journeyman like Savold. About a year later Savold would be pulverised by a way-over-the-hill Joe Louis in America.

Ken Shaw of Dundee had infinitely more class than Porter. Not only was he Scottish heavyweight champion but Malcolm Turner, the then much-revered boxing writer of the *Scottish Daily Express* called Shaw the best Scottish heavyweight he had ever seen. This was in 1951 and Turner's views were widely respected.

Shaw was certainly good enough to dispute with Freddie Mills on 20 April 1948 an eliminating contest for the British and Empire heavyweight title. Yet it was the first contest between this battling duo in 1945 that also determined the outcome of their 1948 scrap. The 1945 bout also proved that whatever qualities Ken Shaw may have lacked, magnificent courage was not one of them. In the very first round Mills split Shaw's lip wide open. It was a horrific injury which would mark him to the extent that he fought thereafter with a bushy moustache to conceal the resulting scar. Top lip flapping around and blood flowing freely, Shaw battled on for another six rounds before the referee mercifully brought the contest to an end.

The 1948 scrap was, mercifully from Shaw's point of view, much briefer than their earlier fight. In the first 15 seconds of round one Mills smashed a left hook on to Shaw's mouth, re-opening the old injury. Even Mills was momentarily taken aback by the sight of Shaw's top lip flapping like a red rag before him. But the rules demand that a fighter keep punching unless ordered to stop so Mills continued in for the kill. Shaw was down on the canvas for another four counts before his cornermen threw in the towel.

Ken Shaw emigrated to New Zealand shortly after this but I had the pleasure of chatting to him briefly in 1983 when he returned home to Dundee. He impressed me as a quiet, self-effacing man yet his courage spoke volumes in his two contests with Freddie Mills. In order to gain the dubious pleasure of sharing a ring with Mills it should not be forgotten that Shaw had to defeat some good class British heavyweights, thus justifying Malcolm Turner's opinion of him.

But finding a British world heavyweight champion is the boxing world's equivalent of alchemy – the elusive science of transforming base metals into gold. Just as the alchemists of old were confounded by the stubborn conservatism of lead molecules so many British fight promoters have discovered throughout the years to their cost that there is more to becoming a world heavyweight boxing champion than possessing a size 18 collar and a physique that would make the average health club narcissist swoon with delight. "Find-a-world-class-heavyweight" competitions were as much a part of the late 1940s and early-to-mid-Fifties as rationing, the crooning of Frankie Laine or classy dribbling of Stanley Mathews on the wing.

The latter-day alchemist who arranged the majority of these competitions was Jolly Jack Solomons, the portly genius of post-war British boxing promotion. Solomons organised many of the most important world-class bouts held in Great Britain between 1946 and 1964. Heavyweight competitions with £500 or £1,000 top prize money were a staple part of such shows. At 1950s values this was a sum considerable enough to attract no end of aspiring would-be scrappers from Britain's big men.

Nor were such aspirants to fistic glory always lacking in some degree of class. Joe Erskine – whom Henry Cooper regards as one of the cleverest men he ever met in the ring and who became British heavyweight champion – came through one such competition – as did Hugh Ferns, Scotland's next heavyweight contender of any note.

The red-haired Ferns forsook the shipyards of Greenock to try his luck in a heavyweight competition in Manchester. On winning this London and Solomons beckoned and the former Scots amateur star went south.

Ferns' London debut was hardly auspicious. In March 1952 he was stopped inside a round at Harringay Arena by another Scots heavyweight from Greenock called Jock McVicar. McVicar who had boxed as an amateur for Scotland had himself been stopped on his professional heavyweight debut by English heavyweight Jack Hobbs in 1950.

On 10 June 1952, Ferns appeared as a reserve only in Jack Solomon's heavyweight competition that backed up the Don Cockell v. Randolph Turpin battle for the British and Empire lightheavyweight battle won by Turpin. This was to be the dominant pattern of Ferns' career. He always moved in the best of British heavyweight company but always in a minor supporting role.

By the 12 May 1953 Jack Solomons had "promoted" him to bottom of a bill that was topped by Don Cockell and Johnny Williams, the former relieving the latter of his heavyweight crown. On this occasion Ferns was scheduled to fight Ron Harman of Brighton.

1953 had in fact been a good year for the lanky redhead from Greenock. He travelled to Belfast to stop both Vic Diamond and Bob Watson inside the distance. He then returned to Scotland to defeat Frank Walshaw. If these boxers were hardly household names liable to crop up in pub conversations on boxing, no such reservation applied to his next opponent, coloured heavyweight Joe Bygraves who would be destined to stop Henry Cooper in 1957.

Bygraves' class told in this particular contest. Undeterred, Ferns bounced back by scoring a cut eye stoppage over old foe Jack Hobbs. This victory won him a place on the bill in the exalted company of British champions Johnny Williams and Ronnie Clayton.

His opponent, Ron Harman, was used to moving in more illustrious company than the Greenock man. He belonged to the stable of John Simpson, manager of former British heavyweight champions Jack Gardner and Don Cockell and he often sparred with these two more illustrious lights. This was to have some bearing on the result of his scrap with Ferns for he was adjudged winner on points.

Ferns returned to the Greenock shipyards but was happy to answer Solomons' call to appear at London's White City on 1 June 1954 for another big heavyweight occasion. This was an eliminating contest for the heavyweight championship of the world between Don Cockell and Harry "Kid" Mathews of Seattle, USA, a contest which won the winner, Cockell, the dubious pleasure of sharing a ring with Rocky Marciano in 1955. For Ferns, however, overcoming Ron Harman over six rounds was quite enough to contend with.

This occasion is also of some interest in that it featured two Scots – Edward Keith, an Edinburgh machine router, and Johnny Veitch, a 6 feet 4 inches engineer, in Jack Solomons' £500 heavyweight competition. Once again heavyweight glory for Scotland was to prove as elusive as a European Cup tie at Stair Park.

Ferns lost on points to Harman. Veitch and Keith both kayoed their first round opponents but Keith in turn was kayoed inside a round by none other than Joe Erskine, the eventual winner of the competition and the man who bothered Henry Cooper so much. In the other semi-final Veitch lost on points to an RAF policeman called Denny Ball of Bedford.

Fern's career petered out gradually and Scots fight fans had to dream anew of heavyweight glory in what they hoped would be the not too distant future. Hopes were raised again from 1957 onwards with the emergence of Chic Calderwood.

Calderwood was beyond dispute one of the finest world-class lightheavyweights ever produced in Britain. The Lanarkshire fighter posted impressive victories over future American world champion Willie Pastrano and world-rated Sonny Ray. He was British and Empire champion at a time when there was plenty of class opposition in Britain at this weight.

However, the bigger money has always been found in boxing's ultimate category so Calderwood was keen to find out if his future lay there rather than in the lighter leagues. His first venture into heavyweight boxing was against Jim Cooper, twin brother of Henry, in 1961. It was not a terribly inspiring performance. Dropped to the canvas in the third round before a national TV audience the Craigneuk "Cruiser" rose to scramble what many thought was a most fortunate draw.

In February 1965 he had another attempt at the big-time heavyweight scene in Wolverhampton when his chosen foe was the American Freddie Mack. Mack was based in Rome, Italy, despite being a stablemate of ex-British heavies king Brian London. He had victories over Italian heavyweight champion Sante Amonti and had also sparred with leading British big men such as Billy Walker and Johnny Prescott.

Despite dropping the Scotsman for six in the second round with a left hook and smashing over a right which sliced Calderwood's left eye the Scots boxer outjabbed and outpointed the American for the next five rounds. But a lightheavyweight fighting a natural heavyweight such as Mack is always handicapped by the relative strength differences in weight of punch and so it was to prove in this case. In round eight Mack dropped Calderwood with a cracking right to the head, forcing him to take a count of six. On regaining his feet the American promptly applied the finisher, not dreaming for one moment that he was also effectively writing the final chapter (for the present at least) on Scottish boxers with heavyweight aspirations.

The story of Scottish heavyweight boxing is hardly an inspiring one, yet in a sense it is a microcosm of all Scottish history. Scots seem to take as perverse a pride in defeat as in victory – Flodden, Culloden, the Darien Scheme are as widely remembered as Bannockburn and Jim Baxter sitting on the ball at Wembley in 1967.

Nevertheless, four rounds of glory in Denver a hundred years ago seems a poor harvest for all the hopes and efforts expended. But just as lack of concrete results has never deterred monster seekers in Loch Ness, so many Scots boxing fans will continue to dream . . . and dream . . . and dream.

Scotland's First Post-War World Title Fight

Scotland's first post-war world championship fight was the contest between Jackie Paterson of Glasgow and Joe Curran of Liverpool for the world's flyweight title. The venue on 10 July 1946 was Hampden Park Stadium in Glasgow. Also at stake were Paterson's British and Empire flyweight titles.

The show was promoted by George P. Grant who has sound claims to being dubbed Scotland's most colourful boxing promoter ever.

George Grant was born in Dundee in 1906 and started selling newspapers at the tender age of five. He continued this vocation until he was fourteen years old and obviously learned much about the value of publicity from it.

His "pitch" in Dundee High Street was by common consent the best in the city and it enabled him to boast throughout his life that he had outsold all other Dundee newsvendors. No mean achievement in those pre-television days.

Hand in glove with an enthusiasm for newspaper selling went an even greater passion for boxing. Yet George Grant's entry into boxing promotion was just as unorthodox as the man himself.

He was spectating at a Dundee soccer match when he found his attention increasingly wandering from the game to a heated argument nearby. An argument between the partisans of two local boxers disputing their respective merits.

Here George Grant revealed the first flash of that opportunism that all boxing promoters must have if they are to succeed. He convinced the owner of a local Dundee stadium to lease it to him and then he matched the two local fistcrivens!

The name of the stadium was "Premierland" and it was to become George P. Grant's base of operations.

However that was yet in the future as George Grant put on his first show. The two local rivals were so keen to do battle they gave their services free.

The result was a whopping profit for young Mr Grant and the beginning of a passion to put Dundee on the same footing as a boxing centre as Glasgow and Edinburgh.

Yet Grant was to discover to his cost that boxing promoters do not live by opportunism and good matchmaking alone.

In 1935 he booked Dundee's prestigious Caird Hall. Topping the bill were coloured Leith heavyweight Manuel Abrew against Ernie Simmons. Also featured was future Scottish champion Jake Kilrain who outpointed Panther Purchase of South Africa. The show succeeded as a boxing spectacle but flopped financially. Undeterred, the doughty Dundonian hired the Caird Hall again in 1936 and promoted Liverpool's Ernie Roderick versus Lefty Flynn.

The Liverpudlian was no doubt delighted by the points decision he obtained as were the two thousand spectators who had witnessed a rousing battle over 15 rounds. Less delighted was George Grant. He had taken another financial bath.

There is something strangely ironic about his next move.

Most would-be promoters having experienced two financial flops in a city's premier indoor venue would have regarded an open air stadium in Dundee – a city never renowned for tropical weather – as the last thing to answer their prayers.

Yet it is his purchase of the open air "Premierland" stadium that proved to be the boxing salvation of George P. Grant!

Capacity crowds of 1,700 turned up to his weekly shows where ringside seats could be had for two shillings. The cheapest seats cost one shilling and no fighter received more than six pounds as a purse. Freddie Tennant a future Scottish flyweight champion learned his trade there as did Jim Brady and scores of lesser fighters.

Not only fortune smiled on George Grant. Good weather was a regular attender at his shows. Yet the evening he finally covered "Premierland" with a circus big top it rained in torrents! This good fortune earned him the nickname "Lucky" Grant.

This then was the man who must have regarded with great pleasure the sun-kissed slopes of Hampden that bright Wednesday of 10 July 1946. (Just how "lucky" Grant was can be testified to by all those who like myself have abiding memories of the persistent downpour that accompanied Glasgow's last outdoor world title fight between Jim Watt and Howard Davis on 7 June 1980.)

Even in negotiating Paterson v. Curran for the world title did George Grant's legendary luck hold. In order to clinch the fight for Glasgow he was forced to make a hectic car journey from Dundee. A journey that resulted in the Dundonian catching Paterson's manager Pat Collins only one hour before he was due to leave for Liverpool to sign for the contest to be staged there.

And what of the defending world champion, Jackie Paterson?

Paterson, a dynamic punching southpaw, was born in 1920 at Springside, Ayrshire. In 1928 he emigrated with his parents to Scranton, Pennsylvania in the United States.

Eventually the teenage Paterson returned to Glasgow where he teamed up with manager Pat Collins.

Considering that many top class pro's in those days never came within sweating distance of any kind of title often after years of battling, Paterson's progress was phenomenal to say the least.

Within a year of his pro' debut he had blasted the Scottish flyweight title from Dundee's Freddie Tennant by eleventh round stoppage. This took place on 31 May 1939.

Four months later the British title was dashed from the eager grasp of Manchester's Paddy Ryan on a 13th round count in Glasgow.

Another six months elapsed then Paterson took the Empire flyweight title from Kid Tanner of British Guyana by a points decision in Manchester.

However, Paterson's finest hour was yet to come – a sensational KO in 61 seconds of Peter Kane. This for the vacant World's flyweight title on 19 June 1943 at Hampden Park, Glasgow.

Kane, the Eddie Cantor clone with the trip hammer punch had given Paterson's boyhood idol Benny Lynch a stern argument before succumbing at Shawfield Stadium back in 1937.

Since that sensational victory in June 1943 Paterson had annexed the European bantamweight title from France's Theo Medina by eighth round disqualification in London in March 1946. He had also outpointed Dundee's Jim Brady for the latter's British and Empire bantamweight laurels.

It is another of the great ironies of George P. Grant's paradox-filled promotional career that he should pay his largest ever purse of £4,500 to Paterson for boxing that July evening. Paterson who had been the scourge of Dundee's fistic stars!

The Glasgow southpaw and Liverpool's Joe Curran were old foes with little love lost between them. They had fought on three previous occasions with Curran leading two to one in the series.

A fourth round disqualification of Paterson in their first contest still rankled with the Scotsman and it was this alleged "needle" and Paterson's reported weight problems that were the main pre-fight talking points.

At the age of 32 Joe Curran was six years Paterson's senior and a veteran of 200 fights. His record going into the Hampden ring was 160 wins, 32 defeats and eight draws.

In their most recent fights Paterson had beaten Jimmy Webster and lost to Rinty Monaghan.

Curran had lost to Webster and beaten Monaghan!

Yet sad to relate any "needle" that did exist between the old rivals seemed to inoculate them against doing each other any further great violence!

In contrast to the blistering excitement of the Peter Kane contest the fifty thousand spectators were "treated" to a fifteen round yawn as the Glaswegian easily outpointed Curran.

By common agreement the best bout of the evening was the bottom of the bill scrap between Clydebank flyweight "Skeets" Gallacher and Glasgow's Frank Tierney.

Gallacher was making his pro' debut and he only out-pointed the Glasgow man by the narrowest of margins. No mean achievement this when you consider that Tierney would go on to outpoint top of the bill Joe Curran.

Also featured that evening at Hampden were Gus Foran of Liverpool who forced late substitute Billy Comeford to retire in the fifth round. Ginger Stewart the Scottish welterweight champion outpointed Kid Marcel of France over ten rounds. To complete the action fans witnessed flyweight Alex Murphy of Port Glasgow against Raoul Degryse of Belgium.

George P. Grant could not be blamed for the poor quality of the fare served up by the top liners.

Besides he had gained adequate compensation for any disappointment suffered in the form of a 50,000 crowd and the usual good weather.

He never did fulfil his promise, made in the official fight programme to "bring the best boxing talent in the world to the city" (Glasgow) – despite an emphatic closing declaration that "plans are already afoot to achieve this object".

The rise of Jack Solomons in the south and Sammy Docherty and Tommy Gilmour Sr. in Scotland saw to that.

But George "Lucky" Grant could add another distinction to his claim that he was the first Dundonian to learn of the 1918 armistice. He was the first and last native of Dundee to promote a world title fight.

The Tayside city has yet to produce anyone to equal his boxing promotion exploits.

Exploits that reached their peak that warm Wednesday in Glasgow in July 1946.

Grant's Promotions
Stop Press News
THANKS

Mr George Grant wishes to thank the magistrates, the Police, the Queen's Park Football Club, the B.B.B. of C. officials, the Press, the Advertisers, and by no means least, the boxing enthusiasts who form the audience, and all who have contributed to the success of this, his first world-championship fight in Glasgow.

In return Mr Grant promises in future shows to bring the best boxing talent in the world to the city.

Plans are already afoot to achieve this object.

The Boxing Booths Remembered, by ARTHUR "TINY" CLEPHANE

Arthur "Tiny" Clephane was born on 28 February 1915 in Kirkcaldy, Fife of mixed racial parentage. Including booth contests he fought something in the region of 370 bouts. The only physical legacy of this extended catalogue of combat is a broken nose and a slightly cauliflowered left ear.

There is certainly no apparent mental legacy, for when I interviewed this sprightly 72-year-old in his Kirkcaldy home in October 1987 he impressed me by his prowess of recall and his shrewd judgement. Having met many former pro' fighters I was not in the least surprised by this. The following interview is the result of one of the most enjoyable evenings I have ever spent in the company of another.

B.D.: "Clephane" is a rather unusual name. Where did your father come from?

T.C.: My grandfather was a Frenchman from Boulogne, France. He emigrated to Kirkcaldy when my Dad was seven years old.

B.D.: And what about your mother?

T.C.: She was a coloured South African. When the Boer War broke out my Dad joined the Royal Scots Fusiliers. He rose to become a regimental Sergeant Major. He met and married my Mum at Bloemfontein, South Africa.

B.D.: Was he a boxer?

T.C.: No, there was no history of boxing in my family – although I think I inherited my father's guts.

B.D.: In what way?

T.C.: When he was 80 years old he was awarded the Carnegie Trust's Life-saving Certificate for diving into Kirkcaldy Harbour and saving a man's life. My Dad couldn't swim but he managed to get the boy who was drowning out of the water!

B.D.: It was also surely brave of him – a white man – to marry across the colour bar at the turn of this century?

T.C.: Aye! I know all about that. That's what made me take to boxing.

B.D.: What do you mean? Prejudice?

T.C.: Aye! You see I was a timid child until I was 12 years old. The other Scots kids used to tease me about my colour, call me "Zulu", "Darkie", even sometimes "You black bastard". I used to run away when they did things like that.

B.D.: What happened when you were 12?

T.C.: Two guys called Frank O'Neill and Alex Penman introduced me to boxing. They ran the East Bank Boxing Club in the Boreland district of Kirkcaldy.

Alex Penman had seen me one Saturday night in the boxing booth fighting.

B.D.: You fought in the boxing booth aged 12?

T.C.: Well, yes and no! What I mean is that when I was 12 we were so hard up that I used to take part in "Battle Royals" for half-a-crown on a Saturday night in Jim Patterson's boxing booth on Kirkcaldy promenade.

B.D.: Were they American style "Battle Royals"?

T.C.: Aye! Same idea – six laddies and myself would be blindfolded and have one boxing glove tied on. We then battled it out and whoever was left standing won the half-crown. I won most times – gave my mother two bob and kept a "tanner" for myself.

B.D.: And Alex Penman liked what he saw?

T.C.: Yes. You must remember I was always very tall for my age. Alex and Frank O'Neill taught me to box with the classic straight left style. I wasn't built to brawl and I rarely did try it.

B.D.: Did you stay with them until you turned pro'?

T.C.: No! I won my first amateur contest in East Wemyss in 1927, had a few more bouts then decided to travel to Leith.

B.D.: But that's 30 miles away. Why did you want to go there?

T.C.: I liked Frank and Alex but Leith Victoria Boxing Club was the best in Scotland. "Tancy" Lee was the coach and trainer. So I travelled through three nights a week.

B.D.: What did you think of the great "Tancy" Lee?

T.C.: "Tancy" was a great wee teacher. He was a great help the night I beat Police Constable Davidson, the amateur heavyweight champion of Europe.

B.D.: But you were only 10 stones!

T.C.: Aye! And he was 18 stones – but we fought in a Scotland v. England Amateur International.

B.D.: And where was this?

T.C.: The show was held in Neaton Baths in Nottingham. I boxed his head off and was leading by a mile when with less than ten seconds to go he finally caught me with a big right hand – I was spark out for three quarters of an hour but I still won on points.

B.D.: How come?

T.C.: The final bell went before I could be counted out, so I was the last person to find out I had won – what with being unconscious for 45 minutes after the decision was given!

B.D.: Did you win any other amateur titles?

T.C.: I was Scottish Eastern District welterweight runner-up twice, and I won but didnae win the Scottish middleweight title against Tommy Smith of Clackmannan.

B.D.: You mean the decision went against you?

T.C.: No! I beat Smith fair and square by decision in the Music Hall, Edinburgh, for the title. So I got up to be presented with the "Hickey Shield" for best stylist. I'm standing there, you understand, with the shield in my hand – it

A typical boxing booth, and the fighter third from the right is former world flyweight champion Benny Lynch, trying to battle his way back to fitness. "Tiny" Clephane is behind the man with the mike.

had just been presented to me – when two SABA officials, a Mr Brown and a Mr Proctor, whisked it out of my hand.

B.D.: Why?

T.C.: Some rat had "shopped" me – you see I had been fighting on the side in Tommy Woods' booth in Perth.

B.D.: So you were unofficially a pro' fighter?

T.C.: I suppose so. When I won the Hickey Shield I had already made my debut in the booths in 1931 against Jim "Young" Todd – he was a good boxer but I outpointed him.

B.D.: So the amateur officials learned of this?

T.C.: That's right! But I had also been fighting for two rival booths in Kirkcaldy – sometimes on the same night.

B.D.: Same night! How did you manage that?!

T.C.: Well, John and James Stewart's booth was at one end of the promenade and Patterson's at the other. I had a bicycle. I would fight in one then cycle along and box in the other one.

B.D.: So someone must have seen you and reported it?

T.C.: Aye, but it didn't matter. I went with Tommy Woods' booth in Perth for four months in the year.

B.D.: Did you fight any well known fighters in this period?

T.C.: Indeed! I outpointed Jackie McLeod, the Scottish middleweight champion from Leith.

B.D.: What was it like in Tommy Woods' booth?

T.C.: Great! I only worked four months in the summer, touring Scotland – a great training! We were paid £4 a week plus our grub and sleeping quarters. We were a four man team. We were also paid a bonus for KOs.

B.D.: How did that operate?

T.C.: We got £2 if we put our opponent away in first round, £1 if he lasted until the second – and if he lasted three rounds we were paid nothing!

B.D.: Who was your toughest opponent in the booths?

T.C.: As a general rule I used to hate when the booth went to the Town Moor in Newcastle. Those "geordies" were tough nuts to fight, I can tell you! But my toughest opponent in the booths was Jim Oliphant from Forfar. He was incredible! Tattooed from head to toe – even his privates were tattooed! I used to outbox him silly but I couldn't put him down. What a hard man!

B.D.: Was he the hardest puncher you ever encountered?

T.C.: No way! The hardest puncher I ever met in a ring was Jock McAvoy, "The Rochdale Thunderbolt". *(Jock McAvoy was British Empire and European middleweight champion between 1936 and 1939; one of the most durable and hardest punching fighters in British fight history.)*

B.D.: Did you fight him?

T.C.: No. I was his sparring partner in 1938 when I was working in Manchester.

B.D.: But let's return to the booths. Was there anyone you didn't like to fight when you were taking on all comers?

T.C.: I would never fight a drunk man – you could have killed them. Remember the ring in the booth was basically only a wooden platform covered in oilcloth. A drunk hitting that head first could have created big problems.

B.D.: What did you consider the toughest arena – the booths or legitimate professional boxing matches?

T.C.: Without a doubt the booths. Remember you had to KO your opponent. Again many of your opponents in a "gee" fight *(a fixed fight)* would be hitting with the open glove. This was notorious for causing cuts – that's why it's illegal today. Another thing was in the "legit" game you could always get some "gen" on your opponent from newspapers or other fighters and trainers. In the booths you didnae ken who you were facing up to.

B.D.: Can you give me an example?

T.C.: Aye. It didnae affect me directly but back in 1927 – I was a 12 year-old laddie at the time – I saw an obvious toff in the crowd, beautifully dressed, talked and looked like a college boy, take up Jim Patterson's challenge. The toff picked

Jim Cowie of Dundee – a brilliant fighter. The crowd thought the toff was crazy and poured in to see him get "leathered."

B.D.: Did he?

T.C.: No, he knocked Jim Cowie spark out – peach of a right hand!

B.D.: Who was this toff?

T.C.: The Marquis of Clydesdale. He became the Duke of Hamilton. He was a good boxer! (*This was the same Duke of Hamilton that Rudolph Hess would fly to see in 1941.*)

B.D.: Did you know that he was a former Scottish middleweight champion at amateur level by 1927?

T.C.: No! I'm not surprised. Jim Cowie was a good wee pro' but that toff was good too. But then you see what I mean about the uncertainty of who you could be facing?

B.D.: Yes, but who introduced you to the legitimate pro' game?

T.C.: A great wee guy from Dundee called Freddie Tennant. (*Freddie Tennant, conqueror of Benny Lynch and Scottish flyweight champion 1937-1939.*) He lost his Scottish title to Jackie Paterson in 1939.

B.D.: Where did you meet Freddie?

T.C.: Up at Brechin in 1936 – in Tommy Woods' booth. Freddie was my best mate, along with a lovely wee boxer from Lochore – a bantam called Johnny Kelly. You see Freddie was a great pal of George Grant who was "Mr Boxing" up in Dundee. Grant had his own stadium called "Premierland". Well, my first "legit" pro' fight was for him against a real tough guy called Davie Ross of Methil. Ross was a blacksmith. Jim Brady who became British and Empire bantam king was on the same bill.

B.D.: Did you win?

T.C.: Aye, but Ross was a toughie – yet he was a slugger and I like them the best. I outjabbed him – won on points.

B.D.: Did you forsake the booths then?

T.C.: No way! I was just getting started! In 1938 Jim Patterson had moved down to Ayr for the races. He gave me a call to join him there. I was working in the pits as a shaft sinker for 30 bob a week, so I got a week's doctor's line off the pit and went down to Patterson's booth in Ayr.

B.D.: Was it worth it financially?

T.C.: I'll say it was! But anyway I arrived at Ayr and immediately I bumped into a Glasgow fighter I knew called "Ricki" Fulton. I liked "Ricki" and I knew his style so I coaxed him to join me in the booth. But to cap it all I was approached by one of the raceowners who was attending the races.

B.D.: Why?

T.C.: He knew Jim and I would be topping the bill at Patterson's three nights that week, so he made a "deal" with us.

B.D.: What kind of "deal"?

T.C.: He gave us "inside" information on three racehorses we could bet on –

if we would tell him in advance the "result" of our "grudge" match on the Saturday night.

B.D.: So that's why you fought three times in the week?

T.C.: Aye. Jim would "win" the first fight, I would "win" the second fight and the third "grudge" or "decider" fight would be held on the Saturday. Mind you, it worked – there were eleven hundred people in that booth tent on the night.

B.D.: How much did you make?

T.C.: Including betting money – nobbins – and boxing money, £130 for the whole week. Much better than 30 bob for sinking pit shafts! (*A tradesman's wage in 1938 was £3.50 per week in Scotland.*)

B.D.: So what happened after you broke up in Ayr?

T.C.: I didnae fancy going back to the pits, so I struck out for Manchester.

B.D.: Why there?

T.C.: I heard they wanted workers in the A.V. Roe Aircraft Factory.

B.D.: Did you box in Manchester?

T.C.: Of course! I got in league with two Manchester bookmakers – Albert and Gus Demmy. They helped me to get an eight round fight against Terry Knowles. They also introduced me to a Jewish businessman called Mr Kaiser. He was boxing daft – he used to pay me £5 just to spar with him. I always took it easy with him.

B.D.: Did the Demmys help you in any other way?

T.C.: Yes. They fixed me up as a sparring partner to a big Canadian heavyweight called Al Delaney.

B.D.: He fought Freddie Mills?

T.C.: Yes, that's the same fellow. Well, this day his manager Jack Hulls tells me to get into the ring. A party of celebrities has arrived to see Big Al show what he can do. It's obvious to me I am supposed to make Delaney look good – but I had different plans. I was a lot faster and trickier than he was. Like a lot of heavy guys he was a bit ponderous to a much lighter fighter like me.

B.D.: Who were the celebrities?

T.C.: Oh! Jimmy Wilde, "The Welsh Wizard" – he was a journalist by this time. And another famous journalist who died in the Manchester United disaster in 1958 – Henry Rose. And there was a famous fighter called "Tiny" Bostick there too. So anyway, the bell went and I ran, ducked, slipped – Big Al couldn't lay a glove on me. So the upshot is I am fired as his sparring partner. In fact he had to be restrained in the end – I'd made a fool of him I suppose.

B.D.: So what happened then?

T.C.: I became a sparring partner for Jock McAvoy. Oh how that boy could punch – I earned every penny with him! But I must tell you how I nearly fought the former world champion, Jackie Brown.

B.D.: The guy whom Benny Lynch took the title from in 1935?

T.C.: One and the same. You see I was working out in front of a mirror when this pugnacious wee customer who I had never seen in my life before tells me to get the **** out of it. I tell him to **** off and he then demands, "Don't you know who I am?" I didn't and told him I didn't have a clue. I think he thought I was being sarcastic – so he charges at me. But a couple of guys in the gym who had been watching us broke it up. Mind you he was a game little so-and-so!

B.D.: So what else did you do in Manchester?

T.C.: My performance against Delancy didn't go unreported so I was asked by Ernie Roderick to spar with him. Jock McAvoy had also recommended me. Roderick went on to fight "Homicide Hank" – Henry Armstrong – for the world crown in 1939.

B.D.: What did you think of Roderick?

T.C.: He was a lovely boxer but not the hardest of punchers.

B.D.: Did you have any booth fights in Manchester?

T.C.: Yes. I was introduced to the great coloured fighter Len Johnson. (*Len Johnson was universally acknowledged as one of the finest fighters of the 1930s. Immensely intelligent and dignified he was nonetheless the victim of the ridiculous colour bar that operated in British boxing until 1948 when Dick Turpin won the British middleweight title.*) Len was a legendary figure – he was as crafty as they come. He made another fighter in his booth and me dress in old clothes from a rag store and grow three days' beard stubble on our faces.

B.D.: Why?

T.C.: Well, he knew the British crowds were suckers for the underdog. We used to pose as *bona fide* unemployed guys. It worked every time – the house would be packed to see if the gallant "unemployed" could beat the professionals. If only they had known. You see when we "miraculously" put on a good show the crowd would throw in more "nobbins" to help the "unemployed" – it never failed.

B.D.: What do you recall about Len Johnson?

T.C.: Len was a beautiful dresser – he usually wore lovely white suits. He also looked after his boxers better than any other booth owners. I had the best of food when I was with Len Johnson. He was one of the best was Len.

B.D.: Then where did you go from there?

T.C.: Oh, the war started in 1939 and I became a soldier in the military intelligence section of the Scots Guards. I became a corporal and picked up speaking Italian from interrogating Italian prisoners in Egypt. I also fought in Italy at the Battle of Monte Cassino.

B.D.: Did you resume boxing after demob in 1945?

T.C.: Aye! I went back to Tommy Woods' booth in 1946. I was one of the last ones to see Benny Lynch alive.

B.D.: Where and when was that?

T.C.: Shortly before his death Benny turned up at Tommy Woods' booth which was on the road between Brechin and Elgin. We were heading for Fort William and Buckie. You know it wasn't the booze that killed him at the end.

B.D.: What makes you say that?

T.C.: It was T.B.. I lay in the same caravan as he for four nights. He was coughing blood into a rolled up pillow case – it was terrible! Especially when you could remember him from the old days.

B.D.: Did he fight then?

T.C.: No. Tommy Woods tried to look after him but he just drifted away.

B.D.: So contrary to the old myth there WERE people in boxing who DID care about him at the end?

T.C.: Aye! I know Tommy Woods wanted to anyway. But what could you do? The wee man had a streak of stubborn pride in him.

B.D.: Do you have any amusing memories of the booths?

T.C.: Oh loads! But two stand out. The first concerned a fight I had with a real hard nut from Perthshire called Dave McLaren. It was in Tommy Woods' booth and it was supposed to be a "gee" fight – you know, not on the level. I had laid bets on myself and McLaren's supporters had been tipped that I was going to "lose" so they bet a bundle at long odds on him.

B.D.: And you rewrote the script?

T.C.: Aye! Well, we had been going at it hammer and tongs when I pulled down McLaren's trunks to his knees. He instinctively put his hands over his privates so I chinned him. He went spark out. McLaren's boys were furious. So I saw the score – they were ready to lynch me. So I jumped right out the ring, sprinted through the crowd and on to my bike – my clothes and my winnings came later thanks to Tommy Woods!

B.D.: You mentioned another incident that amuses you?

T.C.: That was the time when I was boxing at Wishaw in Lanarkshire. The booth owner knew I had picked up the Italian "lingo" during the war – so he tells me to pose as an Italian who just happens to be in the crowd. He figures a lot of folk in Wishaw will pay well to see a cocky foreigner take a hammering. I was with a great old Glasgow fighter called Chick Harkins – he came from the Tollcross area of the town. The game was I had to speak pigeon Italian – you know, "I knocka da block off all youa Scotteesh" kind of thing! – to get the crowd's back up and make them want to come into the tent. Anyway these two girls in the crowd obviously fancied me – I suppose with my dark skin I looked Italian and they were fooled by my "accent". At the end of the scrap and after I am cleaned up one of the girls approached me unawares and overheard me speaking normally, so she says, "Ah thought so, ya chancer! – you sure learned English quickly!"

B.D.: Did you fight any name fighters in this period after the war?

T.C.: Yes. In 1948 I fought Willie Whyte – he was to become Scottish welterweight champion. He was a lovely boxer – fast and with a good left hand. I also fought Bert Gilroy in a "gee" fight on the booths – he fought the British heavyweight champion Bruce Woodcock.

B.D.: When was that?

T.C.: In 1949. Harry Hughes, the Scottish champion – he fought Billy Thomson (*Billy Thomson of Hickleton Main, Yorkshire was British lightweight champion 1947 – 1951, European lightweight champion 1948 – 49. He stopped Scotland's Harry Hughes by KO in round five,*) at Celtic's football ground for the British title the same year – well, Harry Hughes was fighting up at Elgin City FC's football ground and I was offered a "gee" with Gilroy. He was a lightheavyweight – a tough customer too. But the year before that I was down in Southall, Middlesex working.

B.D.: In a booth?

T.C.: Not originally. I went to work as a bath enameller in the British Bath Works at Greenford in Middlesex and I was tipped off that there was a booth owned by Billy Smart – the famous circus man. It was situated in Southall and it featured two of the most famous brothers in British boxing history.

B.D.: Not the Coopers – Jim and Henry?

T.C.: No! This was before their time. It was Alex and Laurie Buxton – Alex was British cruiserweight champion. (*Alex Buxton of Watford was an outstanding performer between 1942 and 1963. He fought 125 times, winning the British lightheavyweight title by a tenth-round KO over Dennis Powell in 1953. He also lost to Randy Turpin twice.*) They were both a pair of "cards". I used to go down and make £3 for four rounds on a Saturday night. But sometimes with the Buxtons being big names locally I could make £10 plus nobbins – aye, happy days indeed!

B.D.: What was your biggest disappointment in boxing?

T.C.: Oh, that would have to be when the big Dundee promoter Mont Leslie reneged on a deal with me.

B.D.: What was the story there?

T.C.: In 1952 I was beginning to want to settle down – I felt I was becoming too old to travel in the booths. So Mont Leslie – he was making a big name for himself as a promoter in Dundee – he approached me and offered to bankroll me if I lent my name to a booth to be erected on Kirkcaldy Promenade. It was to be called "Tiny's Booth". It was actually a big wooden hangar that the RAF had used for storage during the war, but I did it all up and installed 500 seats. I was licensed by the British Board of Boxing Control. I planned to offer four fights for five bob on Saturday nights – there weren't many television sets then.

B.D.: So how did Mont Leslie let you down?

T.C.: Personally, I think he took cold feet about the whole idea. There I was on the opening night – the crowds queueing up, a real gala night in prospect – and then the police come down and tell me I don't have an entertainment licence or a fire clearance certificate.

B.D.: This was Leslie pulling the plug on you?

T.C.: I have no direct proof but he didn't seem sorry either.

B.D.: Any other disappointments?

T.C.: Aye. One of the greatest was the night that Len Harvey (*Len Harvey was a winner of British championships at middle, lightweight and heavyweight. The term "legendary" is an understatement in connection with this great Cornishman,*) stopped my cousin Manuel Abrew of Leith in 1937. I was there and I felt terrible. Strangely enough, Manuel now loathes boxing and is a Buddhist – a total pacifist in fact. He now lives in London. (*Manuel Abrew was born in Leith. He was a coloured lightheavyweight and heavyweight who always flattered to deceive in the ring. He was immensely popular even if he was never quite in the top class of fistic ability.*)

B.D.: Which modern fighters, particularly Scottish fighters, do you admire? Watt? Buchanan?

T.C.: They were both very good but the one I used to admire was young Vernon Sollas of Edinburgh – he won the British featherweight title from Jimmy Revie of London. But it was a pity about his stamina problem at the end. I mean he was doing well against these two guys who beat him at the latter end – what were their names?

B.D.: Les Pickett and Dave Needham.

T.C.: Then he just seemed to collapse. What a brilliant wee boxer – he could jab and move well. Still, that's life.

B.D.: So looking back you have no real regrets about your boxing career?

T.C.: Absolutely none. I would do it all over again – without a doubt!

B.D.: "Tiny" Clephane, thank you.

The Day the Brown Bomber Landed in Glasgow

On the evening of 9 July 1944 a queue of 500 people – many of them women and girls – stood eagerly outside number 560 Sauchiehall Street. There was a buzz of excitement in the air. Excitement that rose in anticipation everytime a car or jeep approached this building in Glasgow's most celebrated thoroughfare.

Under normal circumstances a queue in wartime Glasgow in this the fifth year of war was so common as to be unremarkable. The city's housewives would often stand outside shops for hours at the mere rumour of there being a couple of green tomatoes for sale. However this group were desperately hoping to catch a glance of another valuable "commodity" whose appearance in Scotland was just as severely rationed as any fruit.

Number 560 Sauchiehall Street was the site of the American Red Cross Services Club which was about to become the temporary home for Staff-Sergeant Joseph Louis Barrow. Sergeant Barrow was better known as Joe Louis – "The Brown Bomber" – undisputed heavyweight champion of the world. The famous negro boxer was about to land in Glasgow with a troupe of fighters headed by George Nicholson, his chief sparring partner.

Louis was already a legend by 1944, having defended his heavyweight title no less than 22 times since knocking out James J. Braddock for the latter's crown in 1937.

When America joined the Allied cause in 1941 Joe Louis had not hesitated to enlist in the Army. Prior to his enlistment in 1942 he had donated the purses from his last two title defences to Army and Navy Charities.

Louis was a quiet man who had none of the verbal flamboyance later associated with Muhammad Ali. This led many people to conclude wrongly that he was a typical dumb prizefighter, a view he quickly dispelled when interviewed on arrival in Scotland by the press. He confessed to the assembled journalists that one of the major attractions of Scotland for him was its place as the ancient home of his beloved game of golf. He also expressed sincere regrets that he would be unable to visit the golfing mecca of St Andrews. It is typical of the naturally modest negro fighter that he didn't mention that but for a pledge to visit American war wounded in three Scottish Military Hospitals during his brief stay he may well have been able to include the Fife golf town in his itinerary.

Nevertheless, he did keep his appointment at another St Andrews – the popular Glasgow Halls by that name adjacent to the Mitchell Library. Much to the delight of the thousand service men and women who packed the venue Louis demonstrated his legendry boxing skills there. On two consecutive evenings the Brown Bomber amply showed his fistic prowess in three-round exhibitions with George Nicholson, who had helped him prepare for so many world title fights.

The organisers of the show did everything possible to make the visiting champion feel like the VIP that he was. The "Brown Bomber" was introduced into the ring by Scotland's own world champion, flyweight Jackie Paterson. Also in attendance was Paterson's manager, Pat Collins. On his way into the ring Louis was "squired" by former European flyweight champion and *Daily Record* boxing writer Elky Clark. As a special bonus Sir Harry Lauder stood in the centre of the ring to greet the American champion and welcome him to Scotland. Scotland's premier comedian was introduced by an American officer who expressed the hope that Joe would show "as much business acumen as Sir Harry Lauder". Sir Harry advised the great coloured fighter to "take care of the pennies when you are young and they will take care of you when you are old".

Little could the assembled crowd realise how tragically ironic the Scots comic's words were to become. Just six years later Joe Louis was forced out of retirement into an ill-advised comeback.

By 1950 all the "Brown Bomber" had to show for the five million dollars he had earned from a record 25 world title defences was a tax bill from the US Government for an estimated one and a quarter million dollars!

Many of the Champ's financial woes can be traced to the very game that had made him so keen to come to Scotland – golf. After leaving the US Army in 1945 the popular heavyweight king lost thousands of dollars in golf matches where he backed himself against American pro' golfers – dollars he could ill afford, given his mounting unpaid tax bills. Little credit attaches to those golfing sharks who exploited Louis' weakness in this way.

However, all that was still in the future for the fabulous "Brown Bomber" whose mere presence in the ring enthralled the capacity crowds who turned up on those two July evenings 40-odd years ago.

Less enthralled perhaps were the gallant band who had queued in vain outside the American Services Club in Sauchiehall Street on the evening of 9 July. They never did see the "Brown Bomber". On arriving in Scotland earlier that day he had made straight for Douglas Park Golf Course for a round of golf. As a result his arrival at number 560 Sauchiehall Street was delayed until the wee small hours of the morning of 10 July.

Perhaps Joe Louis had decided to compensate himself for the disappointment of learning that the St Andrew's Halls were not in fact next door to the legendary Old Course but 80 miles west in the heart of Glasgow.

That is speculation. What is certain in the years that followed his visit is that many Glaswegians could tell their children and their grandchildren of the time they actually saw one of America's boxing all-time greats in the flesh.

GEORGE SMITH – the First Scotsman to Referee a World Heavyweight Title Fight

In January 1969 the British Embassy in Madrid was bombarded by angry telephone calls from irate Spaniards. The cause was not Britain's continuing sovereignty over Gibraltar – always a sensitive issue – but the conduct of a certain local government employee from Edinburgh.

The Edinburgh man in question was Scottish "star" class boxing referee George Smith but his conduct was perfectly legal, and not in any way related to the Rock of Gibraltar issue. George recalled his "misconduct" with a wry smile when I spoke to him in his Edinburgh home.

The furore arose after he had refereed the world featherweight title fight between Australia's Johnny Famechon and the flashy Cuban, Jose Legra, in London's Albert Hall. Legra, who was Spanish by adoption, lost on points to the Australian.

George explained: "Legra tried to win each round by producing flashy punches in the closing minutes of each stage. He forgot Famechon had been doing the bulk of the punching throughout the greater part of each round. So there could be only one victor – Famechon". George continued: "Even Legra's Spanish manager told me the decision I gave was just".

This did not stop the Spanish Boxing Federation from trying to ban Mr Smith – a move totally rejected by the BBBC.

Now living peacefully in the north side of Edinburgh, far away from the glare of publicity and controversy, George Smith can look back on an amateur boxing career that was no less interesting than his time as one of Britain's top professional "third men" in the ring. It was an amateur career that gained him a place in the *Guinness Book of Records*.

He explains: "I fought in the only amateur boxing bout in Britain where two different decisions were rendered for the same contest". This was for the Scottish amateur bantamweight championship against Mick Hanlon of the Dalmarnock ABC (Glasgow). The fight took place in the East Claremont Drill Hall, Edinburgh, 1928.

At the end of three rounds George Smith was declared the winner. But after returning to the dressing-room he was yanked from under the shower and told the contest was actually over four rounds – so he had to return to the ring and fight again. The result was a decision for the Glaswegian!

Despite the obvious disappointment of this setback George has few regrets. A year later he was on an all-expenses-paid boxing tour of Norway. Not many working-class laddies from Leith were able to do this in 1929. He won a three-bout series in Oslo and still has the medal which marks this achievement.

In all George boxed for Scotland four times and held Scottish championships at flyweight and bantamweight. Pleasure at these achievements was tempered by the disappointment of losing out on a place in Scotland's 1930 Empire Games boxing team to Tommy Holt of Glasgow. After a keen fight the Edinburgh man was closely outpointed by his west of Scotland rival.

However, his greatest amateur rival was the Dundonian Mickey Whyte of Camperdown ABC: "Mickey and I were deadly rivals inside the ropes". They had a three-bout series – all won by George Smith.

He particularly recalls their contest at St Andrew's University gym on 26 November 1929: "That scrap sums up all our three contests – I couldn't afford to relax for a second with Mickey. He was so game. He kept pressing – pressuring me all the time – but I was always a wee bit better than him. Strangely enough the bitterness of our rivalry brought out the best in both of us."

On retiring from active boxing in 1931 George became a SABA judge and referee until 1939 and the outbreak of war. World War Two saw him join other boxing celebrities such as Len Harvey and Freddie Mills in the Royal Air Force.

Corporal Smith soon found himself in Palestine in charge of a touring RAF boxing team which was not above recruiting American Army personnel. One such American was the Puerto Rican Danny Carabella who was a former protégé of world lightweight champion Lou Ambers – the same Lou Ambers who defeated Henry Armstrong, "Homicide Hank".

George recounts: "We were the guest of the 'Maccabi' and 'Hapoel' clubs and we were royally entertained at the Central Hotel, Tel-Aviv. Whilst there I was constantly being pestered by a swarthy little Yank who was totally unimpressed by my arguments that an RAF boxing team was for United Kingdom citizens enlisted in the Royal Air Force not GI truck drivers! Still, I liked him and let him join the team."

The wisdom of this decision can be gauged from the fact that Danny Carabella received a "Best Boxer Trophy" from Field Marshal Montgomery himself a few years later. The little Puerto Rican went on to fight as a professional on the Marcel Cerdan v. Dick Turpin bill at Earls Court, London, in March 1949.

The return of peace saw George Smith eventually embark on a career as a professional boxing referee in March 1950. When he received his "star" class rating in December 1964 the way was paved for him to become the first Scotsman to referee a world heavyweight title fight. This was the famous bout at the Arsenal Stadium on 21 May 1966 between Muhammad Ali and Henry Cooper.

The thing that George recalls most about this famous fight which ended in the sixth round with Cooper's eye a gory mess, was the power of Ali's left jab: "When I stopped the fight some people booed because they thought Cooper must have been butted, but this was not so. Ali's jab did all the damage – one of the best I have ever seen".

Suprisingly, the Edinburgh man does not think that the Cooper v. Ali fight was the most memorable contest he refereed. That prize goes to the 1967 Albert Hall war between two imported American heavyweights – Thad Spencer and Leotis Martin.

"This fight had the lot," he remembers. "Ferocious punching, toe-to-toe slugging, smart moves and one of the hardest punches I have ever seen thrown." George explains: "Spencer threw a terrific hook which caught Leotis Martin on top of the head as he was ducking. The result was an ugly gash on top of Martin's head. Normally such an injury is the result of a butt – but not this time. Martin's manager who had been partially unsighted when the punch was thrown went crazy when I stopped the fight". Martin, to his credit, told his manager that it was in fact a punch not a butt that caused the damage and that resolved the situation.

George Smith most amusing recollection concerns Brian London, the colourful Blackpool battler. He had just left the ring after giving a draw between Brian London and an American named Henry Clark and was making his way to the dressing-room. On hearing the steady patter of smooth-soled boxing boots behind him he turned to see Brian London, still in full ring gear, pounding towards him. Behind London was another shadowy but large and vaguely familiar figure. The Blackpool boxer was very polite and asked what he had done wrong to only merit a draw.

By the time George Smith had explained his reasons for his decision the shadowy figure had materialised into a Kirkcaldy man who had been the heavyweight star of the RAF boxing team in Palestine – whom George had not seen since the war years. Once London departed the ex-RAF scrapper explained that he had seen Brian London sprinting from the ring after George and he had feared the worst! He had elected himself his old RAF buddy's "minder" in case of trouble!

Other foreign boxers who impressed George Smith were the Basque rock-throwing champion Jose Urtain and the Italian Nino Benevenuti who was two-time world middleweight champion. He first saw Urtain when he refereed the European heavyweight title fight between the Spaniard and Jurgen Blin of Germany. He felt Urtain was game and strong but was tailor-made for Henry Cooper and told promoter Mike Barret so on his return from Spain. The result was Señor Urtain was enticed to Britain where he was kayoed by our 'Enery in nine rounds.

He was also immensely impressed by the Italian Nino Benevenuti, whom he refereed against a German fighter for the European title. "Absolute class," is George's verdict. "No wonder he won two world titles."

George Smith's refereeing career encompassed fights such as Ken Buchanan v. Jim Watt ("Buchanan was definitely the better boxer of the two"); Walter McGowan v. Jackie Brown; Chic Calderwood v. John "Cowboy" McCormack – a veritable *Who's Who* of Scottish boxing greats.

Yet his own place in the boxing history books is no less secure than that of some of his illustrious charges – thanks to his undisputed distinction of being the first Scotsman to referee a world heavyweight title fight.

PETER KEENAN – Combat, Compassion and Commerce

Peter Keenan's fight career and my childhood coalesced like sparring partners doing roadwork. I have a keen recollection of his triumphs and setbacks, especially as he was Scotland's only national boxing champion at one period in the 1950s. This fact made his face as familiar a feature of the boxing pages in the newspapers as the face of a portly Londoner called Jack Solomons.

Two incidents best sum up Keenan's character. The first took place long after Peter Keenan had forsaken boxing gloves for the equally tough world of business.

It was a somewhat drab October Sunday in Glasgow. The year was 1980. I had assembled with other BBBC licence holders in an equally drab gym at Ingram Street for the annual general meeting of the Scottish Area Council.

Only the environment of this draughty fistic academy lacked colour. There was nothing monochromatic about some of the personalities present. Personalities such as wee Jim Maharg, the former 1930s Scottish flyweight champion who had actually EMPLOYED Benny Lynch as a sparring partner and whose losing decision to Walter Lemmon sparked off the kind of riot usually reserved for the Celtic v. Rangers games of the period. Jim Maharg is a man of great natural charm and dignity. A present-day ring whip who is universally admired amongst the Scottish boxing fraternity.

During the order of business the secretary of the area council pointed out – as he was entitled to do – that Mr Maharg's licence fee appeared to be still due for payment. There was a disgusted snort behind me. My eyes focused on an immaculately dressed figure whose wavy dark hair was flecked with grey. To Peter Keenan it appeared that some public affront to Jim Maharg's dignity had taken place.

After some verbal sparring he propelled himself forward towards the chairman's table almost as quickly as one of his left hooks that nearly 30 years previously had made British champion Danny O'Sullivan kiss the earth more times than a Papal prelate on a world tour. Only on this occasion Scotland's former bantam champ was brandishing in his fist nothing more lethal than a £20 note – a sum more than sufficient to restore the imagined compromise to Mr Maharg's dignity. The second incident had taken place eight months before in Glasgow's Locarno Ballroom. The air outside in Sauchiehall Street was positively balmy for late January.

This evening any rawness was confined to the ring in the middle of the ballroom floor, a ring where the sweating and struggling journeymen fighters created the suspicion that distinction was as much in evidence in the audience as in the roped square.

Eventually an interval was declared and Peter Baines, that most amiable of Sassenachs who has "M-Ceed" more Scottish boxing shows than even he cares to remember, announced that a businessman in the crowd would pay a £50 bounty to the boxer he judged to be the best winner of the evening.

Almost instantly Peter Keenan's head appeared through the bottom strand of the ring ropes. He beckoned furiously to Peter Baines. A brief animated conversation ensued, then walking to the middle of the ring the MC announced: "Mr Peter Keenan wishes to declare that he will award ONE HUNDRED POUNDS to the best LOSER!"

This was typical Peter Keenan. A man for the underdog. A man of compassion. A man with heart. In and out of the ring.

Although billed as an Anderston fighter, Peter Keenan was in fact born in Scotstoun but his earliest boxing connections were established and developed in Anderston – as was his early career – so it's fair to say he was an Anderstonian by adoption.

Modern-day Anderston is chiefly noted for being the site of the Kingston Bridge – the longest urban bridge in the world when it opened in 1970 – and the publishing complex which houses the *Daily Record* and the *Sunday Mail.* Much of the old Anderston in which Peter Keenan learned the basics of boxing has been erased in an orgy of civic destruction that might have invoked envious admiration in Goëring and his Luftwaffe cronies. This took place in the 1970s.

Peter Keenan's Anderston – that which existed when he was a freshman fighter – was essentially a creature of Glasgow's industrial revolution when industrial expansion played piggy-back on the shoulders of dispossessed Irishmen, of whom young Keenan's great-grandfather from Dungannon was one.

Yet if Anderston was famed for its industry it was never the clichéd industrial slum so beloved of those whose perceptions of Glasgow owe more to impressionism than fact. Side by side with dingy tenements were erected buildings of real architectural distinction, buildings such as the splendid red sandstone Anderston Savings Bank building or the Clyde Port Authority's HQ at 16 Robertson Street.

However, dingy tenements WERE also part of the area's landscape. Peopled by many who were the disinherited. People like young Keenan who were the descendants of those who had suffered from legitimised acts of mass violence which left not only a feeling of residual bitterness but a lingering feeling extending over generations that such violence used to achieve ends should not be the sole privilege of the ruling classes.

This was the underlying ethos of many of the citizens of Scotstoun and Anderston where young Keenan grew up and learned to defend himself against the violent sub-culture that flourished on the streets. Amongst those who subscribed to this violent ethos pacifism was the ultimate heresy. In Anderston such "heretics" who optimistically considered a shrug or a frantic refusal as being potent antidotes to the boot, bottle or fist soon learned the grievous error of their ways.

Add to this fact that the young Mr Keenan was of short stature – he was by the onset of maturity less than five-and-a-half feet tall – and one can clearly conclude

British
SOUVENIR PROGRAMME
BANTAM WEIGHT
Championship
FIRHILL PARK
MAY 9TH, AT 7.30
PETER KEENAN
DANNY O'SULLIVAN
A SAM DOCHERTY PROMOTION

that the battle lines were drawn early for this young man whose upturned nose and dark good looks gave an almost elfin-like air.

Almost as dangerous as some of the people populating Anderston was a myth that diminutive stature made those afflicted by it open cities ripe for annexation by bigger and more powerfully built conquerors. This myth has never been supported by the facts of Scottish boxing history. In contrast, short stature coupled with natural aggression which was honed and refined by the limitless arenas provided by a particular environment have always been the raw materials from which Scottish fistic greatness has been distilled.

This was true in Anderston in the 1930s where a young man called Jackie Paterson embarked on a fistic career which culminated in his blasting the world flyweight crown from the bemused head of Lancashire's Peter Kane inside a minute. Paterson was the adolescent Keenan's hero. He would devote hours to watching the world-class southpaw work out in the Anderston gym which had helped establish the legitimacy of the latter's claim to the flyweight throne.

Soon young Peter Keenan would embark on his own quest for the celebrity and wealth it had so visibly brought to his hero.

Yet there was another strand in the Keenan character that was just as firmly rooted in the working-class Glasgow of his youth – compassion. Combat and compassion walked hand in hand in a manner of which the youthful Winston Churchill, who gloried in war and vigorously campaigned for old age pensions, would have approved. You might smite your foe hip and thigh but due care had to be given to his wife and weans. The old and the unemployed and bereaved were also aided as often as severely restricted purses would permit.

Add to combat and caring another "C" which complemented them and you have the essential trinity of qualities forming the Keenan character – commerce. In the early days many compared Keenan to Benny Lynch – in boxing terms only was any measure of comparison valid. In terms of business acumen it was no contest. Peter Keenan holds the distinction of actually taking over a promoter financially whilst topping the bill against the coloured South African Jake Tuli.

Again, if recent years have been financially hard for the former bantam champion Peter Keenan was much too shrewd to be exploited ruthlessly as Lynch was by his handlers. Shrewdness in and out of the ring has been as much a hallmark of this battling Scot as the impeccable cut of his suits.

Again, if Anderston provided Keenan with a glimpse of what fistic success could bring it also provided a sharp reminder of what failure could mean. This salutary lesson came in the shape of Scotland's first ever British bantam champion Jim Higgins, winner of a Lonsdale belt in a record 11 months. Higgins was reduced after the glory days were over to eking out his time in Anderston's two model lodging houses in Hydepark Street and the "Popular" Hotel. The little Lanarkshire man would be found dead in an alley off Argyle Street, one of the district's main thoroughfares. He was apparently unmourned. To die friendless in a city like Glasgow is one of life's ultimate obscenities.

Fortunately, the only common ground that Higgins and his younger successor were to have is that they both appeared and fought in the Scottish National Olympic Club in Bridgeton's Olympia Street.

1948 was the year that Keenan entered the pro' ranks as a flyweight. He started in typical no-nonsense fashion by despatching his first foe into dreamland inside the first round; this was in Glasgow on 17 September. Another six victories in places as different as Liverpool, Falkirk, Paisley and Glasgow saw out the year. Three of these victories were by the KO route – ample testimony to the Keenan punching power.

However, an increase in class and experience can frustrate even the most potent puncher and so it proved in his first contest of 1949 – against Jackie Fairclough.

Fairclough was a youthful bantam from Preston, Lancashire, who despite being a brilliant boxer was known to lack a big punch. (In July 1951 Fairclough's lack of clout would lead to his being flattened inside four rounds by Keenan's European arch-rival Luis Romero. Keenan was a spectator at ringside.) Yet despite home-town advantage Keenan could not transform his own talent in this department to conclusive effect. Fairclough lasted the full eight rounds.

No such courtesy was extended to his next two opponents, both of whom were rescued by the referee from the Anderston boy's murderous punching.

Vic Herman was to provide a novel experience. A novel experience at several levels. The word "unorthodox" could easily have been the personal code name of this Jewish fighter from Glasgow. How else can one describe a graduate of the "Jewish Lads' Pipe Band" who played himself into the ring and who has spent his latter days as a personal portrait painter of the rich in the English Home Counties?

In February 1949 however, there was nothing vicarious about Herman's skill in arranging human features to his own satisfaction. Fighting for a side stake of £100 he swept into the attack from rounds one through three. In the fifth round a right hand punch staggered "Wee Peter" and brought a flurry of blows which propelled Keenan head first out of the ring. Amid a chorus of "Hosannas" from the Herman faction the Anderston fighter scrambled back into the ring and only just avoided being counted out.

At this point it is cogent to consider what was to become a recurring feature of the Keenan fighting style. Joe Louis was known by his ominous shuffle; Benny Leonard by his habit of hitching his trunks between blows – trademarks which distinguished each fighter as clearly as his fingerprints. Peter Keenan's trademark appeared to come straight out of Greek mythology.

The ancient Greeks loved to recount the tale of Antaeus – the mythical youth who could perform great feats – but only when he made body contact with the ground. Throughout his career Peter Keenan gave a more than passable imitation of this Greek legend. Three visits to the canvas in the first round against Jake Tuli provoked massive retaliation culminating in a 14th round KO of the South African fighter. Against Luis Romero a similar pattern brought similar results.

So it was with Vic Herman. Frantic efforts by the Jewish boy to end matters were nullified by Keenan's superior boxing skill and this latter-day Antaeus ran out a points winner.

Further victories in 1949 against "name" fighters such as Jackie Briers and Raoul Degryse in Glasgow further boosted the fistic stock of the Glasgow flyweight who was rapidly growing into a bantam.

Another notable victory during that year was achieved at the expense of Emile Famechon even though the manner in which it was achieved – a seventh-round disqualification – could hardly have inspired much satisfaction in the wee Glasgow fighter. Yet his opponent at Paisley was nonetheless Famechon – a member of the fabulous French fistic dynasty which produced Ray and Johnny Famechon, European and world champions respectively at featherweight.

The Anderston Antaeus' progress owed as much to his shrewd handling outside the ropes as his equally shrewd performance within them. Many of the smart moves in this department came from a man for whom the epithet "legendary" is so feeble a tribute that it borders on an insult.

This man was Tommy Gilmour, "The Starmaker" – Bridgeton's one-man Barnum and Bailey, a shrewd and able manipulator of fighters who dominated the 1950s and 1960s in a way that Nat Dresner has ruled supreme in the 1920s. (Interestingly enough, "Tam" Gilmour's father, Jim Gilmour, had been employed by Dresner as a fighter.) Universally known as "Tam" Gilmour there can be little doubt that this greatly respected figure did the early Keenan's career a great deal of good, even though the battling bantam quarrelled with Gilmour and tried to remove him as his manager.

Gilmour told anyone who would listen that in watching the Anderston boy they were witnessing a future world bantamweight champion. The Bridgeton man cannot be blamed for the fact that a quite exceptional South African would eventually frustrate his oft-repeated prophesy in this respect.

Smartness in and out of the hempen square has always been a winning combination and so it was to prove for the Gilmour/Keenan axis. The year 1950 opened with Keenan flattening Dickie O'Sullivan inside three rounds at Paisley. Interviewed by distinguished boxing writer Ron Olver in 1982, O'Sullivan claimed, "It was a disaster – I didn't have a sleeper for the long trip (*from London to Paisley*) and had virtually no rest". From the Anderston man's point of view, however, what mattered most was that he had achieved a victory over a man who had been rated the third best bantam in the world in 1947 – proof indeed that Keenan was on his way.

His next two contests were against Europeans whose pores oozed class and sweat in equal proportion. Jean Sneyers and Maurice Sanderyon were both outpointed. The victory over Sneyers was particularly important in that it marked the Glasgow man's debut in London. This gave Keenan a golden opportunity to fire a second warning shot across the bows of the reigning British bantam champion Danny O'Sullivan, having beaten the latter's younger brother so comprehensively four months before in Paisley.

Less than a month later saw the Anderston man climb through the ropes in Firhill Park, home of Patrick Thistle FC, to fight a rubber match against the little Jewish piper Vic Herman who was clearly determined to play *The Flowers o' the*

Sam Docherty presents
BANTAM WEIGHT CHAMPIONSHIP OF Gt. BRITAIN
OFFICIAL SOUVENIR PROGRAMME
DUNDEE
GLASGOW
Boland
Keenan
PRICE
1/-
AT FIRHILL PARK, JUNE 27th, 1951

Forest over Keenan's progress.

Yet the fight was memorable for other reasons. It marked the Scottish comeback of Edinburgh referee Mr Eugene Henderson who had left the game in disgust after having his decision to stop the Mills v. Lesnevich battle in 1946 questioned by BBBC members. In his book *Box On* Mr Henderson recalled: "The contest was a hard one and difficult to handle". But Keenan won on points sufficiently to provoke this tribute from the Edinburgh third man: "He was a smooth operator, a boxer with class, and whose whole approach to the game had a flourish of the master craftsman . . .".

The Anderston man would need every one of these qualities, for his next two fights were British bantamweight title fight eliminators. Both were held in Paisley, a town whose natives are collectively known as "Buddies", but there was to be nothing convivial about the Keenan scraps with Irishman "Bunty" Doran or Mancunian Tommy Proffit.

Doran was his first adversary. The date was 6 July 1950. Modern readers who think "Bunty" is a surprisingly effeminate title for a ring gladiator should not be deceived. There were many amongst his opponents who must have devoutly wished the diminutive Irish scrapper HAD been more limp-wristed during the bouts.

With so much at stake Keenan could expect no favours from his Ulster rival. Nor did he receive any. Doran's style was so whirlwind that a spectator might have been forgiven for thinking that he had inherited his genes from Sikorski (the inventor of the helicopter). It was a style that in the space of three months brought Doran victory over Jackie Paterson, when the latter was still world kingpin, and European champion Theo Medina.

Add to this potent cocktail the fact that both fighters were bracketed together in the British ratings at number three and four respectively and the scene was set for a good hard scrap.

Keenan used all his coolness and boxing skill to deal with the furious charges of the Irishman. In round one there was a moment of premature ecstasy in the Keenan camp when Doran slipped to the canvas – but the referee indicated that it was not a proper knockdown.

Thus the pattern was set – Doran attacking, Keenan astutely defending, slipping by the merest but most effective of margins blows from all angles, countering effectively himself to such an extent that when the final bell clanged the Anderston warrior was adjudged the winner.

The stage was set for the second leg of this British bantamweight eliminator – against Tommy Proffit of Manchester.

Two things probably sicken Mancunian Tommy Proffit even today: journalistic puns on his name – particularly in connection with the word "loss"; and the memory of his defeat against Peter Keenan on 15 November 1950.

Proffit came to Paisley with a good pedigree, having been ABA champion in 1948 and representing Great Britain in the London Olympic Games in the same year. As a pro', by the time he met Keenan he had notched up victories against top-class Scottish opposition in Bobby Boland and Eddie Carson. Other notable victories had been achieved against top flight Canadians Fernando Gagnon and Charlie Savard. The latter victory had earned Proffit a much coveted *Boxing News* Certificate of Merit. Often described as an "all-action fighter with a punch", that label fitted better his Anderston opponent on this occasion. Proffit was blasted out inside two rounds, thus paving the way for Keenan to administer a double dosage of mayhem to the unlucky O'Sullivan clan.

A tough eight rounds points win again in Paisley over Frenchman Louis Skena concluded 1950.

If 1951 was to become a glorious year for Wee Peter there was little indication of it in his first fight on 14 February.

St Valentine's Day 1951 is remembered in world boxing history as the day that Sugar Ray Robinson laid the foundation stone of a legend by winning the world middleweight title from Jake La Motta of the Bronx. The only connection between the ring in Paisley where Keenan outpointed Spain's Jose Rubio by a wide points margin and the Bronx district in New York lay in the type of cheers that greeted the Scots bantam's victory. *Boxing News* of 21 February 1951 opined, "Keenan unimpressive".

Rubio was another windmill type fighter. Keenan was content to accept many of the Spaniard's blows on his arms and shoulders. In subsequent rounds he may have induced a feeling of homesickness in the little Spaniard by spearing him continually with a left jab in a manner reminiscent of the bull ring. This was followed by heavy body punching that forced Rubio to retreat. When the Spaniard did manage to attack, his punches were woefully mistimed. The remainder of the fight followed this pattern, so with Keenan obviously in command the contest lacked that measure of perilous uncertainty that makes an ordinary contest into a great one.

However, by March some of the old venom had returned and Armand Delanna was stopped inside six rounds at Earl's Court.

Negotiations were now in train for the much coveted title fight with British champion Danny O'Sullivan but first a "warm-up fight", with Italian Amleto Falcinelli at Paisley, was arranged. Peter Keenan recalls: "Falcinelli was tough and amazingly awkward. He was one of the few guys who had beaten Mario D'Agata. It was a tough scrap." (Mario D'Agata was an Italian deaf mute who become European and world bantamweight champion in the late 1950s.) But it made Keenan hard honed and hell bent on destruction for his British title battle with Danny O'Sullivan.

The fight with O'Sullivan took place on 9 May 1951 in Firhill Stadium, Glasgow. It was promoted by Samuel Docherty, a bookmaker, who is remembered with affection by most of the boxers he employed in his capacity as a boxing promoter – a phenomenon rare enough to make him something special. Bobby Boland of Dundee recalls, "Sammy was the fighter's friend".

Falcinelli's showing against Keenan had earned him a recommendation from his erstwhile foe which resulted in his being given second billing against Scottish bantamweight Eddie Carson – another example of the legendary Keenan generosity.

But what of Keenan's opponent – the man from whom he hoped to wrest the British bantam crown? A Londoner from Finsbury Park despite the Irish name, Danny was part of the then famed Benny Huntman stable. In the official programme boxing writer Joe Bromley stated of the Londoner's scrap with Italian Alvaro Nuvoloni: "He (O'Sullivan) is not just a one style battler. He has such an extensive repertoire of punches . . . and so active an intelligence that he is able to expose his opponent's weaknesses in quick time and then fight according to his discoveries". This had been true in O'Sullivan's dealings with Keenan's hero Jackie Paterson. Despite being knocked out by the former world champ from Anderston in October 1948 O'Sullivan had studied the latter's style sufficiently to box his ears off in their February 1949 return.

Certainly O'Sullivan did not lack courage under fire. No better proof of this can be evidenced than by his bout with Stan Rowan in a British title eliminator in May 1948. O'Sullivan had ordered a new pair of boxing boots for this contest. They failed to materialise in time for the fight. The result was that he had to wear a pair belonging to his younger brother, Dickie. These were so ill-fitting that half way through the fight he was forced to take them off and fight barefooted – despite his feet being a mass of blisters. Anyone who has ever traded leather in a ring will readily testify that the assault on one's pain threshold from an opponent is usually more than enough to contend with. To have added to that pain from any other quarter would normally be unbearable – a fact attested to by the ringside doctor who commented, "It was an amazing performance," after seeing O'Sullivan's damaged extremities.

O'Sullivan was to show the same qualities of courage when Peter Keenan sent him sensationally crashing to the boards, not once but six times during the six rounds their contest lasted.

I asked Peter Keenan if he was surprised by the ease with which he despatched O'Sullivan. He replied, "No! I was trained to the minute – and supremely confident. I could have taken anybody that night."

This same confidence was in evidence immediately after the fight. The then Secretary of the British Board of Boxing Control, Mr Teddy Waltham, came to the newly crowned bantam king's dressing-room to take away the Lonsdale belt its new owner had just been presented with in the ring for inscription. Waltham told Keenan that the coveted belt would be returned to him as soon as the engraver had finished his task. Keenan replied, "Why not hold on to it until I have won it outright?"

He was to need all of this confidence in his next fight just seven weeks later. This was his first title defence, against Bobby Boland of Dundee.

As Spain in 1936 – 1939 and the USA between 1861 – 1865 prove, the most vicious wars are civil wars. So it was to prove in this scrap between Clydesider and Taysider. The bloodletting at Firhill park was of such epic proportions that the ring was like the vomitorium at a vampires' convention. Indeed it covered both fighters and the referee to such an extent that it might even have induced an acute attack of dyspepsia in Count Dracula. Bobby Boland recalls: "The blood flowed from a nasty cut on top of my head and from two cuts in Peter's eyes."

The champion forced the Dundonian to retire finally in round 12 – but he required 20 stitches to heal his wounded orbs. These injuries also provided the Anderston man with a prolonged rest during which negotiations with the European champion, Luis Romero – by Samuel Docherty – continued apace.

Luis Perez Romero was born in Spanish Morocco and lived most of his life in Barcelona – both places were greatly different from Anderston where Keenan had developed as a pugilist. Yet both of these very different men had one common thread in their characters apart from prowess within the roped square – a head for business. Romero had shares in the Barcelona Bull Ring and was the owner of a flourishing printing business.

In one major respect he was very different from his Scottish adversary – he was a southpaw, a type of fighter so detested by the Scots boxer that he once declared: "All southpaws should be drowned at birth!" Stockily built, with powerful shoulders, the little Spaniard had been a pro' fighter since 1939. He had over a 100 contests under his belt when he faced Keenan in September 1951 in the ring at Firhill.

Romero had defeated Bobby Boland of Dundee. The Dundee fighter told me: "Being hit by that wee Spaniard made me feel as though I was breaking the sound barrier going backwards." He had also beaten other excellent class fighters such as the Southampton fisherman Ron Draper and Manchester's Ray Fitton.

The Spaniard did not have it all his own way however with Scottish champion Eddie Carson when the two clashed on 23 May 1950 at Earl's Court, London. Many thought the Scot should have had at least a draw but the referee gave the Spaniard the nod. More importantly from Keenan's point of view, the *Boxing News* reporter gave firm pointers as to how the Spaniard might be beaten: "Romero is open to criticism," he wrote, then continued: "He has been so used to slugging his opponents out with that long, looping left hand that he could not vary his approach . . . he rarely used his right with which he normally attempts to cuff his opponents on to a body punch . . .".

Against Keenan a southpaw without a decent right jab was like someone trying to bash a piranha fish with a bluebell. And so it proved before 30,000 wildly cheering Scots fans.

This was Keenan *par excellence*. The *Boxing News* reporter present at ringside informed his readers: "Fighting a cool, calculated battle, Keenan by sheer artistry, had his aggressive opponent baffled, irritated and in the closing rounds desperate in his efforts to land a decisive punch".

For the first ten rounds the Spaniard ate Keenan's jabs like an anorexic on a binge. His frustration showed in a warning he received for kidney punching in the fourth round.

Still Keenan refused to mix it until he had sufficiently softened up his Hispanic foe. From the tenth round onwards the Scotsman outboxed and outpunched his foe. He was positively stingy about consuming his opponent's blows whilst freely providing a glut of his own. There were few dissenters when the Belgian referee declared Peter Keenan the new bantam monarch of Europe.

Now the world title – a crown held by the great Vic Toweel of South Africa – beckoned.

In the meantime, to keep himself up to scratch, on Hallowe'en 1951 he met Maurice Sanderyon in Paisley. But again Keenan's performance owed more to Greek rather than Christian mythology. Antaeus-like, he visited the canvas three times, then came storming back to snatch a draw. Some said he was fortunate to do so. But in any event the stage was now set for the long haul to South Africa to meet world champion Toweel.

Vic Toweel was one of the fighting Toweels, a dynasty whose roots lay in the Lebanon but who were now firmly ensconced as South Africa's leading pugilistic family. Vic had become South Africa's first champ at any weight when he had relieved the Mexican-American Manuel Ortiz of his crown. This was a considerable achievement given that Ortiz had had the crown for nearly six years – apart from a brief period in 1947 when he had "loaned" it for six months to Harold Dade. The little South African was also his country's featherweight champion, one of four crowns he held simultaneously.

Peter Keenan told me, "The altitude beat me – it was so high above sea level."

Toweel had home town advantage when he entered the ring in Johannesburg's Rand Stadium. Keenan, on the other hand, had fought ten times more than his rival. He had also spent eight weeks in South Africa trying to familiarise himself with the very different conditions he would encounter there.

Before 26,000 fans there was the now customary brief Keenan trip to the canvas – in round one for a count of two. The result of this contact with the "soil" was equally familiar. Thus galvanised, Keenan fought back furiously. But Toweel became impressively stronger – like some carnivore who is rejuvenated by the sweat of his prey. However attempts to KO his Scottish foe came to naught as the Anderston man's cool boxing behind his left jab kept him out of further difficulty. Toweel was adjudged winner on points.

Some years in our lives reek with the poisonous smell of personal disaster, leaving a taste of bitterness that frustrates the puny efforts of time to suppress it. Such was 1952, in Peter Keenan's life.

Four months after his unsuccessful African safari he was back again in the familiar territory of a Glasgow ring. Even his opponent's face was familiar – the Frenchman Jean Sneyers whom he had outpointed three years before in London. But there were to be no happy returns in this anniversary. An injured knee forced the Scotsman to retire in round five.

This injury sidelined Keenan for five months. Misfortune seemed to have found a convivial resting place in the Anderston scrapper, for old foe Amleto Falcinelli forced a stoppage by cut eye over his Scottish adversary in Paisley on 15 October of the same year.

The stewards of the BBBC then told Keenan that he would not be permitted to fight again until he had accommodated an English usurper to his British bantam throne – the scouse warrior Frankie Williams from Birkenhead. The fight was fixed for the coronation year of 1953 and the Englishman clearly hoped that he would have something else in common with the soon-to-be crowned Queen Elizabeth other than shared nationality. Such thoughts, though, were treasonable to bantam monarch Keenan who just as clearly sought to put this usurper firmly in his place.

Usurpers to a throne are by nature impatient men but on this score nobody could have blamed the Birkenhead man for being positively frantic about his desire to wrest the crown from Keenan. His title joust had been postponed more times than Danny La Rue's nuptial plans.

What kind of pedigree did this "scouse" bring to bear on his Glasgow rival?

By January 1953 Williams had beaten Hogan "Kid" Bassey, the same Bassey who would become the first Nigerian to win a world boxing title in 1957.

Much was at stake for both men. For Peter Keenan victory would mean the Lonsdale belt would become his own property AND he would be given a match with Maurice Sanderyon to try to regain the European title he had so unluckily surrendered to Jean Sneyers.

Williams was of the Romero mould – a known puncher. This plus Peter Keenan's recent spate of misfortune caused *Boxing News* to speculate that Old Father Time was corroding the Glasgow man's ability "Age May Decide Bantam Championship".

Well, it did. Only Keenan's vastly superior experience proved to be a potent antidote to the rusts of time and it was Williams who was rescued, semi-conscious, by the referee.

Six months later the extended loan of the European crown was terminated by a 15 round points victory over Sanderyon at Paisley in June 1953. There was nothing ambiguous about the Keenan performance on this occasion.

However a new threat to both his titles was looming across the Irish sea. John Kelly of Belfast was another who had beaten future world champion Hogan "Kid" Bassey – as well as common Keenan opponents "Bunty" Doran, Tommy Proffit and Jackie Fairclough, all by stoppage. So he obviously commanded respect when he and his Glasgow rival climbed between the ropes to do battle.

Peter Keenan recalls, "It was one of the few times in my life when you could actually sense the feelings of fear in my supporters at ringside. They were very quiet. The whole scene was scary." He was referring to the sectarianism which informed the partisanship of the Belfast crowd. Kelly was a Protestant in an environment where such a label has implications that the normal 20th century secular man in the street finds hard to fathom.

At any rate Kelly was adjudged the winner after 15 rounds, causing Keenan to clamour for a return.

This wish was to be granted nearly a year later. In the meantime an attempt was made in February 1954 to modify the new-found feeling of nakedness induced by his lack of a title when Peter Keenan signed to fight Eddie "Napoleon" Carson for the latter's Scottish bantamweight crown.

Carson was a former choirboy domiciled in Edinburgh. His "Napoleon" tag came from the fact that he had the same stocky build and hair style (almost bald) of the French Emperor. He had also inherited much of the martial prowess of his more famous namesake. Indeed the famed French general might well have envied Carson's ability to handle the Spaniards in a punch-up – a lack of ability that cost the real Napoleon dear. Luis Romero had experienced fits when fighting this most awkward of southpaws. But then he was a southpaw too. In a ring two southpaws fighting tend to have the conviction and entertainment value of a eunuch lecturing on the finer points of procreation, yet Carson's showing against Romero won universal respect from those who witnessed it.

Peter Keenan's verdict on his 12 round points victory was quite pointed: "Carson was the toughest guy I ever fought. . . tougher than Toweel. . . tougher than Kelly. . . tougher than any of them. He was brutal in the clinches. What a tough, awkward customer. . .".

The Anderston man's compliment merely underscores the quality of his victory.

Return fights in boxing tend to follow one of two main courses. They either exceed the original in thrills and fervour – like the second Leonard v. Duran fight – or they stink out the stadium because familiarity induces not contempt but profound feelings of pacifism in the combatants. The second Conn v. Louis bout was in this category.

So was Keenan's encore with Vic Herman on 26 May 1954 in Glasgow. *Boxing News* reported: "Peter Keenan notched his third victory over Vic Herman . . . at the Kelvin Hall, in what proved to be one of the dullest top-line fights seen in Scotland for a long time."

One can gauge the inadequacy of the fare served up by these cordon bleu fight merchants by the fact that referee Steve McCall, the former Aberdonian Scottish middleweight champion, called for more action.

It was possible that Keenan was conserving his venom for Kelly who signed to meet him in the return at Paisley on the 21 September 1954.

Any comfort Kelly may have derived from Keenan's lacklustre showing against Herman was quickly dispelled. The Irishman's confidence may well have been shattered by his being blown away seven months before inside three rounds by the French-Jewish ace Robert Cohen. In any event Keenan coasted every round except the first when the Anderston man took his usual trip to the canvas with the usual results. Keenan's vicious body punching was but a prelude to the inevitable KO punch which duly arrived in round six. Kelly never fought again as a bantamweight.

This was peak-form Keenan and it is on that high note that we leave the boxing career of the Anderston Antaeus. Further great victories there were: against Jake Tuli and Graham Van Der Walt of South Africa, retribution of a kind for the Toweel defeat; two trips to Australia brought victory over Bobby Sinn and Kevin James. But they are outwith the scope of this volume.

Nor did Peter Keenan's glory days fade after the last crumpled programme from his final contest had been swept up from the arena floor. He was to be highly successful as a boxing promoter. He brought the fabled Sugar Ray Robinson to Scotland in 1962. He also promoted stars such as Willie Pastrano, Chick Calderwood and John "Cowboy" McCormack.

The famed generosity was always in evidence, hand in hand with commercial success. When Dick McTaggart was reported to be working as a rat catcher in Glasgow in 1965 the Keenan response was as instant as it was instinctive. He offered to put up the first £1,000 of a £5,000 sum if the Scottish ABA agreed to a pro-am benefit show for Scotland's most celebrated amateur southpaw.

This was no empty publicity-seeking gesture but a genuine response from a man whose heart outside the ring matched that shown inside the ropes. It is by no means a common equation – although more common than the anti-boxing brigade might allow.

POSTSCRIPT

Jim Maharg has sadly died since this was written. He passed away in January 1988.

The Boy from Gorgie Who Biffed Ali's Brother

Monday, 8 March 1971, in Madison Square Garden, New York. The famous "Big Apple" Stadium was packed to the foyer with people. Rich and famous people. Celebrities such as Tony Bennett and Michael Parkinson. Even Burt Lancaster was in on the act, having assumed a new role as television commentator for the main event.

The main event was Muhammad Ali versus Joe Frazier for the undisputed heavyweight championship of the world. Despite being "stripped" of his title in 1967 for refusing to accept conscription into the US Army, Ali was regarded as being the "true" champion by most of the ringside celebrities and two-thirds of boxing fans throughout the world. Frazier, the new "champion", was a product of rural poverty in South Carolina and urban hardship in Philadelphia where he had been a meat porter.

Yet there was another product of an equally hard school on the bill that evening, a man whose every move in the ring was being watched intently by none other than "The Greatest" himself. For a very good reason. The object of Ali's attentions was Rahman Ali, the younger brother of the "Louisville Lip".

In contrast to his American adversary, this opponent had straw blond hair, a baby pink skin and piercing blue eyes. The blond bomber had learned the rudiments of his tough trade not in the meat halls of Philadelphia nor the police gyms of Louisville, but in the back greens of Gorgie, Edinburgh, in the early 1950s – particularly that strip of back green adjacent to his tenement home at 21 Wardlaw Place, Edinburgh.

His name was Danny McAlinden.

Despite billing himself as the "Coventry Irishman" – he was born in Northern Ireland – Danny spent the bulk of his childhood living in Wardlaw Place. I lived in neighbouring Wardlaw Street. I was six years his senior and I can remember him clearly.

As a child Danny had a positively cherubic air, due to his rosy cheeks and the blond hair he had inherited from his mother. For a child he had a remarkably deep voice, a voice that reverberated from the surrounding Gorgie tenements as he shouted to his constant companion, a huge alsatian named "Dante". When Dan wasn't wrestling with "Dante" he found himself increasingly engaged in combats of a different and more serious kind – due to a combination of his precociously stocky build and the love of a fist fight, which was as common as measles amongst the younger citizens of Gorgie.

In retrospect, the most remarkable thing about Dan's basic fighting style which was on display in Madison Square Garden was how little it had changed from his back green battling days. Danny simply waded in fists flying until his opponent, be it back green contender or experienced professional, had been beaten.

These were the methods that had captured the British heavyweight title from Jack Bodell, the Derbyshire farmer who had taken the crown from Joe Bugner. These were now the methods behind the eight-round shellacking being handed out to the younger Clay.

Yet, 20 years previously, as I hauled the young McAlinden off some unfortunate with more valour than good sense, I did not realise that I would perform a similar function many times when I became a professional boxing referee.

It would be wrong to conclude that young McAlinden was some kind of junior thug as a child. Nothing could be further from the truth. Like many who embrace the fistic trade, Dan was a good-natured individual with a hearty laugh and an impish sense of humour. But if anyone tried to pick on him or test his growing fistic reputation, then watch out!

After losing his British title to Bunny Sterling in 1972 Dan eventually made amends of a kind by winning the Irish heavyweight title in 1979.

Whilst he was no great boxing artist, he could claim that he had beaten Muhammad Ali's brother in what was virtually the latter's own backyard.

I have often wondered what he was thinking about as he looked out of his corner in the Madison Square Garden ring at the sea of famous ringside faces. The faces of Diana Ross, Mayor Lindsay of New York, Robert Redford and Frank Sinatra. One thing is certain, these world-famous stars paid a whole lot more than we did. We who had sat cross-legged almost 20 years before, watching our blond battler in the back green of 21 Wardlaw Place, Gorgie.

BOBBY NEIL
Scotland's Svengali of Sock

One of the least plausible theories as to why men take up the hardest game is the hunger theory – the idea that a socially deprived background is a must for fistic greatness. Whatever it was that impelled Muhammad Ali, "The Greatest", to enter a boxing ring it certainly wasn't hunger. Ali came from a prosperous middle-class family.

Some will point at Benny Lynch or Rocky Graziano as exemplars of the socially deprived fighters school but Fidel La Barba who held the same world flyweight crown as Lynch at one point, also came from a solid middle-class background.

Numerous studies of social deprivation have in fact shown that unemployment and hunger induce in the vast majority of human beings an apathy that would be positively dangerous inside the roped square. In his classic, *The Road to Wigan Pier,* Orwell was amazed at the overwhelming apathy and the resignation of the masses of socially deprived notherners he encountered. In this connection, whilst it is true that depression in the north-east of England coincided with the rise of such fistic terrors as Sunderland's "Cast Iron" Jack Casey, the majority of his hungry northern compatriots in Jarrow marched south with nothing more aggressive in their hands than harmonicas.

Individual skill, God and/or genetics make great fighters great – not the number of patches on their pants. So it was with the resolutely middle-class Italian Nino Benevenuti, world middleweight champion twice in the 1960s, and so it was with Scotland's Bobby Neil.

At one stage Bobby Neil was as famed for his bowler hatted "city gent" image as he was for his fistic exploits. Deprivation for this handsome Glasgow-born but Edinburgh-raised fighter was not being able to travel first-class to a chosen destination. Yet Neil had to battle injury both in and out of the ring. A motorcycle accident at the age of 18 very nearly ended his boxing career before it had begun.

In his fight on 13 April 1959 in Nottingham against Cambuslang's Charlie Hill, for the latter's British featherweight title, Neil survived cuts to both eyes – one requiring eight stitches – before halting Hill. A cut eye also cost him the decision against Aberdeen's Johnny Kidd in 1960.

Again, there were other ways in which this impeccably bourgeois scrapper from Edinburgh showed he had as much courage and fighting spirit as any ragged kid from a Mexican barrio or European slum. On 27 September 1960 Bobby Neil entered the ring in London to defend his British featherweight title against Londoner Terry Spinks. Spinks had been one of the Olympic heroes of the 1956

Melbourne Games. Then he had won Olympic gold at flyweight. In 1959, in their first meeting as professionals, Bobby Neil had KO'd Spinks and therefore must have been confident of his chances as the bell signalled the beginning of their fight in London's Royal Albert Hall.

Neil had unsuccessfully tested the water at world featherweight championship level the year before. In a non-title bout he lost inside a round to the reigning American world champ, Davey Moore. This and other factors made the Edinburgh boxer regard the second Spinks bout as his last as an active fighter. However events inside the ring made Neil's retiral an impossibility.

The second Spinks v. Neil joust was unusual in that it was for a purse of £5,000 – on a winner-take-all basis. Normally championship purses are divided on a percentage basis and this without doubt aggravated the Scottish champion's sense of injustice at what happened during the contest.

Welsh referee Ike Powell stopped the bout at the end of the seventh round because of a "cut" eye – an injury that was so small as to be invisible, as Neil made clear to ringside scribes who visited his dressing-room. Pointing to the nick, he demanded, "Do you think the fight should have been stopped for this?" To a man they agreed it should not.

Such adversity was not new to this brave fighter from Edinburgh. In September 1958, despite having a broken jaw, he had gone on to stop his Belgian opponent Aime Devisch – and this after having been injured in a car crash!

The return match with Spinks was duly held in the Empire Pool, Wembley, on Tuesday, 22 November 1960, and it was to present Bobby Neil with the biggest struggle any man can have – the battle to stay alive.

In the 14th round a superb Spinks left hook high on the temple left Bobby Neil a thoroughly beaten fighter, draped over the bottom rope of the Wembley ring. Although only half-conscious, the Scot bravely tottered to his feet before the count of ten. Spinks put Neil down for the full count with a fusilade of blows.

Allan Hubbard the then *Edinburgh Evening News* boxing correspondent was in Neil's dressing-room and graphically described the scene that followed: "I was with Neil in his dressing-room when he whispered half-dazed that he had fought his last fight. 'I just wanted to see who was really the better out of Terry and myself. Now I know. . .' Then he lapsed into unconsciousness again," Hubbard continued. "A little later Neil roused himself and asked visitors to leave his dressing-room while he dressed." He did so – and then collapsed into the arms of his father. An ambulance was called and the Scots fighter was spirited away to Wembley hospital where he was immediately operated on for a blood clot in the head.

Neil's manager Sam Burns (who would guide Terry Downes to a world middleweight title crown) was obviously relieved when he told waiting newsmen that his fighter had made a remarkable recovery. Nobody was more relieved than his opponent Terry Spinks. The little Cockney scrapper and Neil were, ironically, as good mates outside the ring as they were deadly foes inside it. Spinks was quoted as saying, "Bobby couldn't help laughing when I took off my dark glasses and showed him the black eye that he gave me in the fight". Bobby Neil told the relieved Londoner, "Don't worry Terry, it is just one of those things. . .".

Bobby Neil never fought again but in truth this near tragedy was the catalyst that made him one of the shredwest and most knowledgeable trainers and managers in British, and indeed world, boxing.

Neil had a Svengali-like effect on Alan Rudkin whom he transformed from a skilful amateur into a British and European bantam champion who so nearly won world honours. The Neil presence in Alan Minter's corner was a potent factor in the Englishman from Crawley winning the undisputed world middleweight crown from Vito Antuofermo early in 1980.

Neil's skills as a conditioner and coach of fighters were recognised by his country's amateur ruling body. The Scottish Amateur Boxing Association appointed him coach and national team supremo in the early 1980s. It was in this capacity that I first met him in the celebrity-full foyer of Dundee's Angus Hotel. His methods bore fruit that evening too: the Scots defeated the Americans.

Bobby Neil was a "former pupil" of the Sparta Amateur Boxing Club in Edinburgh's McDonald Road. This fistic academy includes among its protégés Ken Buchanan, former world lightweight champion, and Ian McLeod, who is currently fighting as a pro' in Scotland.

After recovering from the motorcycle accident that very nearly spelled an end to his boxing career Bobby Neil turned professional and in September 1956 he won the vacant Scottish featherweight title by stopping Matt Fulton of Coatbridge inside eight rounds. In December 1956 he defeated the reigning British featherweight champion Charlie Hill in a non-title bout. Hill was totally helpless after only two minutes and 45 seconds of the first round. In April 1959, in their second meeting with his title at stake Hill was floored no less than ten times as Neil took his British featherweight crown.

Six months later the bourgeois battler secured a non-title bout against the reigning world featherweight champion, the American negro Davey Moore. Moore was himself to die tragically from brain injuries received in the ring but when he met Neil he was at the peak of a career that had already established him as an all-time fistic great. Moore defeated Nigeria's first-ever world champion Hogan Bassey in 1959. He held the title for four years before his fatal clash with Cuban ace Sugar Ramos in 1963. Bobby Neil was stopped in two minutes 55 seconds by the American champion.

Now resident in London, Bobby Neil granted me an interview.

B.D.: Where were you born and raised in Edinburgh?

B.N.: I was in fact born in Ibrox, Glasgow, on 15 October 1933.

B.D.: What was your father's occupation? Was he a boxer?

B.N.: My father never boxed. He printed a tipster's racing programme.

B.D.: When and why were you introduced to boxing?

B.N.: As a kid – because I was a strong and big-shouldered boy and everybody kept saying what a good boxer I would make.

B.D.: What were your achievements as an amateur boxer?

B.N.: I won titles at Eastern District and Scottish ABA level. I also boxed for Scotland in internationals.

B.D.: What was the story behind you deciding to become a professional?

B.N.: I always intended that boxing amateur was just a step before becoming a professional. But for my motorcycle accident I would have turned professional at 18.

B.D.: You have expressed the opinion that "the deprived background" theory about making boxers climb inside the ring is basically a false one. Could you expand on this idea?

B.N.: I come from a middle-class background, attended a fee paying school and progressed to finishing my education at college in London.

B.D.: As an articulate, intelligent guy did you encounter any open hostility/cynicism to your fistic aspirations when you turned pro'?

B.N.: Never! When you take off the bowler hat and lay aside the attaché case you are just another boxer.

B.D.: Do you still feel that referee Ike Powell was out of order in the first Neil v. Spinks fight?

B.N.: Ike Powell WAS out of order. The Board knew it and ordered a rematch!

B.D.: Whose idea was it to have a £5,000 winner-take-all purse arrangement in the first fight with Terry Spinks?

B.N.: To be honest I can't remember!

B.D.: Did you have any hard feelings towards Spinks after your recovery?

B.N.: Never. Terry is a nice fellow, was a nice fellow, and always will be a nice fellow.

B.D.: Who was your toughest opponent as a pro'?

B.N.: Brown in Belfast. (*Jimmy Brown was a tall curly-haired Ulster featherweight famed for his power punching. A protégé of Belfast promoter George Connell, Brown massacred Bobby Neil in a British featherweight title eliminator inside a round when they met in 1957.*)

B.D.: You tried commendably to guarantee boxers' post-career financial security by selling insurance packages to them. Do you still do this? Did you receive a good initial response to this idea?

B.N.: It took me many months to work out an insurance type policy with retiral benefits which were good for boxers. I advertised my scheme through the trade paper, *Boxing News,* and did not get ONE enquiry. One cannot complain when people say, "Boxers are stupid!"

B.D.: Whom would you nominate as your favourite Scottish fighter of any era and why?

B.N.: Peter Keenan. He was charismatic and had for a little man "big balls".

B.D.: When you are dealing with fighters in your training/coaching capacity what basic things do you try to instil in them?

B.N.: I instil into them that boxing is a learning process that goes on throughout their career.

B.D.: Further to that, to what extent did you think you influenced Alan Minter in moving from his old "boom-boom" days to world champion?

B.N.: I altered Minter from bottom to top. He lost the "boom-boom" when I taught him to eliminate this pre-punching sound by properly controlled breathing.

B.D.: Any thoughts on the current Scottish amateur game?

B.N.: It was a sad day for me when I resigned as national coach to the SABA. I should like Scotland to keep from looking backwards as has often been the case in Scottish amateur boxing.

B.D.: Do you think government funding through Youth Training Schemes would be feasible or desirable?

B.N.: It is something, along with private sponsorship, I have advocated for many years.

B.D.: Would you say London management or training was a "must" for any promising Scottish pro' boxer, bearing in mind Vernon Sollas and Jim Watt, to name two?

B.N.: Yes, because the hub of British boxing, TV, radio, newspapers etc. is in London and I feel that to make it you must come south. To Sollas and Watt you can add Alex Dickson, a boy I took with me from the Scottish Amateur Boxing Association. From the original SABA team in which he appeared he was the only one to become British champion.

B.D.: Who was the greatest American fighter you have ever seen? Why was he so?

B.N.: Sugar Ray Robinson, because he could fight, box, punch, box attacking, box in defence. He epitomised the word "boxer".

B.D.: How would you rate Pat Clinton as a pro' fighter amongst today's modern breed of Scottish boxers?

B.N.: Very good!

B.D.: Who in your opinion was the best American trainer/manager you ever met? Why?

B.N.: (1) Angelo Dundee (2) Simple. He had all the champs. (3) I never rated Angelo as a great trainer, but certainly a great corner man.

B.D.: When you boxed the world featherweight champion was Davey Moore (*a coloured American nicknamed the Springfield Rifle*). How do you think he would have coped with Barry McGuigan, Eusebio Pedroza and co.?

B.N.: He would have KO'd them all.

B.D.: Any theories as to why Scotland has failed to produce a world heavyweight fighter of even contender status?

B.N.: We have big caber tossers, heavy ball throwers, the biggest police force in Great Britain and – who knows? – the smallest hearts!

B.D.: What would you say has been the biggest single change in the fight game of your active days and the boxing world today?

B.N.: In a word – television.

WALTER McGOWAN MBE
The Boy Wonder from Burnbank

Ever since the Middle Ages the Royal Burgh of Hamilton and neighbouring Burnbank have been part of the hereditary domain of the Dukes of Hamilton, Scotland's premier aristocratic family. Yet in boxing terms Burnbank has an equally strong connection with another noble but English family – the Lonsdales – for it was a native of Burnbank called Jim Higgins who won a Lonsdale belt in a record 11 months and 16 days in 1920 – 21.

In addition, it was another native of Burnbank, who, in May 1966, established another Lonsdale belt record. On this occasion the coveted trophy was awarded for the first time in boxing history to a boxer who had made only one stipulated defence of his title. The name of this Burnbank battler was Walter McGowan and this distinction was but one of many that were to stud his life like diamonds, causing many to call him "The Burnbank Boy Wonder".

I first met Walter McGowan MBE in 1983 in the foyer of the Angus Hotel in Dundee. I was the boxing correspondent for Radio Tay, sent to interview an army of Scottish boxing celebrities that included Bobby Neil, Dick McTaggart and "Wee Walter".

The occasion was an amateur international between Scotland and the United States. In the ring the outstanding performance was provided by light-middleweight David Milligan of Methil, Fife – a performance that won him "The Fighter of the Evening" award and that rarest of accolades, a standing ovation for beating one of their compatriots, from some dozen US naval officers from a nearby base!

Outside the ring the undoubted star of all the celebrities I interviewed that evening was Walter McGowan. So engrossed did I become in what this Lanarkshire boxer turned publican had to say about the noble art and life in general that my portable radio recording machine ran on. . . and on. . . and on.

It had been that same intelligence transmitted into action in the ring that was to make Walter McGowan the flyweight champion of the world.

The fighting saga of Walter McGowan did not simply begin in Hamilton on Saturday, 13 October 1942, when he was born into a family of five brothers and five sisters. Genetically speaking, it began much earlier.

The *Edinburgh Evening Dispatch* of Saturday, 14 March 1936, announced on its sports pages: "Connolly taken distance – magnificent display of pluck by Gans". This report went on to outline how Bathgate featherweight star Joe Connolly had appeared for the first time as a top-of-the-bill fighter at Hamilton over 12 three-minute rounds. However, it was his opponent, Hamilton's Joe Gans, who really stole the show by his fighting display of guts. The *Dispatch* reported: "Connolly was taken the full distance not because he boxed badly or hit without power, but because of a magnificent display of pluck on the part of his opponent . . .".

The remainder of the fight report is worth reproducing because it reads in many respects like a dress rehearsal for young Walter McGowan's career 30 years later, although that was to be characterised by success at the highest level AS WELL AS pluck in the face of adversity. The report continued: "By the end of the seventh session Gans' face was badly puffed, but he was full of pluck, in a contest which was going consistently against him . . . there was no doubting Connolly's intention to win by the decisive route if possible . . . a right then a left dropped Gans for another long count, but although groggy, he lasted the session. Gans, before terrific punishment, went down in the tenth for eight, staggering right across the ring before being brought up by the ropes. Another count of nine came the way of Gans in the final round, but Connolly could not put him out. Gans had served up an amazing display of stamina and courage."

It was pluck of a similar kind displayed at the early age of ten years that made Joe Gans decide that the "bairn" of the family – Walter – would be his heir apparent within the ropes.

But how, one might ask, can someone called "Gans" produce a family called McGowan?

"Joe Gans" and Thomas McGowan were one and the same person. McGowan Senior took his ring name from one of the fistic greats among early lightweights – Joe Gans, a negro known as "The Barbados Demon" who won the world lightweight title on 12 May 1902 by knocking out the reigning champion Frank Erne in one minute 40 seconds of the first round. The original Joe Gans held the world title for six years – a fact that clearly impressed the young Scots fighter Thomas McGowan, who elected to perpetuate the great negro boxer's name by adopting it.

As anyone who witnessed the appalling massacre of Marvis Frazier by Mike Tyson will agree, having a father with an illustrious ring pedigree is no guarantee of success in the fight game. Indeed the latter example would tend to point to the fact that a father's best place during a fight is as far away from his son's corner as possible. Cases that support this contention are those of Bob Fitzsimmons who, having won three world titles himself, failed utterly to impart the knack to his son who also had fistic aspirations. Mike Rossman, who was for a short time WBA light-heavyweight champion in 1978, ascribed his loss in the return fight with Argentinian Victor Galindez to constant pre-fight bickering with his father and chief second Jimmy DePiano.

In Scotland though, on the whole, father and son fistic relationships seem to have operated without some of the pitfalls evident across the Atlantic. In the 1920s a certain Mr Hill of Strathmiglo guided his son Johnny's career so that he was not only British and European flyweight champion, but was also, in October 1929, on the verge of fighting Frankie Genaro for the world title when he tragically died. No

Walter McGowan (right) in typically devastating form. Cut eyes would be his downfall.

such stain of tragedy afflicted the combination of Ken and Tommy Buchanan – or Joe Gans and Walter McGowan.

Hamilton is as famous for its racecourse as it is as a cradle for distinguished boxers, so not surprisingly young Walter McGowan had aspirations towards becoming a jockey – aspirations that gradually faded as his amateur boxing career gained impetus.

And what a brilliant amateur career it became. He suffered only two defeats in 124 bouts. Amongst the illustrious scalps he collected as a vested warrior was that of future pro' opponent, Liverpudlian Alan Rudkin. In 1961 he won the ABA flyweight title – only one of a crop of titles, yet for any amateur the pinnacle of domestic boxing prizes. Shortly after winning the ABA title the decision was taken to turn pro' under the management of his father Joe Gans.

"Wee Walter's" pro' career started well enough. George McDade was forced to retire inside three rounds on 9 August 1961. Six weeks later Eddie Barraclough was beaten on points over eight rounds at Hamilton. It was with his third contest that the cynics and knockers who said that a father managing a son in boxing is poison were given the opportunity to have a field day. Gans agreed to let his son fight Jackie Brown of Edinburgh.

Raised in the Abbeyhill district of Scotland's capital city, Jackie Brown had a brilliant amateur career behind him. By the time he climbed into the Paisley ring to face McGowan Brown was an experienced pro' campaigner with 19 contests under his belt. His class of opponents had been nothing but the best. He had outpointed the former world champion and Italian deaf mute, Mario d'Agata, and good class fighters in Alex Ambrose and Brian Cartwright. Brown was a beautiful boxer, a master craftsman who relied on poise and punch rather than power and pulverising to defeat an opponent.

As a professional McGowan was to become known for the power of his punch as well as consummate ring skill. But it was Brown using his superior pro' experience to the full and his classy left jab who emerged as the victor on points at the end of eight rounds.

Confidence was restored in the McGowan camp by the end of 1961. On 16 December in that year the Burnbank battler outpointed Brian Bissmire over eight rounds at Glasgow.

In the McGowan fistic calendar 1962 was characterised by increased evidence of punch power. After outpointing Port Glasgow's Danny Lee, continentals Jacques Jacob and Rene Libeer were both pounded to defeat in Glasgow and in Wembley respectively inside six rounds.

Next to feel the paralytic sting of the McGowan venom was Ray Jutras, an American from Boston who, Walter McGowan recalls, "was a real Boston street fighter type – a real tough guy". Tough guy or not Jutras fell in six to the Scots flyweight's skill and weight of punch.

1963 opened as the previous year had closed with a victory over Frenchman Bernard Jubert who was outpointed in eight. But his tenth fight was to be the most important one thus far in Walter's career.

The first defeat by Brown had rankled inside the wee Lanarkshire man's breast in the same way that defeat by Schemling had rankled inside Joe Louis for the two years it took him to get Schemling back inside the ropes. Jackie Brown had not been idle either since their last meeting 18 months before. In this period he had acquired a Lonsdale belt and the British flyweight title by outpointing Englishman Brian Cartwright over 15 rounds in Birmingham. Eight months later at London's National Sporting Club in December 1962 – in the depths of one of the worst British winters this century – Brown was almost iced in the second round by his Nigerian opponent Orizu Obilaso who put him down for a count of nine in their Commonwealth flyweight title fight. Brown replied by getting on his bicycle and jabbing and moving for the remainder of the contest like a pocket version of that great American exponent of "stick and move", Willie Pastrano. He was thus adjudged winner and new champion.

Titles and revenge, therefore, were the incentives for Walter McGowan when they met in Paisley on 2 May 1963. Walter McGowan recalls: "Jackie had the psychological disadvantage of knowing that this time he would be facing a professional, not an inexperienced boy, and that's how it went."

Peter Keenan, who promoted the fight as well as McGowan's other Paisley bouts, recalls: "It was close in the early rounds but gradually Wee Walter gained the upper hand from the halfway stage of the fight." A 12th-round left hook ensured that the British and Empire flyweight crown had acquired a new owner.

Perhaps the only person more overjoyed than the new champion himself was his father/manager Joe Gans. He had gone a long way to confounding the critics who shook their heads about the wisdom of keeping McGowan's managerial reins firmly in the hands of the family.

That Gans fought as fiercely outside the ring for his son as the latter did inside the ropes cannot be disputed. Peter Keenan who negotiated with McGowan Senior in his capacity as promoter at Paisley Ice Rink recalls: "People used to criticise Gans but Joe was a good negotiator – tough – but he knew the business and got a good deal for his son."

That Joe Gans could be downright rude to critics, especially the press, is a well catalogued fact. Writing in the aftermath of the Chartchai Chionoi contest in 1967 (lost by Walter McGowan on a cut eye) Hugh McIlvanney was moved to comment: "Joe (Gans) does not go much on the pleasures of debate. Conversation with him tends to be like attempting to travel in the wrong direction along a one-way street in the rush hour".

Yet in defeat Joe Gans displayed a dignity and integrity that was wholly admirable and a far cry from the "we wuz robbed" sour grapes school. When Walter McGowan lost in Bangkok's Kittikachorn Stadium on a cut eye to the Thai Chionoi Gans said, "It was an accidental butt. The referee did the right thing . . .".

Certainly the father/son partnership gave the critics another bloody nose on 12 September 1963 in Paisley. On that date Walter McGowan met the Jamaican Kid Solomon for the British Empire flyweight title. McGowan was clearly the superior boxer in this fight and in the ninth an all-out attack drove Solomon to the canvas for two counts, forcing the referee to signify that Scotland had a new Empire champion.

One of the outstanding features of the evening was the appearance in the ring of the then world heavyweight champion, Charles "Sonny" Liston, who did his famous "night train" skipping routine to the delight of the fans. However, almost as significant as the victory gained was the first pointer to a factor that was to become an increasingly prominent feature of the Burnbank battler's career – a tendency to cut and bleed. In the case of the Solomons fight the nasty gash that opened up had fortunately been located below the left eye and therefore was easier to contain.

Not all future injuries would prove so biddable.

After a slight break it was back to training in the converted byre rigged out as a gym by Joe Gans. There were no frills in this makeshift fistic school – a "shower" was taken in a tin bath. Again Wee Walter's training was somewhat unorthodox in that his five-mile stint of roadwork was completed most days by a swim.

Unusual or not, 1963 was completed by a points win over Ric Magramo in ten rounds. Despite the knockers the family firm of McGowan and Son was prospering with an even brighter future ahead of it.

Throughout European sporting history Finland has been more noted for its runners than its fighters – men like Pavel Nurmi and in more recent times Lasse Viren, athletes that have shot this northern country that straddles the Arctic Circle into world prominence in the Olympic Games. However in the late 1950s and early 1960s Finnish boxers emerged as a new force in world boxing – boxers such as lightweights Elis Ask and Olli Maeki or lightheavyweight Pekka Kokkonen who fought a draw with top Empire rated lightheavyweight Johnny Halafihi. But arguably the best of the bunch was the balding customs officer Risto Luukonnen.

"Risto" won the European bantamweight title from Mimoun Ben Ali of Spain in Helsinki, the Finnish capital, just 11 days after Walter McGowan's defeat of Ric Magramo in Paisley on 28 November 1963.

By the time he met Walter McGowan "Risto" had already acquired two Scottish scalps on his belt – Jackie Brown and tough Glasgow bantam Alex Ambrose were both victims of the flailing Finn.

Meanwhile Joe Gans had been fighting on another front far to the south of Finland. Gans was having an extremely trying time pinning an Italian promoter down to a date for his son's challenge for the European flyweight title in Rome's Olympic Stadium. There were purists and old-timers who thought Gans was crazy putting his son, a fourteen-fight pro', in with a tough Sardinian who was on a 43-fight winning streak, but McGowan Senior would have reminded them that his son was not called the "Boy Wonder" for nothing.

On the morning of the fight with Luukonnen tempers in the McGowan training camp became considerably frayed on receipt of a cable from the Italian promoter Reno Tomassi informing them that due to unforeseen rental problems with

Rome's Olympic Stadium the proposed European title battle would have to be postponed from 3 April to 24 April. This three-week delay infuriated Wee Walter. Dick Currie, boxing writer of Glasgow's *Daily Record,* reported on Wednesday, 4 March 1964: "A midnight cable from Rome has made Walter McGowan fighting mad".

As it turned out the Burnbank boxer needed all his aggression to conquer the tough Finn.

Writing in the *Daily Record* of Thursday, 5 March 1964, the celebrated British boxing writer Peter Wilson headed his article: "This was McGowan's Finest Win" – although to underline how tough it had been for the Scots boxer there was a photograph beneath the caption of McGowan on the canvas where the Finn had put him briefly early in the fight. It is not surprising that the Finn did not lack aggression, for his corner man on this occasion was the "Aldgate Tiger", Al Philips, a former British and European featherweight champion whose ring ferocity made his feline namesakes look like pussycats in comparison.

In the first two rounds of the contest Luukonnen attacked strongly with left hooks to the body and whiplash right crosses to McGowan's head. Yet this fierce attack revealed just how fine a ring tactician McGowan was. It is axiomatic in boxing that you do not stand and trade with a known puncher unless or until you have worn him down somewhat. McGowan, sensing that the Finn's left hooks carried more power than his own punches, stayed away from the Finn by boxing on the retreat.

Towards the end of the third round McGowan received help from a strange quarter – the Finn's own nose! A previous nose injury meant that every time "Risto" blew his nose from his exertions in the ring a swelling developed on his left eye. From the end of the third round onwards the Finn's left eye rapidly disappeared under this self-inflicted swelling. So bad did the swelling become that at the start of round four Al Philips angrily told his Scandinavian charge to stop blowing his nose!

McGowan once again showed the shrewdness of his tactics by circling to the Finn's blind side once the eye had completely closed and popping him with right crosses.

Nevertheless, as Peter Wilson testified, it was still by no means an easy contest for "Wee Mac". The English scribe wrote: "I say it was a clear victory – and so it was. But at the end of the seventh round I had the men dead level on points with both having two rounds – three being even. It was then McGowan put in a really storming finish to take the last three rounds and put the decision beyond dispute."

The way was now clear to Italy and the tough European champion Salvatore Burruni. But boxing politics had created a new difficulty, should the Burbank battler defeat his more experienced Sardinian foe. The British Board of Boxing Control, sickened by what it considered to be the inconsistency of the European Boxing Union had seceded from the latter body. This meant that if McGowan won the title he would have to travel to Europe to defend it because the EBU had retorted to the British secession by stipulating that ALL European title fights could only be held in countries under their jurisdiction.

This problem clearly exercised the mind of Peter Wilson who put it to father/manager Joe Gans. The patrician Wilson always had difficulty in understanding the hard-boiled logic of the Scottish working class and he was clearly bemused by Gans' attitude in an interview just before Walter McGowan was due to do battle in the Roman ring. The interview is also interesting in that it reveals just how uncompromising Joe Gans was with media men – particularly those whose questions he considered not to his taste.

The patrician Peter opined: "What curious characters you do meet in boxing. Take Joe Gans – father and manager of Walter McGowan . . . who is challenging Salvatore Burruni here tomorrow . . . for the European flyweight title. Today Mr Gans was asked what he felt about the regulation of the European Boxing Union – from which our own BBBC has seceded – which says that European title fights must take place in countries affiliated only to the EBU. . . . To this point Mr Gans was supremely disinterested . . . . We're not interested in the championship. All we want is to get Burruni in the square and get the money . . . he can buy the title back for a few pounds. When in Rome do as you do in Glasgow."

This provoked Mr Wilson to reply: "The sum of £2,660 which McGowan will receive is a plummy reward for a European flyweight challenger . . . but do patriotism, prestige and honour count for zero? Surely 'Scots wha hae wi' Walter bled' must feel slightly different?"

Having met Walter McGowan personally I can say that all these things did matter to the Burnbank boxer as his subsequent performance against Burruni was to prove.

But what of McGowan's opponent Salvatore Burruni?

Burruni was born into humble circumstances in Alghero, a part of Sardinia as rugged as this young man was to become, first in the streets where he learned to fight and then in the amateur ring. By 1955 he had twice won the Italian amateur flyweight championship as well as two army championships gleaned during his stint of national service.

In the European amateur championships of 1955 Burruni lost to a future pro' opponent and victim, the Londoner Derek Lloyd. This setback did not deter the Italian selectors when they chose their 1956 Melbourne Olympics boxing squad. There, a second-round defeat by a Russian may have won Burruni no medals but it proved to be the catalyst which propelled the young Sardinian into the pro' ranks in April 1957, first under Frank Klaus, then with the legendary Umberto Branchini.

Branchini was and is in Italian terms a combination of Jack Solomons, Angelo Dundee and Don King – a man of enormous power with a multitude of important contacts. Contacts that were to prove invaluable to Burruni, for shortly after joining Branchini the Sardinian scrapper annexed the Italian flyweight title in September 1958 from Giacomo Spano.

Four successful defences of this domestic title prompted Branchini to tempt the European champion Risto Luukonnen to Sardinia in June 1961. The pale

Scandinavian customs officer certainly acquired a suntan in the broiling Sardinian sun but at considerable expense to himself as he left his title in the keeping of Burruni.

In contrast to McGowan's 14 pro' fights the Italian champion who faced him at 11 p.m. on 25 April 1964 had a total of 66 fights and had run up that impressive 43-victory winning streak referred to earlier. In the end the Sardinian's greater experience was to be the decisive factor.

As with Risto Luukonnen, McGowan shrewdly decided not to trade with his harder punching opponent and indeed he appeared to baffle the Sardinian by his retreating tactics in the first three rounds – tactics which did not prevent McGowan from scoring with some smart shots to the head.

Scottish hopes reached a crescendo in the third round when the Burnbank boy cut the Italian champion's right eye. But Burruni was not the kind of fighter to wilt under pressure and he came storming back so that by the sixth round it was the Scot who appeared to be in trouble from some hard rights from Burruni.

The ding-dong nature of the battle was emphasised by the fact that in the seventh round it was the champion who now appeared troubled by McGowan's left jab which was finding his nose with worrying regularity.

From the eighth round onwards Burruni slowly gained ascendancy with fierce attacks that ultimately guaranteed his crown would remain in Italy for the time being at least.

Nevertheless, in losing Walter McGowan had equally emphasised his right to be there with the best in the world at flyweight – an opinion accentuated by the fact that Burruni left the Rome ring looking as though he, not McGowan, had been vanquished. The Italian had four facial cuts, cuts above each eye and a single cut under the right eye as well as a cut nose. In contrast McGowan's swollen face looked comparatively unmarked.

Both combatants were generous to each other after the contest. McGowan said, "I lost to a great champion... Burruni is a well-trained fighter with infinite experience and he put up a good fight throughout the fifteen rounds". The Sardinian commented, "He's a good boxer".

As events were to prove McGowan had learned several valuable lessons which would prove decisive the second time they met.

It was to be just over four months before "Wee Walter" returned to the ring but these months were exciting ones for several reasons. A lifelong devotee of Glasgow Rangers Football Club, the Burnbank boy had the thrill of being permitted to train with his heroes, men who have since become sporting legends themselves – John Grieg, Jim Baxter, Willie Henderson and Ralph Brand. Yet thrilling as this must have been even greater excitement was to ensue with the arrival in Scotland in August 1964 of the fabulous Sugar Ray Robinson, the man most fight fans agree was "pound for pound" the greatest fighter ever under Marquis of Queensberry Rules.

Not only did McGowan share a gym with "Sugar Ray" but he was scheduled to appear on the same Paisley fight bill as the great man. His opponent was to be an 18-year-old West Indian from the Dominican Republic called Natalio Jiminez – a youthful pugilist whose Scottish safari was to be memorable for several reasons, not all of them directly connected to his ring performance.

For a start the youthful Dominican scrapper had been a fully fledged professional since the age of 15 – in Dominica pro' boxing licences were then granted to anyone of the age of 14 years or over!

Trained by "Sugar Ray" Robinson's manager George Gainsford, Jiminez astonished his Scottish hosts and even Robinson by refusing to rest after a 20 hour, 5,000 mile flight from the West Indies, opting instead for an immediate training session!

Jiminez had won 18 of his 21 contests and a few weeks prior to meeting his Scottish foe he had been narrowly outpointed in Turin by Salvatore Burruni – but not before he had decked the Sardinian champion.

Clearly then Jiminez was no soft touch. But equally he was not hard enough to stand up to "Super Mac" – as some of the newspapers called him. Walter outpointed this tough youth who fought to help support a family of 11 brothers and sisters.

This victory kept Walter McGowan amongst the world's top contenders and a rather easy win over Luis Rodriguez at Solihull closed out the eventful year of 1964 – a year of disappointment certainly but disappointment that was a pale imitation of what was to follow in 1965.

For the wee battler from Burnbank 1965 started in swashbuckling style. On 20 January he met English bantamweight Mick Hussey. Hussey was a "trial horse" in more ways than one. The defeat of European bantam champion Luukonnen whilst conceding half a stone had given Gans a pointer as to the future path to be followed by his son – alternating between the flyweight and bantam divisions. Consequently, for the bout with Hussey Wee Walter came into the ring at eight stones three and a half pounds, his heaviest ever weight as a pro'. This increased poundage also enhanced the ferocity of his puching, as is evident from the fact that he decked Hussey three times in the three rounds that the fight lasted.

However, just over a month later McGowan Junior was faced with an entirely different proposition in the ferocious bantam Felix Brami.

Brami, a Tunisian-born Jew, was based in Paris where he was handled by Gaston Charles Ramond who had guided Robert Cohen to a world bantamweight championship in the 1950s. Brami was undefeated in 28 contests. Three of these had been draws but amongst the 25 victories there were triumphs over Ben Ali of Spain who was European champion, stoppage victories over Englishman Brian Cartwright and a KO victory over Edinburgh's own Jackie Brown. Glasgow's Alex Ambrose had also been outpointed by the little Paris-based Tunisian who rejoiced in the name of the "Patent Leather Kid", due to the highly polished black boxing boots he wore in the ring.

Yet on this occasion all the gloss came from McGowan.

The *Boxing News* correspondent present at the Albert Hall wrote: "In one of the finest and fastest contests between 'the little men' seen for some time, British and

Empire champion Walter McGowan from Hamilton. . .clearly outpointed Felix Brami. . .over ten rounds. . .this was Brami's first defeat either as an amateur or a professional". The *Boxing News* writer continued: "The Scot's all-round performance was little short of a revelation. His speed and variety of punches restored our faith in British boxing."

Wee Walter started in whirlwind fashion in the first round, constantly punishing Brami to the head with multiple jabs. A hard left to the body had the Tunisian crashing into the ropes at the end of the round.

Brami mounted a two-fisted attack throughout the second but much of his venom was nullified by McGowan's slick slipping and feinting.

In the third round Brami drew earned applause from the London crowd by stepping back when McGowan slipped, leaving him vulnerable to a hefty counter. The French-based boxer must have felt just a little aggrieved that his reward for this gallantry came in the shape of a beautifully executed uppercut by McGowan which crashed into the former's jaw at the end of the round.

Another feature of the fight at this stage, which was to continue throughout the contest, was the Frenchman's apparent inability to avoid McGowan's right cross over his own left lead.

Yet in the fifth round that old bogey of the Burnbank battler – cuts – reared its ugly head. A toe-to-toe fistic exchange in mid-ring saw the Scot emerge with a diagonal forehead gash just above the left eye. This wound appeared sufficiently serious to warrant a referee's inspection between rounds five and six.

The sixth saw a Brami rejuvenated by McGowan's optical misfortunes charging forward but ironically the reward for this additional aggression was an eye problem of his own. A slight bruising on his own left eye began to swell considerably, causing the referee Jack Hart to inspect it at the end of the session.

The next two rounds saw McGowan attempt to aggravate the Frenchman's optical discomfort, thus provoking the handicapped but incredibly brave Brami to pursue McGowan relentlessly. McGowan back-pedalled, slipped and feinted, but even so when the final bell rang it was discerned that he had another cut near his left eye.

So euphoric was the wee Lanarkshire man at his victory that he actually bodily lifted Brami around the ring in his arms. *Boxing News* commented: "Having beaten the world's No. 5 bantamweight McGowan can confidently look forward to the best of both worlds. . .".

However, future events often make present euphoria appear like the plush velvet silencer on a Russian roulette revolver – the sensation of pleasure encountered a cruel deception for what might, and often does, follow. So it proved for Walter McGowan.

Firstly, there was Italian Tomasso Galli – a man who must have caused the Gans-McGowan partnership more frustration than Churchill did to Adolf Hitler. Galli and his mentor Rino Tomassi originally agreed to fight with Wee Walter in Rome on 23 April 1965. Yet shortly before this engagement was due to take place Galli withdrew leaving the Burnbank man to fight a Ghanaian called Benny Lee whom he outpointed over ten rounds. It was a poor substitute, though, for the European title fight originally promised.

Yet worse was to follow.

Joe Gans had been attracting considerable flak from the omnipresent critics for making his son fight at bantamweight. The knockers were not convinced by the Gans arguments that lack of decent opponents forced his boy to fight at the heavier weight. (This, incidentally, was a judgement vindicated by the British Board of Boxing Control's decision to give McGowan his Lonsdale belt after only one flyweight defence.)

The date Tuesday, 1 June 1965, must have appeared to the critics as the fruition of the Doomsday scenario they had been predicting for so long. On that day Walter McGowan stepped into the ring with Mexico's Jose Medel.

Stepping into a ring with a Mexican bantam is a pastime only slightly less perilous than putting a pint of nitroglycerine into a cement mixer. In boxing Mexican bantamweights are to the noble art what Fred Astaire is to dancing – the ultimate in excellence. Alfonso Zamoro, Carlos Zarate, Lupe Pintor are immortals in boxing's hall of fame. Even second line Mexican bantams are a hot handful as Charlie Magri discovered to his cost on at least two occasions.

Jose Medel proved to be straight out of the classic Mexican mould. For the first five rounds it was obvious that McGowan was being outpointed but the end, when it came in round six, was highly controversial. To many the Mexican appeared to half-punch half-push McGowan to the canvas. The McGowan camp were incensed at referee Ike Powell's decision to stop the fight there and then.

Certainly, the photographic evidence shows McGowan sitting upright on the ring floor with a look of amazement directed at his Mexican foe. There is scant evidence of daze or pain in his eyes yet a referee under British rules can stop a contest at any time if he feels a boxer's stay in the ring is pointless in the face of his opponent's strength or better class.

The remainder of that summer of 1965 was to prove no happier for the clan McGowan.

In an effort to restore some lost prestige for his son, Gans signed Walter to fight an American from Chicago called Ronnie Jones on a Peter Keenan promotion at Paisley on 20 August. The Chicagoan was not in the same league as his Mexican cousins from south of the Rio Grande and was in the process of being comprehensively outpointed by his Scottish adversary when disaster stuck in a boringly familiar form – a horribly lacerated eye forced the referee's intervention in favour of the American. Nor was this the kind of injury that liberal dosages of 1/1000th adrenalin and a couple of weeks rest would heal. At first the medics spoke of four to six months complete rest from the ring – a disaster given that Joe Gans had been communing with his old friend, the Italian promoter Rino Tomassi, on the subject of a crack at the European bantamweight title now held by another Italian, Tomasso Galli.

Just 24 hours before the Paisley débâcle with Ron Jones, Galli had taken the European title from the Spaniard, Mimoun Ben Ali, in San Remo on 19 August 1965. Galli was a clever boxer and counter-puncher whose preferred tactics were to permit his opponents to burn themselves out in the early rounds of a contest, when he would avoid their blows by clever feinting and slipping. The Italian then mounted a strong counter-attack in the latter half of a contest against normally tired foes. These were precisely the tactics that brought him victory over Ben Ali although it must also be stressed that the Spanish champion's pre-fight equilibrium could not have been helped by the furious rows he had with promoter Rino Tomassi over a cut of the television receipts for the contest.

In any event the eye injury suffered by "Wee Walter" at Paisley responded to treatment in a fashion much better than expected. *Boxing News* of 1 October 1965 reported: "The doctor is so pleased with McGowan's progress that he may allow the Scot to fight again before the end of October." In fact the fight with Galli did not take place until 3 December in Rome.

The best that can be said for Belgian referee Jean Deswert's verdict of a draw was it was the biggest act of legalised larceny since a certain Dutchman bought the island of Manhattan from the Indians for a pokeful of trinkets. Even the Italian crowd, normally so nationalistic, booed the decision. The Burbank battler had outboxed and outfought Galli yet was left with little other than plaudits for his efforts.

1965 had not been a happy year for the McGowans. 1966 was to be on the whole, better. Much Better.

Just over a month after the Roman robbery "Wee Walter" faced another Italian – the non-stop punching pocket bantam dynamo, Nevio Carbi. Joe Gans was clearly not picking "patsys" to re-establish his son's value in world fistic circles. Carbi had the reputation of being a perpetual motion fighter like the fabled American negro, Henry "Homicide Hank" Armstrong.

The Scot and the Italian whirlwind met over eight rounds at the grand gala opening of the London-based "World Sporting Club" in Park Lane. Watching at ringside was one of boxing's all time greats, Barney Ross, who won world titles at light, light-welter and welterweight in the 1930s and who won his greatest battle of all – to overcome heroin addiction – subsequent to his being wounded in action in World War Two. Ross wrote a best selling autobiography entitled *No Man Stands Alone* but Nevio Carbi would have disputed this as he was pummelled from pillar to post by Walter McGowan. Poor Carbi had nowhere to run but to the arms of the referee who rescued him in the sixth round.

Whilst his son practised mayhem on Italians in the ring Gans was already sounding out old Italian foe Salvatore Burruni who had become world flyweight champion since last trading leather with the Burbank Boy Wonder. The Sardinian had made history by becoming the first Italian to win the title. This he had achieved in Rome before 18,000 rabid fans of whom 3,000 were fellow Sardinians. His opponent that 23 April 1965 had been the sleek Thai world champion Pone Kingpetch. Kingpetch had taken the title in 1960 from arguably one of the greatest flyweights who ever fought – the Argentinian Pascual Perez. Constant hammering aggression by Burruni wrested the world crown from his Oriental foe.

In December 1965 Burruni accentuated his class by kayoing the tough Italian-Australian terror Rocky Gattellari in the 15th and final round. This bout did not have universal recognition as a world title fight due to the murky politics of international boxing. In November 1965 the World Boxing Association had ordered Burruni to fight the Argentinian Horacio Accavallo. The Sardinian refused and was stripped of recognition by that body. He was still recognised as world champ by Britain, Europe and the USA.

However, before the Burbank boxer could fight Burruni he had to overcome a countryman of the Argentinian usurper Accavallo – a tough bantam called Ernesto Miranda who was five and a quarter pounds heavier than his Scottish foe. That was the only advantage he enjoyed that evening of 28 March 1965 in London. He was comprehensively thrashed by "Wee Walter" who had now forced himself back into serious world contention for Burruni's flyweight title.

Although illustrious London boxing promoter Jack Solomons was entering the twilight of his fabulous career as Britain's number one world title fight impresario he still retained sufficient clout and cash in 1966 to command international respect. "Jolly Jack" as he loved to call himself – and be thus addressed – won the right to stage the world title bout between the Burbank "Boy Wonder" and the Sardinian for the Empire Pool, Wembley. It cost him £14,000 yet despite a heat-wave in London that day of 14 June 1966 the attendance was as meagre as the fighters' pre-fight meal. Solomons lost £12,000, thus making him rue his decision not to put the fight on in Scotland before McGowan's ain folk where the attendance could hardly have been worse.

That is speculation. What is certain is that McGowan trained for this contest as never before. Glenlee House, where he prepared himself for the fight, was a 30-odd roomed mansion in Lanarkshire that had been the childhood home of the Emperor Haile Selassie of Ethiopia, the same Haile Selassie who had to flee from Italian poison gas and bombs in 1935 when the Fascist dictator Mussolini had conquered his country in one of the most disreputable episodes in Italian history. However, Walter McGowan had little time to reflect on world history as he prepared to follow in the footsteps of Benny Lynch and Jackie Paterson.

The Burruni who entered the Wembley ring on that hot June night in London was now at the veteran stage, aged 33. Ominously, he had lost three of his last five fights before meeting McGowan. Yet he was still regarded as a stern test for any flyweight.

There was a mini-drama before the fight when at the weigh-in Burruni was adjudged to be five ounces overweight. He had to then carry out a vigorous training routine during the hour permitted for him to come in at the stipulated weight. This pre-fight struggle with the scales almost certainly affected the Sardinian, who was a pale imitation of the comprehensive fighting machine which had outpointed McGowan 18 months before. Yet for all that the McGowan propensity to cut produced suspense of Steven Spielberg proportions for the Scots boy's fans.

From the first bell the Burbank boy made it clear he would not stand and trade with the Italian who was noted for his right hand clout. Wee Walter danced, feinted, slipped and counter-punched the Italian who at one stage vented his frustration by making a histrionic gesture to McGowan to come in and mix it.

McGowan was well ahead in the eighth when a left hook from Burruni opened a nasty gash over his right eye. Fortunately the blood ran down the outside of the wee Scot's face thus not affecting his vision – a fact accentuated by the massive counter-attack McGowan mounted in rounds nine and ten. In the latter round Burruni suffered a cut to his own right eye.

In the 11th the best punch was a McGowan right cross that sent shudders of apprehension all the way back to the Italian's corner. If McGowan could protect his eye from further aggravation then it was clear Britain would have a new world flyweight champion.

Rounds 12,13 and 14 followed the same pattern – Burruni anxiously seeking a knockout and being both denied it and punished by the Scot's counter-punching and ringcraft. The 14th did reveal the depth of the Italian's frustration for in an otherwise sporting contest referee Harry Gibbs had to warn the soon-to-be-ex-champion for an alleged butt. It was at the end of this round that the real drama began as Walter's eye began to "greet" blood as though it had been deeply moved by his opponent's plight.

For the 15th and final round it became a case of a four-sided contest between McGowan's skill at evasion, the Sardinian's left swing, referee Harry Gibbs' sense of duty as a referee to prevent serious injury and the timekeeper's bell. Three times Harry Gibbs halted the action to look at the eye. But as if to stress that he was not totally handicapped by the afflicted orb, Walter was in the process of attacking Burruni when the bell went. Scotland had a new world flyweight champion.

What followed anticipated the *Rocky* movies by a clear decade. Joe Gans and Walter McGowan wept openly in each other's arms. Unlike the movie tears, there was no glycerine quality about this emotion. They had confounded the critics and knockers and vindicated the methods of Joe Gans.

The British press was both unanimous and generous in its praise of the new Scottish world champion. George Whiting of the *Evening Standard* opined: "Only one thing was gloriously different on this occasion. When they had wiped away the blood, it was the Briton who had won!" Des Hackett of the *Daily Express* wrote: "When the journalists, cameramen and officials rise to applaud a winner, then you know you are in the presence of greatness".

The "Boy Wonder" had come of age in championship terms.

It has become a long established convention in boxing that a world champion interlards hectic battles for his crown with either exhibition bouts or title "defences" against soft touches who are willing to accept inglorious defeat in exchange for a reasonably hefty sum of cash. For every Billy Conn he fought, Joe Louis also amused himself by kayoing Jack Roper and Nathan Mann, fairly mediocre talents who belonged to what became known as "The Bum of the Month Club". Similarly, Joe Frazier followed up his epic and victorious 15 round battle with Muhammad Ali in March 1971 with a couple of easy title "defences" in 1972 against Ron Stander and Terry Daniels.

However, Joe Gans would have no truck with this philosophy as is evident from his next choice of opponent – the Liverpudlian bantam hotshot Alan Rudkin.

Neither was this a prestige only fight – the British and Empire bantamweight titles were up for grabs on Tuesday, 6 September 1966, at London's Wembley Pool.

The contest had also been invested with a significance not foreseen when it was first contracted earlier that year. Shortly before Rudkin and McGowan met to join battle British boxing had witnessed another heavyweight fiasco when Brian London had virtually surrendered any attempt to win the world crown without throwing a decent punch throughout the three rounds his "fight" lasted. Considerable odour had attached itself to the British game in world terms and it was hoped the two little men would redeem the tarnished image of the sport.

Actually there was an element of that old Scottish boxing civil war between east and west in this contest. Alan Rudkin had been induced to turn professional in May 1962 by former Edinburgh featherweight ace Bobby Neil, who at that stage had really just embarked on an illustrious career as a manager and trainer. Neil's inducement to turn pro' – £100 a fight and a job as a janitor in a London school – might seem modest by today's standards but it was sufficient for the little Liverpool scrapper, who promptly repaid his Scots mentor by knocking out his opponent Dickie Hanna inside two rounds. Scottish brains and Liverpool grit subsequently proved a winning combination although Rudkin was to have something in common with McGowan in that when he lost his second pro' fight to one Carl Taylor despite being streets ahead on points, the cause was the old McGowan bogey of a cut eye.

Before meeting "Wee Walter", who had beaten him twice in the amateurs, Rudkin himself reckoned that his toughest battle had been in his 13th bout, against old Burruni foe, the Frenchman Pierre Vetroff. This had taken place in London in 1963 and Rudkin had triumphed by the slimmest of points margins.

The spring of 1965 saw him share a ring with former Joe Aitchison protégé and world bantamweight champion Johnny Caldwell of Belfast. Yet it was the scouse who looked the world beater in the Nottingham ring. From the third round onwards Rudkin gradually eroded Caldwell's strength and fighting spirit to such an extent that the referee called a halt in round ten in favour of the Liverpool boy.

Just to prove this was no fluke four weeks later the geordies in St James' Hall, Newcastle, acclaimed the little scouse scrapper after he had produced a scintillating performance in outpointing the European bantam champion, Moumin Ben Ali of Spain, in ten rounds. Unfortunately it was a non-title affair but this performance did at least play a large part in securing Alan Rudkin a shot at the world bantamweight crown in Tokyo on 30 November 1965.

Bobby Neil, his Scottish manager, probably told Rudkin this was St Andrew's Day in the Scottish calendar. Scotland's patron saint was crucified and that is precisely what happened to Rudkin in his fight with world champ Fighting Harada – thanks to the judges. Only one of the judges was not Japanese, but even he, an American called ironically enough Dick Pope, saw it the way of his Japenese hosts, although his score was markedly fairer than that of his colleagues.

Anyway, soft touch Alan Rudkin was most certainly not and so it proved that torrid Tuesday evening. *Boxing News* of 9 September 1966 stated it was "the finest battle between 'little men' for years".

The first eight rounds belonged to Alan Rudkin. The scouse fighter was the aggressor, attempting to coax his Scottish adversary into a close quarters punch-up, but the Burnbank battler was too shrewd to risk this whilst Rudkin was fresh and fit.

Rudkin concentrated his attack to the body, paying particular attention to McGowan's rib cage – when he could hit it for McGowan was boxing beautifully on the retreat at this stage. When Rudkin did pin McGowan momentarily the Scot took a lot of blows on his elbows and arms or tied up Rudkin so that he totally lacked sufficient leverage for his big punches.

From the ninth round onwards McGowan took the attacking initiative, catching Rudkin with hurtful hooks and crosses although Rudkin did his share of retaliating.

The tenth round saw an ominous nick appear on McGowan's right eye but this simply spurred the Burnbank battler to retaliate with a couple of smashing hooks to the Liverpudlian's jaw.

McGowan's eye and nose were now bleeding copiously and this provoked him to even greater action for the remainder of the contest. When the bell for the 15th round ended the bout there were storms of booing when the Welsh referee raised McGowan's hand in victory. Many felt a draw would have been a fairer result but the fact remained that Walter McGowan of Burnbank had emulated fellow townsman Jim Higgins who 45 years earlier had won the same title and the accompanying Lonsdale belt in record time.

After a brief respite from ring warfare, negotiations in connection with Walter McGowan's world flyweight title took a somewhat exotic turn, for a lucrative offer came from Bangkok, capital of the Oriental kingdom of Thailand. Thailand was formerly known as Siam and Thomas McGowan and his son were cordially invited to play leading parts in their own version of *The King and I,* although Gans would have claimed they had been doing this ever since Walter had beaten Jackie Brown for the British flyweight throne in 1963. The Thais ensured there would be a bleak Hogmanay in Burnbank if Walter was forced to abdicate by insisting that the bout be held on 30 December 1966.

Joe Gans showed he had learned something from the Tomasso Galli heist and the Rudkin experience in Tokyo by insisting that one of the ringside judges be much-respected *Scottish Daily Express* boxing scribe, the late James Sanderson. This was agreed, but before the various jabs from a hypodermic that always precede such visits to the Orient had to he endured, jabs of a different order were lined up for 16 November in the London World Sporting Club.

Wee Walter's original opponent was another from Italy called Tony Sassarini. He called off and was replaced by the Spaniard Jose Bisbal, a points victim of old McGowan foe, Alan Rudkin. This was a "warm-up" bout for the Burnbank man and the heat was too much for the Spaniard who retired in the fifth – thoroughly beaten.

The McGowan camp then experienced a loss before they had even put foot on an Orient-bound plane. The British Board of Boxing Control reminded them that under their rules McGowan could not hold two national titles, so he was forced to relinquish his British flyweight crown.

But this was a mere pinprick compared to what was to follow in Bangkok.

Chartchai Chinoi was a private in the Thai army by day, drawing 62½ pence per week by day. By night he was a tough little scrapper who had alternatively quaint and horrifically named opponents on his record – men like the quaintly named Terry Go (whom he stopped in eight) or the horrifically named Chaihtong Singshuepiering (whom he stopped in three rounds) – but he clearly could fight. Ten months before, he had avenged his countryman Pone Kingpetch by outpointing Salvatore Burruni over ten rounds in Bangkok. Former McGowan foe, the Argentinian Ernesto Miranda had also been beaten over the same distance. So Chinoi – who had been born only three days before the Burnbank boy – clearly commanded respect.

Gans and McGowan were fêted and treated with great courtesy by the naturally hospitable Thais who had even consented to two non-Siamese judges. Joining Jimmy Sanderson was Nat Fleischer, world boxing authority and editor of the influential *Ring* magazine. The third judge was a Thai referee. The contest was held in the 20,000 seat Kittikachorn Stadium in a humid 80 degree temperature.

Boxing fans in Britain have become blasé about trumpet fanfares heralding ersatz kings of the roped square into the stadium but there was nothing ersatz about His Royal Highness King Bhumibol of Thailand, who was heralded into the stadium by his own royal trumpeters. Some 15,000 loyal Thais packed into the arena to join their king to see if Chinoi could pull off a bloody coup against Scotland's world flyweight boxing monarch.

The first round belonged to the challenger, who scored well with right crosses which caused noticeable reddening of the Scot's features.

The second round was one of high drama and low fortune for the defending Scottish champion. Right at the start McGowan floored the Thai with a hard left but no count ensued. Chinoi was however hurt and was subjected to a severe shellacking before disaster struck. A clash of heads resulted in a horrific cut across McGowan's nose. McGowan had won the round but lost the battle at this point.

From this stage two of the judges – Nat Fleischer and his Thai counterpart – had Chinoi ahead.

In round five Scottish hopes rose as McGowan scored with right-left combinations to the head, shaking his Oriental opponent. But Chinoi proved his own championship calibre by coming back with a series of jabs which cut McGowan's nose again. The Thai then relentlessly pursued the Burnbank battler and punished his already afflicted nose with more left jabs.

In rounds six and seven McGowan's concentration on the task at hand was affected by the constant drip of blood – evident by the continual wiping he interspersed with punches. These rounds were won by the Thai challenger who kept winging fast hurtful punches, particularly at the bleeding nose of the champion.

In round eight the same spirit that had frustrated Bathgate's Joe Connolly 30 years before when Joe Gans had impressed all with his guts now surfaced in his son. In this penultimate round "Wee Walter" actually had the Thai dazed from a ferocious counter-attack, but the nose injury that had been such a handicap had now reached crisis proportions.

Early in round nine the continued attention paid to his injured nose forced the referee's intervention. The ringside doctor was called and the fight stopped in favour of the new world flyweight champion – Thailand's Chartchai Chinoi.

What was especially heartbreaking for the wee Burnbank man – who knelt for a time weeping in his corner – was the knowledge that but for a skin with an "Andrex-like" resiliency he could have continued fighting, although two judges, Nat Fleischer and the Thai referee, had him behind at that stage.

Stating that the cut was the result of an accidental butt, manager Joe Gans scorned any sour grapes or histrionics concerning his son's loss. Gans praised the Thai referee's decision and indeed emphasised he would have pulled his son out had the official not so acted.

Although it was poor compensation for losing his own world diadem "Wee Walter", ex-flyweight king of the world, was presented along with Joe Gans to the King of Thailand. The Burnbank boy also left the stadium smartly, head damaged but held high as he exited between two pipers. It had after all not been an abject surrender but a gallant losing battle more against inherent physical deficiencies than the Thai challenger, who in fairness cannot be condemned for exploiting them to his advantage.

When the McGowans arrived back in Scotland a new year had dawned – 1967 – a year in which their first priority was to regain the title they had left behind some 6,000 miles away.

As former Scots world lightweight champion, Ken Buchanan, could testify, losing one's crown in a foreign field can sometimes make it well-nigh impossible for the deposed champ to get the boxer who has taken it to meet him again. Edinburgh's WBA lightweight king tried everything short of an appeal to the United Nations to get Roberto Duran back into ring contention, but the Panama "macho" man declined each and every offer.

There were similar ominous rumblings of reticence from Chinoi's manager, Colonel Boonlert Lerpreecha. Immediately after the Bangkok battle the good colonel stated, "There is the possibility of a return match with McGowan but definitely not in England". Colonel Lerpreecha also stated he did not much fancy the British scoring system of a home-grown referee being the sole arbiter, nor did he think his charge would find the food or climate to his advantage.

However, all these obstacles were to prove somewhat less than insurmountable when "Jolly Jack" Solomons started to speak the Esperanto of big money to the Thai colonel – although it took £16,000 to convince Lerpreecha that a little coldness and possible indigestion were tolerable diversions given the cash involved. Only the July 1951 Sugar Ray Robinson v. Randolph Turpin world middleweight title fight cost Solomons more to stage.

Yet all this was firmly in the future as the McGowans took stock of their situation now the world title was gone.

At this point a considerable body of British fight *cognoscenti* began to question "Pa" McGowan's reluctance to employ a professional cuts man such as another famous British bleeder, Henry Cooper, did for much of his career when Danny Holland had helped him. Londoner Holland was touted to Joe Gans by Hugh McIlvanney amongst others but the former's refusal to incorporate strangers into the firm was expressed in a highly coloured Scots vernacular that made *The Observer*'s top boxing writer despair of having a dialogue with his fellow countryman. Certainly cuts men can save world titles. Italian-American Adolph Ritacco saved American negro Saad Muhammad's world light-heavyweight title (on 18 August 1979) in his contest with Britain's John Conteh. However, Ritacco stopped Muhammad's horrific eye injuries by applying a substance that would not have been permitted for use in Britain.

Gans for his part could also have pointed out that Danny Holland could do nothing with the injuries that cost Henry Cooper a possible victory in June 1963 against the then Cassius Clay. Whatever the critics might say, Gans and McGowan were Gans and there the matter would rest. Indeed, some vindication of the elder McGowan's own skill in containing eye injuries came in his son's first post-championship fight on 15 March 1967.

The venue was London's World Sporting Club and the opponent was Japan's Osamu Miyashita, a tough bantam imbued fully with the Samurai spirit of his ancestors. But even though referee Harry Gibbs awarded McGowan the decision by a clear enough points margin of 49.75 to 48.5 there were times when the conclusion looked anything but foregone for the Scots boy.

Throughout the contest McGowan had to be on top form. It was evident from round one that any major mistakes would bring instant retribution. The Japanese invader had a four-pound weight advantage and a heavy punch that McGowan treated with due respect. Fortunately, Walter McGowan was highly skilled at rolling with many of the heavy right hand counters that rammed through his guard. Yet it was not all one-way traffic. As with Burruni the Burnbank boy had no intention of presenting a static target to a heavy hitter. He used the ring by constant lateral movement jabbing and hooking his charging foe as he went.

The seventh round is chiefly remembered for providing an answer to sponsors of the Danny Holland idea and for the usual drama associated with cuts that had now almost become synonymous with a McGowan fight. In this round a spate of in-fighting produced a cut above Walter's right eyebrow, forcing a referee's inspection. Harry Gibbs repeated his inspection at the end of the round but it was clear that Joe Gans had learned from his past experiences of dealing with his son's involuntary haemorrhaging. Gibbs waved the fight on.

The Japanese boxer was no tactical slouch either. From the seventh round onwards he tried to cut off McGowan's exits by moving where he moved and throwing body punches calculated to bring down Walter's guard so that he could assault the eye injury with his heavy rights. Nevertheless, all these tactics were ultimately in vain. It was McGowan not Miyashita who had his hand raised in victory, although the Hiroshima hitter received a standing ovation for making the victor earn his purse money the hard way.

Two months later a somewhat similar task was set and accomplished when Frenchman Giancarlo Centa was outpointed over eight rounds at Solihull. This too was a tough battle, highlighting another part of Joe Gans' philosophy which some modern managers in the contemporary fight game clearly do not share – that there is little to be gained by putting your protégés against what a BBC commentator once called "deckchair" opponents (one hit and they fold). Gans belonged to the school which believed that one does not get sharp fistic teeth by being fed "soft meat".

On another front promotional ally Jack Solomons was busy negotiating with the Thais to bring Chartchoi Chinoi to London. Few human motives have the pureness of distilled water and Jack Solomons had reasons of his own for making such a lucrative offer to Chinoi's management. "Jolly Jack" was in the middle of a protracted promotional civil war with arch-rivals Harry Levene and Jarvis Astaire, who had successfully introduced close circuit pay-television to British boxing in the 1960s. In securing the McGowan-Chinoi scrap for himself in London, Solomons could demonstrate that he was far from down and out to his rivals. So this, his 22nd world championship cost him £25,000 to stage. Victory – and a grateful Gans and McGowan – could do Solomons nothing but good in his own scrap with fellow London promoters.

In their Bangkok battle a familiar European face had been in the victorious Thai's corner – none other than Salvatore Burruni's ex-manager, Umberto Branchini, by now quite an expert on McGowan's strengths and weaknesses. Branchini indeed arrived in London as the Thai world champion's co-manager, thus giving him the distinction of having managed two world flyweight champions.

Chinoi trained in Jack Solomons' London gym and whilst he was there a little Branchini-inspired gamesmanship over the gloves to be worn kept the boxing scribes busy. Chinoi had at first expressed satisfaction with the British mitts shown him by the BBBC secretary Teddy Waltham, but then changed his mind and demanded American gloves.

McGowan meanwhile had prepared for the big battle that September by having a highly paid sparring session with French bantamweight champion Antoine Porcel at London's World Sporting Club on 10 July 1967. Actually it was billed as a *bona fide* contest but McGowan was so far above Porcel – who had lost to old McGowan foe Felix Brami – that it is difficult to regard the gallic scrapper seriously. It is indeed a sign of the lopsided nature of this "contest" that all the high drama associated with cuts was confined to the Frenchman's corner. Porcel emerged from a sixth round head clash with a split eyebrow, yet he was being comprehensively beaten anyway and he never won a single round of the ten contested.

The McGowans could not be blamed for this mismatch as Porcel was the European Boxing Union's nominee to fight the reigning champion, Mimoun Ben

Ali of Spain. Ironically, the EBU had chosen Porcel in preference to McGowan for this task, which suggests that as judges of fighting ability the EBU left much to be desired.

Chinoi, as the battling Burbank duo knew only too well, was going to be a difficult proposition – even with "home" advantage.

In what was to be a night of disappointment the first sense of loss that evening of 19 September 1967 was experienced by promoter Jack Solomons who saw only 7,000 spectators turn up for a world championship when he had confidently expected 10,000.

The referee was Welshman Ike Powell who had angered the McGowans so when he had stopped the Jose Medel scrap two years before. Again the night was not to be without controversy for the Welshman.

Wee Walter came storming out of his corner like a demented tornado and started fast, accurate punching that caused a neutral observer – the American Nat Fleischer – to have McGowan ahead by four rounds to two when the end came.

Leading on points at the beginning of the fourth round, the Scots boy seemed to be heading towards regaining his crown. But it was in the fourth that Chinoi began to get into top gear himself – a point he emphasised by jolting the challenger's head with a stiff right hand. This provoked a toe-to-toe exchange which produced the inevitable cut on the McGowan forehead, just above the right eye.

By this stage in his career Wee Walter knew only too well what the salty taste of his own blood now normally signified. So it was no surprise when, in the next stanza, he pursed the Thai champion like a homicidal miser in pursuit of his wallet. Punch after punch rained down on Chinoi – to the obvious concern of his corner. The champion pumped in lefts to the afflicted optic on those few occasions when McGowan paused from delivering his sustained barrage of leather.

In the sixth, blood still oozing from his cut, the Scots challenger resumed his assault on the Thai champion. There were times in this round when Chinoi seemed to be doing a passable imitation of an aerosol-affected fly as he staggered under the weight of leather poured on him by McGowan, who now realised a KO was the only road to victory. Yet it speaks volumes for the Thai world title holder that he did not collapse under this orchestrated mayhem.

The start of the seventh was but a continuation of the previous round. McGowan charged forward. Premature roars of triumph from the crowd greeted a slip by the Thai, who promptly rose to jab away at his Scottish tormentor, opening up another cut over his right eye. This forced the Scots fighter to up the stakes by close-quarters slugging – a desperate ploy that left the way wide open for the Thai's slashing punches to prompt referee Ike Powell's intervention at one minute four seconds of the round.

What made this stoppage doubly tragic was that, unlike their Bangkok battle when the Scots challenger was trailing, McGowan was clearly ahead and looking set to regain his crown.

Gans was incensed by the third man's action. He declared angrily: "The referee should have waited at least one more round. My boy was ahead and doing well and would have knocked out his man if the referee had not stepped in . . . the cuts were not so bad". Neutral observer Nat Fleischer clearly did not share this viewpoint as he wrote: "One can fully understand the feeling of Walter's father, but I doubt that many spectators agreed with him".

Chartchai Chinoi ascribed his victory to the punch in the fourth round that had opened the cut on McGowan's left forehead. He said, "I hit him so hard in the fourth round that it turned the tide for me. I felt it right down to the calves of my legs".

Referee Ike Powell, whilst conceding that he had McGowan ahead on points at the time of the stoppage, totally rejected the McGowans' complaints about his actions.

But the fact remained that "Wee Walter" was still an ex-world champion. He still held the Empire flyweight and the British and Empire bantamweight titles and a firm refusal by Chinoi's management to countenance a third battle meant the wee Burnbank battler would have to address himself to domestic rather than international issues, especially as an old McGowan foe had not been exactly inactive himself since their last meeting. Since his last battle with McGowan, Rudkin had kayoed Ron Jones, who had gained that lucky cut eye win over the Scottish boxer in Paisley, outpointed Japanese Yoshici Tzuganezewa, and also run up other victories against lesser known adversaries.

Before their second meeting for McGowan's British and Empire bantam titles on 13 May 1968, at Manchester's Belle Vue Stadium, the Scots boxer had not fought at all. Thus he had the problem of ring rust to contend with.

Belle Vue was the venue where Benny Lynch had so unceremoniously ripped the world flyweight title from Manchester's own Jackie Brown in 1935. For the McGowans it was to be the sepulchre of their championship days from which there was to be no resurrection.

Another change was that the fight was promoted on this occasion by Jack Solomons' arch-rival Harry Levene. "Jolly Jack's" smile must have been nonetheless fairly wide on this occasion. The stadium was barely two-thirds full and Levene was probably saved from a financial débâcle by the large scouse support Rudkin brought with him.

Yet, this could hardly be classed as a solely Liverpool victory over a Scotsman. Rudkin had had in wily Scots manager/trainer Bobby Neil one of the best coaches and ring tacticians in the business, a man whose hallmark was indelibly printed on the little Liverpudlian battler wherever and whenever he fought.

From round one it was Rudkin who dictated matters. He prevented McGowan from mounting his own offensive by forcing the champion back continuously. A warning to Rudkin for careless use of the head in the second round simply prompted him to greater aggression. The third stanza was better for McGowan. He inflicted a cut above Rudkin's left eye and scored with some other useful blows. However, up to the half-way stage Rudkin was clearly in the lead.

In the ninth the McGowan left optic started to bleed once again, prompting "Wee Walter" to fight furiously. He had Rudkin troubled by a left-right combination to the head and this was to be the shape of things to come in rounds ten to 13, when the Scots champion handed out punishment to his Scouse challenger in liberal doses. The purpose of this fistic philanthropy was of course to pull the fight out of the fire, but it was not to be. From the 14th round onwards Rudkin reasserted himself by boxing smartly on the retreat and amassing more points.

When the final bell sounded it was to the Liverpudlian's corner that referee Harry Gibbs went to indicate that Britain and the Commonwealth had a new bantamweight champion.

Time was to prove that this was the end of the fighting salad days for the clan firm of McGowan and Son. Certainly "Wee Walter" went on winning in the ring after the battle of Belle Vue. In 1968 there were points victories over Messaoud Boussabova; stoppage victories over Gerard Macrez and Marc Van Domme. 1969 saw points victories scored over Umberto Simbola and Antonio Chiloiro and a stoppage win over Michel Houdeau. But the vital spark of enthusiasm was slowly beginning to wane.

The end came abruptly at the close of 1970. The catalyst was the decision of the Rudkin camp not to grant a third "rubber" match to McGowan but to opt for a title defence against Johnny Clark. But despite being in line for a European bantamweight title shot against Franco Zurlo, "Fighting Mac" had simply lost interest in boxing. He had lived for and in nothing but a boxing milieu for 14 of his 24 years so it was in a sense natural he should want to try something else in life.

One of the most vivid remarks he made to me during our fascinating tête-à-tête in the foyer of Dundee's Angus Hotel was, "It is just as important to be a success in life as it is in boxing – maybe more so". On that score "Wee Walter" was certainly a winner all the way. Unlike fellow Burnbank bantam champ Jim Higgins, Walter McGowan will never become a walking Gethsemane. Recognition at the highest level outside the ring came in 1966 when he was awarded an MBE in the Queen's Birthday Honours List. When he comprehensively beat Burruni for the world title the then editor of *Boxing News* – the late Tim Reilly – presented him with the first *Boxing News* Certificate of Merit to be presented to a British fighter for 15 years.

In business success has been his also. "The Walter McGowan" bar and grill dominates the main street of the Lanarkshire town of Carluke in the same way that its owner once dominated the world's flyweights and bantams, its clientèle, in a public bar festooned with McGowan memorabilia, tough but decent, as my wife and I discovered on our visit there early in December 1987.

Toughness and decency were attributes possessed by the late Joe Gans who in turn passed them on to his son who, mixing them with his unique and outstanding boxing skills, produced a stunning cocktail which pleased the palates worldwide of all true aficionados of flyweight boxing at its ultimate best.

Walter McGowan MBE fully deserved the many plaudits he received in the ring and out – such is not always the case.

JOHN "COWBOY" McCORMACK
the Boxer who Outpointed Himself

Question? Who is the only fighter in the entire history of Scottish boxing to be defeated in his final contest by a man with an identical name? This unorthodox event was the fate of the equally unorthodox John "Cowboy" McCormack, who lost on points to John McCormack of Ireland on 28 June 1966. Yet this contest was highly symbolic of "Cowboy" McCormack's career, for if ever a boxer outpointed himself in terms of a contest between potential and actual performance then it was this bow-legged warrior from Maryhill.

Punch for Pay playboys were not a novel phenomenon when McCormack made his pro' debut in 1957 and pursuing pleasure as ruthlessly as one's ring opponents has never been a bar to attainment in the professional boxing ring. In the 1930s Max Baer's habit of spending as much time under nightclub lights as ring klieg lights did not prevent him from winning the world heavyweight title in 1934. Another good-time gladiator was Lee Oma of the USA. Whilst enjoying the multiple pleasures of wine, women and song Oma was nonetheless capable of posting victories over opponents of the calibre of world lightheavyweight champion Gus Lesnevich. Oma had a minor speaking role in the classic 1954 film *On the Waterfront* starring Marlon Brando as a mob exploited fistic has-been. Appropriately Oma played the bartender in "Johnny Friendly's" Bar – even in the world of fantasy he couldn't escape his ever present companion, the bottle.

However, if there is one element normally lacking in the makeup of such good-time gladiators it is consistency – a lack that is normally associated with the hectic pace of their social lives. In this connection, the Max Baer who decked Primo Carnera 12 times *en route* to the world heavyweight crown was hard to reconcile with the Max Baer who tamely surrendered to Joe Louis in 1936. The Lee Oma who behaved in 1948 like a seven-stone weakling with a fetish for being hit hard and often by Britain's Bruce Woodcock bore absolutely no relation to the tiger who had decisioned world champ Gus Lesnevich.

In the same mould was Scotland's own John "Cowboy" McCormack. Yet when I spoke to this charming and intelligent ex-boxer during one of his rest periods from the oilrigs where he now makes his living, he was commendably free from any hypocrisy on this score. "I never really liked boxing," he told me, then added, "to be truthful, boxing was just a job – a means to an end to me. It gave me lots of money to spend and a certain fame. I loathed the training – it was a grind."

These sentiments only confirmed what celebrated Scots boxing trainer Joe Aitchison had told me, that "'Cowboy' McCormack could have gone to the very top if only he had trained". Peter Keenan also confirmed this during my conversations with him. He said, "'Cowboy' McCormack's philosophy was, 'I'm only young once and I mean to enjoy life to the full.' I used to tell him I could put him all the way up the ladder but he would just laugh."

Another excellent judge of fistic talent was "Emperor" George Gainsford, the pilot who steered a skinny but talented Detroit negro called Walker Smith to ring immortality as Sugar Ray Robinson. The *Daily Record* of Tuesday, 18 August 1964, reported: "John 'Cowboy' McCormack, former British and Empire middleweight champion has been asked to go to America and join up with Sugar Ray Robinson. Said John, 'This is a great chance for me . . . I will have to talk it over with my wife and then come to some agreement'."

The offer came from Robinson's manager George "The Emperor" Gainsford. Gainsford would look after McCormack in America and would get him fights in New York and Philadelphia. Said George, "'Cowboy' would do all right in America. He is a good looking kid and they would just love him in the ring."

Peter Keenan even offered to pay his return air fares to the United States. After due discussion with his wife McCormack declined the offer. Nevertheless it underlines just how much potential this bow-legged battler from Maryhill had.

Ample testimony to McCormack's southpaw awkwardness is contained in an anecdote he told me concerning the first time he sparred with "Sugar" Ray in Peter Keenan's Charing Cross basement gym in Glasgow. After about a minute of fistic activity the great "Sugar" Ray stopped the action and asked quizzically, "What's with this guy? What is he doing to me?" John McCormack then informed Gainsford and Robinson that he was a southpaw – a snippet of information that caused Gainsford to say, "Hell! If we had known that we wouldn't even have talked to you let alone employed you!" "Cowboy" ceased to spar with Robinson from that point onwards but there were obviously no hard feelings for John told me, "'Sugar' Ray was a real gentleman – I liked him a lot."

John "Cowboy" McCormack was born on 9 January 1935, the son of a professional soldier in the Cameronians. The young McCormack's father boxed at regimental level.

Today the Glasgow district of Maryhill where "Cowboy" McCormack was born and raised is an extremely pleasant and considerably refurbished and rebuilt area of grey and red sandstone tenements, of sparkling new shopping centres that straddle the hill that gives the district its name. Maryhill in the 1930s was a very different place. Although flanked to the south by the River Kelvin and the swankier districts of Kelvinside and Hillhead, Maryhill took its ambience from the industrial artery of the Forth and Clyde Canal that runs parallel along the district's northern boundary.

Maryhill was a tough industrial suburb whose residents were literally packed into grim tenements, yet it is doubtful if this environment in itself would have made a boxer out of John "Cowboy" McCormack because he was a bright pupil and became head boy at St Marie's Primary School. Yet fate was to terminate this promising academic career. In 1947 when John was 12 years old his father died, making it imperative for "Cowboy" to leave school at the first available opportunity and take a job.

The Maryhill youth discovered boxing via the North British Loco Club and its trainer (and his future pro' manager) Charlie Kerr.

A distinguished amateur career culminated in 1956 when "Cowboy" won the ABA and Scottish amateur light-middleweight titles. In recognition of this achievement he was selected to represent Great Britain in the light-middleweight class at the Melbourne Olympic Games. He emulated Scotland's original Olympic battler Hugh Roddin by winning a bronze medal.

The man who halted "Cowboy's" progress on points was none other than Jose "Chequi" Torres who would win the world light-heavyweight crown via a KO win over Willie Pastrano in 1965. Torres has since gone on to author a successful biography of Muhammad Ali – *Sting Like a Bee* – and become Boxing Commissioner for New York State.

"Cowboy" told me, "I was convinced that I had outpointed Torres – a French judge came up to me after I had left the ring and apologised. He said, 'I'm very sorry – but too many British fighters are in the finals. It is politics – it happens, you know?' " Torres went on to lose in the final to Laslo Papp of Hungary – the first man to win three gold medals for boxing in consecutive Olympics, 1948, 1952, 1956.

Undeterred, John McCormack returned to Scotland where the decision to turn pro' was made in the same NB Loco gym where he spent his days as a vested warrior. As he explains, "I went up to the NB Loco and promoter/manager Sammy Docherty was there with Charlie Kerr and Len Mullen . . . ".

Len Mullen and the present writer shared a ring many times in the early 1980s when we were both rostered to referee the same professional shows in places such as the St Andrew's Sporting Club or the John Wilson Hall in Airdrie. An extremely affable man outside the ring, Len Mullen was a lightmiddle and middleweight terror inside the ropes as an amateur with the famous LMS Rovers Club. Mullen boxed for Scotland and has several unusual distinctions to his name.

One of his major rivals for European amateur honours was the top class Englishman Bruce Wells, yet Mullen and Wells were so matey that they even shared the same shower after practising ring mayhem on each other! Again Len Mullen is probably the first referee to make a pair of trunks for an American world title challenger. In June 1980 former American Olympic star Howard Davis entered the ring in a rain sodden Ibrox Park in Glasgow to challenge Jim Watt for the latter's world lightweight crown. The salmon pink trunks that encased the American fighter's flanks were made by bespoke tailor Len Mullen who refereed some bouts on the undercard!

Again, Len Mullen holds another unusual distinction – winning a coveted boxing honour and not finding out about it until 27 years later! In 1956 the "Bible of Boxing" – the *Ring* magazine – nominated Len Mullen as one of their "prospects of the month" for the light-heavyweight class. Len knew nothing about this until an evening in 1983 when I told him of it at the St Andrew's Sporting Club. Despite the time lapse he was justifiably proud. More so when on our next refereeing assignment at the Albany Hotel I presented him with a copy of the *Ring* ratings that had honoured him thus without his knowing it all those years before.

So this, then, was the man that Charlie Kerr and Sam Docherty asked "Cowboy"

McCormack to spar with that fateful day in the NB Loco gym. "Cowboy" told me, "Charlie Kerr admitted later that he thought Lenny Mullen would murder me – but I shocked them all, including Len."

The result of this fistic tête-à-tête was that Kerr signed McCormack as a professional middleweight in 1957.

In only his second pro' contest, on 26 March 1957 at Leith's El Dorado Stadium, Cowboy gave a hint of some of the powerful punching that was to come. His opponent was Cliff Garvey of Dundalk, billed as the middleweight champion of the Irish Republic. Garvey lasted all of one minute and 52 seconds. *Boxing News* of 5 April 1957 reported: "Southpaw McCormack jabbed his opponent with a succession of powerful rights to the head that forced Garvey to cover up and go on the retreat. . .Garvey made one feeble effort to fight back but as soon as he advanced McCormack stepped in with a perfectly timed right hook to the temple that floored the Irishman for the full count."

This was the second instalment of a winning streak that was to see only one loss in 14 contests – to Coventry's Jimmy Lynas, who stopped "Cowboy". I asked John McCormack about his stoppage loss to Lynas in their first contest in October 1957. "Cowboy" told me, "October 1957 was the time of an Asian flu' epidemic and I had been hit badly by the bug. . . I had also just married and bought a house. . . I know now I shouldn't have fought him but I needed the money."

It was a different story when the pair were rematched in 1958. The Maryhill southpaw recalls, "Lynas' face was so badly cut up I asked the referee to stop the contest. . . but I had to fight on to beat him on points . . .". He continued, "Years later when I was on my way back north from a Scotland v. England game I decided to stop over at Jimmy Lynas's club in Coventry. Jimmy recognised me all right and, pointing to me, declared, 'Cowboy, you were too kind hearted to be a fighter. . .fancy asking that referee to save me from further punishment!' "

Somebody had to pay for the October 1957 setback at Lynas' hands and that "somebody" was ironically one of John McCormack's best friends outside the ropes, the West African Vincent O'Kine.

The late Vincent O'Kine settled in Glasgow and was a very popular man at the after-battle dances that used to follow some of Peter Keenan's promotions in the "Locarno" Ballroom in Glasgow's Sauchiehall Street. The ever-smiling Vincent was a very good dancer but in his 5 February 1958 battle with "Cowboy" McCormack in Glasgow's Kelvin Hall he was given very little opportunity to show any nifty footwork in the ring.

Admittedly, McCormack had half-a-stone weight advantage but his firepower was awesome that evening and he sent the brave O'Kine crashing to the canvas from a vicious left hook in the fifth round. In the sixth more power punching by the Maryhill southpaw had the brave African on the deck for a count of seven. Three short trips to the canvas by O'Kine in the seventh round forced the referee to halt the contest in favour of McCormack.

The Maryhill ex-champion told me, "I had injured my hand from banging Vincent around so often. It was typical of the man (O'Kine) that the next day he came into my mother's wee corner shop in Maryhill and asked, 'Missy Cowboy' – he always called my mother 'Missy Cowboy' – 'how is your son's hand?' My mother was so appalled at the state of Vincent's face after our fracas that she tore into me verbally when she saw me later that evening! She liked Vincent a lot, you see."

It was in that same year of 1958 that the bow-legged scrapper from Glasgow destroyed – for a time at least – the dreams of a young but ambitious trainer/manager called Terry Lawless from London. Lawless thought he had found, in one Harry Dodoo, a real world class contender. The "Cowboy" expressed his disagreement with this notion in a rather devastating fashion, knocking Dodoo cold inside a round!

John McCormack told me, "Years later – in April 1979, the night Jim Watt won the world lightweight title – I was having a drink with Terry Lawless who, pointing to me, told the assembled company, 'This is the so-and-so who wrecked Harry Dodoo . . . and my dreams for a while.' "

1958 was also to be the year that John McCormack won his very first title – the Scottish middleweight title held by his old mate Len Mullen. Strangely enough this title-winning performance is not remembered with any affection by the Maryhill man who recalls, "This fight was a 12-round bore. I mean, I won on points – but I liked Lenny Mullen too much. I just couldn't get fired up or feel mean towards him."

When I repeated "Cowboy's" interpretation of the fight to Len Mullen his reaction was a gust of incredulous but affectionate laughter. Said Len, "Cowboy was hurting me all right . . . but do you know people still come up to me who were at that fight and tell me they still think I won the decision? Yet as a serving referee I accept that if the ref thought 'Cowboy' won that's good enough for me." Then Len added, "Besides I won an order from 'Cowboy' immediately after the fight for a dinner jacket and trousers – which I think he still has!"

Another opponent John McCormack recalls from 1958 was the Liverpool Dane Martin Hansen. "Cowboy" outpointed Hansen but recalls he was "very good . . . it was a hard fight . . . I had to earn my victory there".

If 1958 had been a memorable year then 1959 is probably the one year in "Cowboy's" life that would defy the severest of all possible attacks of amnesia were he to be so afflicted. 1959 was for the Maryhill scrapper a year of the "Ds" – Diouf and Downes. Michel Diouf was a rough tough Senegalese brawler who had stopped future world champion Terry Downes on cuts. John McCormack recalls, "Diouf was one of my toughest opponents – he would have been a hot handful for most boxers . . . After my scrap with Diouf – who was a real whirlwind type – I even had bruises on my knees! The French guy just threw punches irrespective of where they landed." "Cowboy" still won.

Then there was Terry Downes. "Terry Downes of Paddington" was how he was billed but he had in fact lived for a time in the USA where he joined the US Marines and developed his boxing talents.

Gilbert Odd, the great English boxing historian, has called Downes, "The gutsiest fighter I have ever seen." Certainly Downes had had his share of early ring adversity. A proneness to injury cost him decisions against future world middle and light-heavyweight champion Dick Tiger, Welsh-born Freddie Cross, Michel Diouf and in what was to prove Downes' biggest shellacking by an American fighter – Ellesworth "Spider" Webb.

Downes was an all-action fighter who favoured body punching and an unconquerable spirit to see him through against better boxers. Such had been the case when he had stopped Welshman Phil Edwards on 30 September 1958 inside 13 rounds. "Cowboy" McCormack nominated Edwards as one of the cleverest ring warriors he had ever encountered yet this ringcraft and skill had been nullified by Downes outgaming the Welsh boxer to take the British middleweight title and the attendant Lonsdale belt.

Ironically enough, in view of what was to happen at Wembley's Empire Pool, the betting odds and many newspapermen favoured John "Cowboy" McCormack. The *Daily Record* of Tuesday, 1 September 1959, opined: "It should be said that the odds of 11 – 10 on the Scot are just about right." The reasons for the *Record*'s optimism were clearly enough stated. McCormack had beaten Diouf who had beaten Downes. Such logic has a nasty habit of beating even the seconds out of the ring once the bell rings and action commences. Still, the *Record* continued in optimistic vein: "Downes' eyes must have it... in 1957 he was stopped in five rounds by Dick Tiger with cuts... in 1958 Freddie Cross did the same job in six and Spider Webb in eight rounds."

When the gong signalled the start of this middleweight championship battle it looked as though the bookies and the Glasgow Press knew the score exactly. McCormack won the first round but the real shape of things to come was established in the fourth. In that round McCormack was dropped for a count of nine by a peach of a right hand punch – the traditional "cure" for southpaws. Ironically enough it was the only time a head punch put "Cowboy" down.

In a memorable phrase English boxing scribe Peter Wilson described the ten visits "Cowboy" made to the canvas thus: "The Scots boxer was up and down like a busy lift in the rush hour." Yet when I asked John McCormack to account for his yo-yo like visits to the canvas he was quite specific, "Oh yes, Downes was whacking me to the body all right – right between the legs!" This is certainly borne out by the actions of Welsh referee Ike Powell who had warned Downes several times for low blows.

With only three seconds of the eighth stanza left "Cowboy" McCormack dropped to the canvas in obvious agony. Eyewitnesses at ringside, among them Peter Wilson, were sure the Downes blow was accidental. Wilson stated: "The way it happened was particularly unfortunate – McCormack had been driven back on the ropes... he bound off them with unexpected speed and ran into a Downes right hander which had not reached its maximum elevation."

Referee Powell caused uproar by disqualifying the Paddington-based British title holder and gave the decision and the Lonsdale belt to "Cowboy" McCormack.

"Cowboy" McCormack versus Chic Calderwood.

Never a man to let something as banal as furious controversy mar his pleasure, the Maryhill southpaw was reported to have greeted his triumph thus: "It feels wonderful to be champion even though I won it this way." And British middleweight champion he surely was – despite the howls of execration coming from Paddington and similar points south.

Downes and his backers clamoured for a return as did most of the media. Winning championships sitting on the canvas is, after all, only slightly less absurd than Heinrich Himmler being awarded the Nobel Peace Prize. Yet, as "Cowboy" told me, he was one of the last people to learn of the return date and the venue, fixed for 3 November 1959 in the Empire Pool, Wembley: "After the controversy and hubbub I decided to take my wife for a continental holiday. Charlie Kerr my manager meanwhile went ahead and fixed the return without my approval. I felt I needed a longer break than the time I got (49 days) – I split with Charlie after this. I never spoke to him for at least ten years – when we finally shook hands at a boxing show!"

Besides losing a manager "Cowboy" McCormack lost his recently acquired middleweight crown but in so doing he displayed courage of the highest order.

Peter Wilson's verdict on John McCormack's superb bravery was declared thus: "I would like to strike a special medal for some of the greatest raw courage I have ever seen displayed in a ring in any part of the world." Praise indeed for a man who was noted for the frankness of his views. Nevertheless, given Downes' successful body punching tactics in their first meeting the Paddington ex-Marine's strategy was difficult to understand during the first three rounds of the fight.

It was not until the end of the third stanza that one of the famed Downes body shots was fired. In the next round McCormack showed he could punch some too when he opened up a cut on the Englishman's nose which exposed the bone. Downes was only too aware of the consequences of such an injury, given his past record which had resulted in his features having received more stitches than the Bayeux Tapestry. It galvanised him into furious retaliation. In the sixth round the famed body punches shook his Maryhill foe. From then onwards it was only a contest in real terms between Belfast referee Andy Smyth's compassion and "Cowboy" McCormack's rib cage, stomach and liver's ability to absorb Downes' lusty bangs.

At two minutes 30 seconds of the eighth round the end came. Peter Wilson described it: "The pallid Scot who I thought was going to roll under the bottom strand of the blood-stained ropes and onto my typewriter hauled himself wearily, hopelessly, agonisingly upright for the fifth time to face the fearsome figure in front of him. . . Belfast referee Andrew Smyth stopped it with McCormack hanging dead over the top rope."

For many fighters losing a championship and a trusted manager might have been a trauma that adversely affected their future ring performance but to a devil-may-care playboy like the Maryhill southpaw adversity was something to be treated like a spittoon – and with just about the same measure of respect.

The proof of this came the following year – 1960 – against an American negro called George Benton from Philadelphia. "Cowboy" McCormack told me, "After the fight with Benton in Paisley was over, Peter Keenan showed me an international telegram from a guy called Dewey Fragetta. Fragetta was one of the top boxing matchmakers in the USA – a man who knew the game from A to Z. This cable said, 'Don't let your boy fight Benton. Stop. He'll get murdered. Stop.' Peter told me that he had received the cable BEFORE the fight but hadn't showed it to me in case it affected my morale or made me feel too apprehensive."

The Maryhill boxer outpointed Benton over ten rounds – a superb achievement when one considers that George Benton was highly rated in world terms as a superb ring tactician and consummately skilled boxer. Today, Benton is highly regarded for his coaching skills in America but that evening all the smart moves came from the Maryhill Cowboy who recalls, "Benton was classy, okay – but like most American fighters he had problems with my southpaw stance."

Still, this fight confirmed McCormack's own class at world level despite the traumatic Downes affairs. It is interesting to note that, subsequent to losing to "Cowboy" McCormack, Benton went on to outpoint Joey Giardello who 12 months later would win the world middleweight crown from Dick Tiger. Yet sweet as his

John "Cowboy" McCormack in action.

victory over such an accomplished ring craftsman as Benton was, John McCormack does not rate the sepia socker from Philadelphia as the best ring technician he encountered in serious combat. That honour he accords to an opponent he had in common with Terry Downes – the Welshman Phil Edwards.

"Edwards never won any titles. But I thought he was a very clever guy indeed – the smartest I ever met." The Welshman's composite ring skills were, however, not enough to bring him victory against John McCormack who outpointed him in 1961.

Yet it was the year following the Edwards bout that saw "Cowboy" McCormack gain what was arguably the finest triumph of his career and certainly his best performance as a middleweight – his 14 June 1962 victory over Henry Hank of Detroit.

Many boxing fans will recall the BBC *Fight of the Week* series which was screened every Saturday just after lunch during the early Sixties. This excellent series showcased the top-rated world contenders in America who would otherwise have remained simply names in the ratings lists to the vast majority of British boxing fans. One of my favourite and oft-featured "stars" of these black and white television days was a Detroit negro named Henry Hank.

Subsequent to fighting "Cowboy" McCormack Hank would go on to defeat a then middleweight named Jimmy Ellis in September 1962. This was the same Jimmy Ellis from Louisville, Kentucky, who would become famous as Cassius Clay/Muhammad Ali's sparring partner and WBA world heavyweight champion. The Detroit negro would also defeat world-rated Scot Chic Calderwood – who would play a vital though unconscious part in ensuring John McCormack's victory over the American at Glasgow's Kelvin Hall.

This contest was unusual in that it was over the relatively short distance of eight rounds – world-ranked fighters normally fight at a minimum of ten rounds per contest. Hank was number five in the world middleweight ratings. He had had 70 professional contests of which he had won 57. Thirty-six of these victories had been by KO so he was by any standards a dangerous opponent.

"Cowboy" told me, "I was down on the canvas three times in the first two rounds (*for counts of eight, nine and nine*) and I couldn't figure out what was different about the guy – until I twigged! He had the longest arms of any fighter I had ever seen."

The third knockdown was the catalyst that turned the Maryhill southpaw into a fighting fury. As he explains, "When I hit the deck the third time I happened to glance through the ropes and saw Chic Calderwood (*whom "Cowboy" detests even today*) and his brother standing up acclaiming what they wrongly thought was Hank's kayo victory. 'That's it,' I thought, 'I'll show those so-and-sos . . .'."

And show them he surely did, although it must also be stated that "Cowboy" had an advantage that nullified Hank's reach superiority – "Cowboy" was a southpaw, the first the American had ever met as a pro'. That McCormack's "wrong-way-round" style caused the Detroit fighter no end of trouble was evident throughout the contest because it was McCormack's southpaw right jab which won the contest. His left hand was not idle either for he decked Hank with it for a five count in the action-packed first round. So desperate did the American become in round six that he switched himself to a southpaw stance, but all to no avail – "Cowboy" was declared the winner by a convincing margin. It was one of his finest hours as a middleweight boxer, even if it had taken the gloating faces of two of his enemies to inspire him!

As we have earlier mentioned, one of the hallmarks of good-time gladiators who like to be social lions as well as ring tigers is that they are not noted for their consistency of performance. So it was to prove time and time again in the career of John "Cowboy" McCormack. And so it proved just a few months later after the marvellous Hank triumph.

The good times in Glasgow's nightclubs – such as the "Chevalier" at the top of Buchanan Street – paved the way for bad times on the scales, which is what happened before "Cowboy" was due to meet American negro slugger Ike White on 13 September 1962 in the Kelvin Hall. The torture of weight-making was translated into a tortuous time against White who cut the "Cowboy" midway through the ninth round. Twice the "Cowboy's" lacklustre display drew slow hand-clapping from the crowd who had acclaimed him only two months before. Only an all-out performance in the tenth and final round when he sliced a gash on White's eye made the spectators inclined to forget what had gone before.

The press were rather less forgiving. To some extent this was understandable, for the Maryhill southpaw had begun the year 1962 in fine style. Championship-winning style in fact.

During the previous year – on 17 October 1961 – the Glasgow boxer had followed such illustrious Scots as Tommy Milligan by annexing the European middleweight title. Of his opponent, Harko Kokmeyer, the "Cowboy" recalls little other than, "He was strong, tough, game – but unexceptional compared to some of the guys I have fought."

By this stage John McCormack had acquired London management in the form of the old "Aldgate Tiger" Al Philips, a former British featherweight champion. Once McCormack had acquired the European crown manager Philips drafted an ambitious plan calculated to thrust the "Cowboy" further up the world ratings ladder and garner them both £11,000 in cash – a huge sum at today's values. Philips had penned in title defences against Germans Heini Freytag and Peter Muller (Muller had been suspended for "life" at one stage for flattening a referee whose decisions he did not like), the Dane Chris Christiansen and the great Hungarian Lazlo Papp in Vienna.

But first there was Herr Freytag to be taken care of. The fight was fixed for Frankfurt, West Germany, on 6 January 1962, but it was one of several "Cowboy" McCormack contests where the action outside the ring was arguably more entertaining than that in it.

The tone for the whole affair was set by the German fight posters which described the resolutely Glaswegian McCormack as being from "England". German confusion was also evident at Frankfurt when the immigration officials were confronted by a Scottish pugilist trying to enter their country on the strength of his golf club membership card – "Cowboy" having forgotten his passport! Only the timely intervention by promoter Joachim Gottert saved the Maryhill fighter from the embarrassment of being deported.

Soon it was the German "bookies'" turn to be confused by the unorthodox Scotsman in their midst. Having installed the 29-year-old Offenbach carpenter Freytag as a two-to-one favourite, they then had to watch him being comprehensively beaten by the Scots boy. Their optimism before the match is hard to understand given that Freytag had never gone more than eight rounds before and he had only had 19 fights – although he was undefeated when he clashed with McCormack. Freytag was a no-frills slugger but in the "Cowboy", who was a composite boxer, he more than met his match. Indeed, "Freytag" is German for "Friday" but poor Heini must have thought he was at a violent Sabbath convention given the number of McCormack's Sunday punches that rained down on him. Only once – briefly in the tenth round – did Freytag threaten, when he decked McCormack without a count, but when decision time came there was little controversy at the verdict – a points win for the Glasgow man.

Sitting at ringside with his wife was McCormack's next scheduled opponent in the Philip's plan – the Dane Chris Christiansen. The Danish veteran was accompanied by the man who was and still is the Danish Don King/Jack Solomons/Mike Barret rolled into one – Mogens Palle. It was agreed that "Cowboy" would present himself in Copenhagen on 8 February – just a month later – to do battle with Christiansen.

In the meantime the Maryhill fighter decided to sample some of the many pleasures offered by a West Germany which was fast becoming the most prosperous nation in Europe. However, liverwurst and late nights are not recommended, especially for a boxer with increasing weight problems and an imminent championship fight on the horizon. So it proved.

On arrival in Copenhagen from Germany Mogens Palle asked the Scottish champion to undergo a test weight-in. McCormack agreed and was promptly found to be nine pounds over the stipulated middleweight poundage. The result was that the Scots fighter had to resort to sauna baths and training in a hotel room that had been transformed into a sweat cabin. Finally, in desperation, a call went out to Glasgow to his wife Margaret to bring over a special American polythene sweat suit. Actually, in view of what transpired in the ring the move to bring over Mrs McCormack can be seen as being providential.

The Danes, like the Swiss, are a peace-loving people. Apart from the German occupation of 1940 – 1945 Denmark last fought a war in 1864 – the so-called "Six Weeks War" when the Prussian Otto Von Bismarck had ruthlessly wrested Schleswig-Holstein from Denmark by force of arms. Now another German, Herr Rudolfe Drust was instrumental in inducing a state of war between a citizen of Glasgow and a goodly portion of Denmark's population who were at ringside for this international fracas.

But what of "Cowboy's" opponent Chris Christiansen?

Christiansen was a veteran but as the Chatteris slugger Dave "Boy" Green discovered to his cost in the summer of 1979 Danish veterans on their home patch can become Tartars. (Jorgen Hansen a reputedly over-the-hill veteran blasted Green's European crown from his head.) Christiansen had turned professional in 1948 after an 88-victory amateur career. He was a big hit in the United States where he defeated world rated Billy Graham (the puncher not the preacher) in his US television debut. He also had fought a draw with the world-rated German Gustav "Bubi" Scholz and had beaten a good class English fighter in Manchester's Jacky Braddock.

Certainly the *Ring* had considered him the goods in 1955 when they allotted him an entry in their *TV Fights Annual* magazine. In those days Christiansen's speedy boxing had made him Danish welterweight champion. Even if he was now reaching the veteran stage it speaks volumes for "Cowboy" McCormack's own class that by round four of their contest he was well ahead on points thanks to the famous southpaw right jab which had made the Dane look like a mumps victim, so swollen were his features.

During the fateful fourth round "Cowboy" hit Christiansen with a peach of a right hook which felled him. The Dane rose, then contrary to the agreed rules Herr Drust started to give him a standing eight count.

John McCormack told me: "It was a disgrace! No standing eight count was allowed so I went in and smashed him with a left cross." Christiansen was draped by this punch over the bottom rope of the ring – out to the world.

Because of the confusion created by the German official the Danish fans were outraged at what they thought was a vicious foul on their hero and promptly forgot their traditional pacifism. British journalists were punched and kicked. So much glass rained into the ring that it looked more like the champagne-glass strewn fireplace at a debutantes' ball than a place for dual combat.

"Cowboy" recalls, "My wife tried to defuse the situation by placing the traditional laurel victory wreath round the now recovered Dane's neck." This placatory gesture was interpreted by some Danes as another outrageous assault by the female half of the clan McCormack upon their Nordic hero. More punches and kicks were aimed at the McCormacks as they struggled to the sanctuary of their dressing-room.

It was by any accounts an outrage on the Scottish ex-champion but the result was allowed to stand. Nor did the ructions end there.

Peter Keenan demanded a return bout in Paisley and claimed there was a return clause to that effect in the original contract. This was flatly rejected by Palle who ultimately received backing from the European Boxing Union and the British Board of Boxing Control, who reminded Keenan that return clauses were outlawed in championship contests held under their jurisdiction.

This rift between Dane and Scot was happily only a temporary one. Later Mogens Palle, who was a great admirer of Ken Buchanan, employed the Edinburgh lightweight towards the end of his career. Yet there can be little doubt that "Cowboy" McCormack was robbed of his title.

If the quality of the Maryhill southpaw's performance against Ike White signalled a retreat from the top drawer quality of the Hank contest, even worse was to follow.

Joe Aitchison had been training the "Cowboy" at this stage and whilst the Bridgeton trainer had a profound respect for John McCormack's great abilities he told me, "He would disappear for a couple of days – to the 'Chevalier' nightclub and then reappear . . . I liked him – still do – but he drifted away from me."

Meanwhile rumblings of discontent south of the border were to have far-reaching consequences on "Cowboy's" career as a middleweight. Old foe Terry Downes was decidedly unhappy about the purse sanctioned by the British Board of Boxing Control to be paid to him for defending his British middleweight title for a third time against John McCormack. Indeed, so unhappy was the Paddington ex-United States Marine that he relinquished his middleweight title, leaving the way open for the Board to nominate Hoxton-born-but-Market-Harborough-based George Aldridge for the vacant crown.

Never was the old cliché, "What's one man's meat is another's poison," so true as on this occasion. Whilst Aldridge had been in serious training for a proposed but ultimately abortive bout with the great "Sugar" Ray Robinson, "Cowboy" had been tangoing with *La Dolce Vita* – a fact that left him with the bitter prospect of losing 21 pounds in weight to make the middleweight limit.

George Aldridge was not rated too highly by many contemporary boxing scribes of the time. This is evident in the *Daily Record*'s judgement that: "The whole affair is a sad reflection on the present state of British boxing . . . call it a fairy tale if you like but two weeks ago Aldridge was not within reaching distance of a championship fight let alone the title."

Whatever Aldridge's merits as a fighter I can personally testify to his exemplary sportsmanship. In April 1983 I refereed a contest involving one of the Market Harborough man's young fistic protégés and a local Glasgow boxer at "Morley's Night Spot" adjacent to Ibrox Park. There was considerable dissension at my verdict in favour of the Scottish fighter. Indeed, the then Scottish correspondent of *Boxing News*, Mr Gavin Lafferty, opined: "This was a good fight marred only by the ridiculous scoring of referee Brian Donald." (Lest readers draw the wrong conclusions from Mr Lafferty's criticisms let it be stated that even my sternest critics within the Scottish Area Council freely conceded that my scoring of fights was normally "spot-on".)

After the fight I met George Aldridge and he asked me calmly and politely if I did not think I was wrong in my scoring. There were no angry histrionics or recrimination. I firmly but equally politely told him that I scored as I saw it. Whereupon we embarked on an interesting and extremely cordial chat about his career and his losing battle with the three-time Olympic gold medallist Lazlo Papp. We parted by shaking hands – a refreshing change from the antics of some fight managers who seem to think a referee is a convenient scapegoat for their own or their fighter's deficiencies.

In any event, the torture endured by John "Cowboy" McCormack in the ring was nothing to what he went through in losing the stone-and-a-half of unwanted poundage. "Cowboy" informed me, "It was murder... I was so weakened by weight loss I hadn't a lot left."

Normally, "Cowboy" would have been favourite against the grocer from Market Harborough whose only title to date in a 46-fight (11 losses) career had been that of Midlands area championship at middleweight. McCormack had also stopped his English foe inside nine rounds when they had previously met in 1960.

Aldridge's manager was the former British heavyweight champion Johnny Williams of Rugby and he clearly had the previous meeting in mind when he assured ringside scribes that things would be definitely different this time. So they were. Those who attended this Harry Levene promotion at Manchester's Bellevue witnessed the crowning of a new champion – George Aldridge stopping the Maryhill "Cowboy" inside six rounds.

It was one of John McCormack's poorest performances, as he readily conceded to me. Aldridge's tactics cannot be faulted. He bombarded McCormack's body whenever he could. Only in the fourth round did the undoubted McCormack talent shrug off its malnutrition-induced hibernation and flicker briefly into life. McCormack charged forward and sliced open Aldridge's left eyebrow with three good punches. The end came in the sixth when a vicious Aldridge right hook smashed into "Cowboy's" body, felling him. Referee Billy James' count reached six when John McCormack rose weakly – to be met with another vicious blow to the body which terminated the contest.

It was a sad postscript to a year that had seen his greatest triumph as a middleweight – against Harry Hank.

Many, especially those who were aware of the Maryhill man's addiction to pleasure, were inclined to roll out the obituaries and make the inevitable comparisons between Max Baer and other playboys whose potential for greatness had been stunted by various forms of dissipation. Such comparisons had some validity but they were premature – throughout his career "Cowboy" would be written off as many times as the crew of the *Marie Celeste.*

Nevertheless if 1962 ended on a bleak note 1963 was to prove little better.

Ever since modern professional boxing evolved there has been a time-honoured tradition that middleweights with weight problems move up to a higher division. Many have done so, with varying degrees of success. Some, such as Randolph Turpin, made a literally stunning switch from middleweight to light-heavyweight. Turpin began in a blaze of glory by stopping weight-worried Don Cockell for the British light-heavyweight title in 1952. He lost the Empire portion of this crown in miserable circumstances to a totally undistinguished brawler named Gordon Wallace in 1955.

In global terms, after a distinguished career as world middleweight champion, Carl "Bobo" Olson invaded the light-heavies with some initial success but it all came unstuck when he disputed the world title with "Ancient Archie" Moore who dumped him in three rounds in 1955.

It was so typical of John "Cowboy" McCormack that he did things the opposite way round. His light-heavyweight invasion began disastrously and then provided him with one of the sweetest victories of his career – the victory he prized above all others – against Chic Calderwood.

The initial disaster occurred against Harry Scott from Bootle. I can vividly recall sitting in the gallery of the now demolished St James' Hall in Newcastle-upon-Tyne the previous year, on 12 July 1962, watching the dour bruiser Scott fighting a tough battle with Nottingham's Wally Swift.

The Bootle brawler was too tough for his Maryhill rival, sending him crashing to the canvas no less than TEN TIMES during the five rounds the contest lasted. That this defeat was traumatic can be gauged from the fact that even today "Cowboy" prefers not to discuss it – when I raised it he was obviously not prepared to dwell on the affair.

Yet as long as a certain native of a Lanarkshire mining village called Craigneuk was active there could be no thoughts of retiral. That person was Chic Calderwood, a man thoroughly detested by his Maryhill counterpart – sentiments heartily reciprocated by Calderwood. This hate had been rooted in a youthful amateur sparring session that had gone sour, leaving both men sharing a mutual resentment that endures to this day. As "Cowboy" told me recently, "Calderwood was a bully. I loathed him." However the culmination of this hateful rivalry was still two years away. Fate was to intervene in a way that seemed cruel at first but on reflection was more providential than it initially appeared.

The aftermath of the Harry Scott affair was a time for deep reflection and stock-taking. Out of the soul searching came a resolution to train harder and prove that the Harry Scott mess had been a fistic aberration of the same order as the first amateur contest of a young Detroit negro who was decked seven times. His name? – Joe Louis.

"Joe Louis" was in fact the name of one of "Cowboy's" first comeback opponents in 1964. This "Joe Louis" was a Nigerian whose only resemblance to his more illustrious American namesake was the colour of his skin and the boxing boots and trunks he sported in the ring. "Cowboy" jabbed Louis silly with the famed right jab before finishing him off within a round.

Next for the McCormack summary dismissal was light-heavyweight Malcolm Worthington of Crewe. At Paisley in March 1964 a short right hook – the only real punch seen in the contest – ended Mr Worthington's interest in matters in only one minute and 40 seconds of the first round.

In two bouts the Maryhill boxer's comeback amounted to three and a third minutes of actual combat. This was sensational stuff and it gave credence to "Cowboy's" continued taunts at the hated Calderwood – taunts he backed up with an offer of a £500-a-side challenge and some tart remarks about Calderwood's valour. That this rattled the normally taciturn Craigneuk man cannot be doubted. *Boxing News* of 11 December 1964 reported: "Calderwood has told me to tell McCormack to cough up or shut up."

As stated earlier, misfortune was to prevent any possibility of an immediate response to this challenge. Ruptured achilles tendons acquired during training put McCormack out of action for nearly a year.

Calderwood, as though to rub salt into his Maryhill tormentor's wound ran up a very impressive win over America's world-rated Johnny Persol – a win that had top American promoters clamouring for his services. Meanwhile "Cowboy" could only fret and plan for the day when he would finally trade punches with Calderwood.

If *The Guinness Book of Records* ever has a section under "comebacks" then the Maryhill southpaw will surely be up there with Frank Sinatra. Govan Town Hall, where "Cowboy" made his return on 29 April 1965 may have been a bit more prosaic than the "Reprise" or "Capitol" recording studios in sunny California but the sweet music of a crowd acclaiming victory in his ears made it a happy homecoming for McCormack. His opponent was 32-year-old Frenchman Bernard Quellier, a former champion of his country with a reputation for stiff punching. However the bulk of that came from the Scots light-heavyweight who was a clear points winner. Any lingering doubts about "Cowboy's" fitness to share a ring with Calderwood – a Calderwood still basking in his highly creditable win over Johnny Persol – had been dispelled.

One of those who was utterly convinced by the "new" McCormack was promoter Peter Keenan who signed him to fight Calderwood on 10 June 1965 at Paisley Ice Rink. The stage was now firmly set for what promised to be the grudge fight of the century in Scottish boxing annals. This was no ersatz emotion calculated to jam a few extra bottoms into seats. This was a conflict fuelled by real – very real – hatred.

In one sense, the battle for supremacy between John "Cowboy" McCormack and Chic Calderwood was like the scenario from a Robert Louis Stevenson novel where each major character depicts one half of the conflicting Scottish soul and temperament. In one corner there was the "Alan Breck" figure of John "Cowboy" McCormack – flamboyant, colourful, reckless and controversial. In the opposite corner stood Chic Calderwood, whose attitude and demeanour suggested he was an honours graduate of the Knox-Calvin Academy of Personality Repression, outwardly dour and taciturn to those outwith his immediate ken. Five thousand fans came to Paisley Ice Rink to see if they could fulfil their promise of mutual mayhem that Wednesday evening.

Fortunately for Calderwood, in view of the result, his British light-heavyweight title was not at stake on this occasion.

When both contestants entered the ring the atmosphere was charged with anticipation and excitement. After pre-fight instructions from Edinburgh referee George Smith the bell clanged and at last the great grudge match was on.

Calderwood was an infamously slow starter but McCormack stormed into him from the opening bell, forcing the Craigneuk man to cover up. "Cowboy" kept up his two-fisted assault as Calderwood jabbed on the retreat – a tactic that suited the bow-legged battler from Maryhill for it nullified the Craigneuk fighter's greatest weapon, his powerful left jab. A left jab thrown on the retreat is never as potent as one delivered going forward with the full body-weight behind it.

Just before the round ended "Cowboy's" pressure tactics paid handsome dividends when a short left cross opened a cut above Calderwood's right eye. This provoked Chic Calderwood into a counter-attack that made both fighters oblivious to the bell ending the session. Only referee George Smith's intervention forced a respite in the action.

The second stanza saw Calderwood try to come forward and plant the left jab that had carried the day against world-rated Johnny Persol firmly on "Cowboy's" features. Immediate two-handed retaliation from the Maryhill fighter forced Calderwood back to the ropes where a left hook to the head opened the eye cut further, prompting an intervention by referee Smith who decided the injury was too severe to permit matters to continue. Calderwood protested – his vehemence given a certain piquancy by the sight of John McCormack doing a victory jig with trainer Andy Gant and chief second Hugh Burke.

Large sections of the crowd echoed the *Daily Record*'s sentiments of "Big Fight Flops". There were even shouts of "Liston" – a reference to the farcical goings on in Lewiston, Maine, earlier that year when Sonny Liston had appeared to take a dive against Muhammad Ali in their return contest. A beer can thrown into the ring was further proof of punter disenchantment. But once the din and gnashing of teeth abated, the fact remained that John "Cowboy" McCormack had beaten a deadly rival and put himself firmly back on the world fistic map.

Less than three weeks after this victory *Boxing News* was testifying to "Cowboy's" risen fistic stock in world markets. The trade paper informed its readers on 2 July 1965: "Former British and European middleweight champion John "Cowboy" McCormack of Glasgow who created quite a sensation when he stopped British cruiserweight titleholder Chic Calderwood of Craigneuk, inside two rounds at Paisley Ice Rink on 10 June has been inundated with offers for his services."

Apart from fight offers from Germany, Italy and even Denmark, McCormack's manager Al Philips received a call from Madison Square Garden's Teddy Brenner, who was keen to match the "Maryhill Cowboy" with a top-rated American.

John McCormack was naturally more interested in a return against Calderwood with the latter's crown at stake. It was never to be. Calderwood was to join that unenviable band of fistic warriors who met their end on the roads in a grossly unequal confrontation with another vehicle – Jack Johnson, William "Young" Stribling and Mexican featherweight great Salvador Sanchez are others who died in a similar fashion.

John "Cowboy" McCormack was to have only one further contest, on 28 June 1966 in London's Royal Albert Hall in a British light-heavyweight title final eliminator. He was beaten somewhat uniquely by a boxer with an identical name, a man who was nine years his junior. In my view the record book entry "28 June 1966. Lost Points v. John McCormack" was a highly symbolic epitaph on the career of this extraordinary man, for it was almost as though he was being confronted by the squandered talent of his youth which had come back to haunt him.

However, this "John McCormack" to whom the Maryhill boxer lost was an Irishman from Eire who had assumed British citizenship to fight for a British title. It is to the elder McCormack's credit that he gave his youthful Irish tormentor a tough battle – indeed in round eight of this ten round scrap the Irishman was nearly swamped by a flood of punches. But in the end the resilience of youth won the day.

In retrospect, the Scottish fight game would have been a poorer place had the "Maryhill Cowboy" not graced its rings between 1957 and 1966. This is a view shared by former WBC lightweight champion of the world, Jim Watt. Interviewed on a television programme made to celebrate 30 years of the ever-popular *Scotsport* programme produced by Scottish Television, the blond southpaw-turned-TV-commentator from Bridgeton was asked to nominate his favourite Scottish fighter. Without hesitation he replied, "John 'Cowboy' McCormack." When asked to elaborate further Watt gave an affectionate smile and replied, "He was a great character!"

That must rate as one of the great sporting understatements of this or any other decade. The "Maryhill Cowboy" WAS a character... and then some.

JOE AITCHISON
The Boxing Bard of Bridgeton

To write a book – any book – on Scottish boxing and omit Joe Aitchison would be the equivalent of a Hebrew scholar translating the Old Testament and omitting any reference to God or Moses. If Charles Cotter of Edinburgh was Scotland's finest boxing trainer for the first 30 years of this century then Joe Aitchison was without peer as his successor for the following 50 years.

Any man who can attract unsolicited testimonials from individuals as diversely talented as former British and European middleweight champion John "Cowboy" McCormack and TV and stage comedian Bob Monkhouse has to be a bit special. During my visit to Mr Aitchison's neat bungalow home in Glasgow he showed me a letter dated 27 September 1963 from the celebrated English "showbiz" personality. In this testimonial Mr Monkhouse thanked Joe profusely for training him in keep-fit sessions at the latter's Dalmarnock gym, sessions arrranged by the comedian whilst he was appearing at the Alhambra Theatre in Glasgow.

Earlier that same month – on 5 September – another glowing tribute arrived from England where its author was training for a British middleweight title eliminator against George Aldridge of Market Harborough. John "Cowboy" McCormack wrote: "When I left Glasgow I left with the thought that you were the best and most knowledgeable trainer I ever had . . . and having been down here for some time now and seen what they had to offer I must say it has only strengthened my opinion of you." There were many other boxers who, for lack of McCormack's eloquence, expressed the sheer poetry of movement instilled in them by Joe Aitchison only in their ring performances.

To call Joe Aitchison the fistic bard of Bridgeton is less fanciful than appearances might at first allow. Joe Aitchison stressed in all his fighters – be it amateur novice or world champion bantam John Caldwell – the necessity for balance and movement, that fluid physical versification in the ring which made Muhammad Ali and Sugar Ray Leonard as different from street-fighters as Michaelangelo is from your average public "loo" graffiti monger.

The laws that govern the boxing ring and the writing of poetry are virtually synonymous. Poetry, like any form of creative writing, requires a ruthlessness with time and one's family that makes an "acknowledgement" page as obligatory in most published works as an index. In boxing this is reflected in Rocky Marciano forsaking wife and child for three-month stretches and living like an ascetic but very violent monk in a cabin in the Catskill mountains.

Trainers in boxing are the bards – the men like Joe Aitchison and Angelo Dundee who teach, really teach, rhythm and movement and the syntax of socking in lethal combinations. Both Aitchison and Dundee have a shared contempt for trainers who do not or cannot teach the poetry of ring movement – those whose conception of "training" goes no further than chewing a designer cotton bud and whose greatest concern is not to get blood or vaseline on sweaters that might have been filched from the set of Rocky IV. Such charlatans – the Chattertons of the prize ring – do exist. Joe Aitchison is most decidedly not one of them.

Poetry and violence were always blood brothers in the Bridgeton district of Glasgow where Joe Aitchison was born, on 11 March 1902, the eldest son of a family of five children.

Not only did William Wordsworth and Robert Burns choose to reside for short periods in Bridgeton but the district also boasted the largest Burns Club anywhere in the world. The author of the well-known Scottish song The Muckin' O' Geordie's Byre *was a Bridgeton poet Alex Rodger (1784 – 1836). So Bridgeton was a place of bards and battlers.*

In the first half of the 20th century the battling took two distinct forms. On the streets the gangs – the "Norman Conks", "The Billy Boys" and the "Baltic Fleet" – practised vicious partisanship with razors, bottles and bicycle chains. Some like Billy Fullerton, legendary leader of the "Billy Boys" recharged their batteries for further street mayhem by occasional forays into the boxing ring. (Fullerton was, according to some, a fairly good operator under Marquis of Queensberry rules). Even in May 1961 when some of the benefits of Harold McMillan's "affluent society" had percolated to the inhabitants of Bridgeton, American screen tough guy Richard Widmark called Bridgeton a place "worse than Chicago" – not that fighting citizens of Chicago were strangers to the streets of Glasgow. In 1912 Jim Fitzgerald, a Chicago negro, became one of the first coloured professional boxers to appear in Scotland from the USA at the Govan Athletic Club where he was outpointed by Govan's Jack McKinnon over ten rounds. Fitzgerald had trained in Bridgeton.

Fortunately from the authorities' point of view the majority of Bridgeton inhabitants embraced boxing as an outlet for their aggressive impulses – either as spectators or participants at the Scottish National Club in Olympia Street.

Joe Aitchison's father, George, was a steel driller at Beardmore's by day and the secretary of "The Scottish National" in the evening. He was abetted by Tommy Colquhoun – soon to become famous as the manager of Scotland's first contender for world flyweight honours, Elky Clark, who would lose in his bid for the world crown against America's Fidel La Barba in 1927. George Aitchison was also a highly respected trainer and it was he who introduced the young Joe to the game to which he was destined to make such a large contribution.

Joe Aitchison's talent was not restricted to training, motivating and coaching fighters. His youthful friendship with a medical student resulted in his acquiring a knowledge of physiology and massage. His services in this department were sought by a wide spectrum of people. This then is the man I interviewed in late November 1987.

B.D.: Your father was a prominent trainer before you. Did he handle any outstanding men?

J.A.: Of course! He helped train Billy Marchant of Salford, a leading featherweight who fought for the Lonsdale belt in 1920. (*Bat Masterton, the former famous Western Marshal turned journalist, described Marchant's New York debut in 1912 as a "decided hit". Marchant was cold-shouldered by the NSC who never let him fight the British champion Jem Driscoll. After the First World War he finally got his chance.*) He also trained Eddie Beattie of Castlecary who was one of the few men to force that great Welsh fighter Frank Moody of Pontypridd to throw in the towel. Don't forget Moody put Tommy Milligan, a world-rated middleweight, away inside a round.

B.D.: Did your father confine himself to the "Scottish National" at Bridgeton?

J.A.: No. After the First World War he became matchmaker at a famous professional boxing venue called the "Parkhead School of Physical Culture" – this was in fact an old converted billiard room which could accommodate around 750 people. I was employed as a round boy, but I didn't carry cards into the ring – I had a "magic lantern" and I projected the numbers on to a screen at one end of the hall. Another unusual thing about the place was that the fighters' seats in the ring were not diagonal but directly opposite each other on the same side of the ring!

B.D.: Which fighters do you remember appearing there?

J.A.: "Hamilton" Johnny Brown who fought Ted "Kid" Lewis later. Tommy Milligan made his professional debut there too. I also saw future British featherweight champion George McKenzie box there. I also saw Tancy Lee refereeing there.

B.D.: What did you make of Tancy as a referee?

J.A.: I didn't think very highly of him I'm afraid. He was inconsistent in his scoring and he definitely favoured boxers who displayed a style similar to his own – a frequent fault amongst former boxing champions who became "third men".

B.D.: What about your own career as a boxer, Joe?

J.A.: Well, as you can see for yourself I have very short arms – but I was quite useful. My father encouraged me to go to night school. From there I graduated to the "Dennistoun Palais". I loved dancing – I still dance. I was also a good skipper. This is why I believe in balance and movement being absolutely essential to any successful boxer. My dad encouraged me to take up training and coaching when he opened up his own gym in Bridgeton – the Dalmarnock ABC. He also opened a small gym in Clydebank – so I gradually became increasingly involved in training.

B.D.: Who was the first "great" fighter you saw in this period?

J.A.: Without doubt Elky Clark. I saw his professional debut on 14 November 1921 in the Parkhead School of Physical Culture against Boyles. Elky was knocked out in three rounds but a week later he gained a draw over ten rounds – against Boyles. Then three months later he finally beat Boyles on points. (*Elky Clark [1898-1956] was the Glasgow flyweight who won the British flyweight title on 31 March 1924 by outpointing Kid Kelly in London. He won the Empire title from Belfast's Jim Hanna by a tenth-round KO in Glasgow. The European crown was annexed in 1925 on points in Glasgow from Michel Montreuil. He was the first Scotsman to dispute the world flyweight title in 1927 – losing in New York.*)

B.D.: Tell me more about Elky Clark.

J.A.: "Elky" was an enigma – he was incredibly introverted. Do you know that when he went on his roadwork up the Cathkin Braes he was so shy that the minute he saw anyone coming he would take out an old pipe and stop – make as though he was just sitting having a quiet smoke!

B.D.: Your father trained him, I believe?

J.A.: Yes, part of the time. But my father got on Elky's nerves by always telling the boys in the gym to avoid Elky's left hook. Elky was an amateur at this time

– so Elky walked out in a huff one day and became a professional musician. He played the Dulcimer for five shillings a time.

B.D.: How did he come back into boxing?

J.A.: He drifted back to the Southern Amateur Athletic Club where he started sparring again. He gradually came under the influence of a grand old man called Jim Morton. Morton became his first professional manager. I liked Jim Morton but he was a better second than a manager – anyway Elky started as a professional fighting for "sausage money".

B.D.: What was "sausage money?"

J.A.: "Sausage money" was 50 shillings (*£2.50*) for ten two-minute rounds of boxing. So Elky told my father that he originally was only fighting for "sausage money". Elky was a great trainer – he actually got better. Elky's ideal fighting distance would have been over 45 rounds.

B.D.: Forty-five rounds?

J.A.: Definitely. That's what beat him in his world title fight with Fidel La Barba in 1927 – the fight was only over 12 rounds. Elky would have defeated any man over a long, really long distance. His stamina was phenomenal.

B.D.: When did he first catch your eye and make you think, "He could go all the way"?

J.A.: His great rival was Willie Woods. Elky's problem was he had an inferiority complex about Willie Woods – he thought the latter was actually better than he really was. The first time they fought (*3 July 1922 in Glasgow*) they drew over 15 rounds.

B.D.: Were they rivals outside the ring as well?

J.A.: Bitter rivals – they had a real feud going. Wood was an extrovert – Elky was painfully shy.Anyway, the second time they met (*20 November 1922*) it was over 15 rounds again. Woods bet his manager a bunnet he would win. Yet everyone agreed that whilst Woods had won the first half of the fight, Elky won the decision. But Woods was adjudged the winner.

B.D.: How good was Woods?

J.A.: He was good enough to go to New York and fight the Filipino Pincho Villa, who took the world flyweight title from the immortal Jimmy Wilde in 1923.

B.D.: Did Clark ever beat Woods?

J.A.: Four months after losing that hotly disputed decision to Woods he knocked him out in the ninth round – so he finally caught up with him.

B.D.: How would you compare Elky Clark to Benny Lynch?

J.A.: Elky wasn't as fast as Lynch but he had far greater stamina.

B.D.: What about Clark's world title bid against the American Fidel La Barba in 1927?

J.A.: Elky was sick with food poisoning when he boarded that liner for the USA. Dr. William Kivlichan (*who played for Celtic and Rangers in his pre-medical days*) gave instructions to his manager on how to treat him before he left. He was weakened by this on the way over – then, and Elky told me this himself, he had managerial problems with Colquhoun. To get the world title shot Colquhoun agreed to cut in an American agent – Charles J. Harvey – for eight-and-a-half per cent. Colquhoun took 33 and-a-third per cent. This left Elky with £500 for a world title fight. (*This was precisely the sum Nat Dresner paid "Hamilton" Johnny Brown in 1923 for a non-title fight against Augie Ratner.*) The twelve-round distance did not favour Elky either. Then, to cap it all, the Americans wouldn't let Elky wear his special double gum shield – this weakened Elky's jaw considerably. Then to make matters worse La Barba thumbed him in the eye – Elky lost the sight of this eye.

B.D.: He never fought after La Barba did he ?

J.A.: No. He was finished after that but he did quite well for himself. He was a very likeable person – opened "The Lonsdale Bar" for a time, then became a very good boxing writer with the *Daily Record.* He lost his licence for the pub – but he certainly didn't die as a pauper.

B.D.: What about someone who did – I mean Benny Lynch?

J.A.: I first saw Benny Lynch at the "Dumbarton Star Palace". I was seconding a fighter called Jim Cameron. Benny was fighting a boxer called Young Griffo from Dumbarton over six two-minute rounds. Funny thing I recall was that after the contest he was wearing a suit made up of an odd jacket and trousers that didn't match up.

B.D.: What were your impressions of him as a fighter then?

J.A.: I formed the opinion that he was very balanced. He danced like a man on a trampoline – yet I didn't think he would be strong enough for an eight-stone fighter at that point. It was Len Johnson's booth in Manchester that was the making of him.

B.D.: What do you mean?

J.A.: Johnson built up Lynch with good feeding. He also taught him good moves and made him physically much stronger at Manchester. He also emerged much more confident.

B.D.: When did you first notice the difference?

J.A.: I was seconding a guy at the "Gallowgate Ring" in 1932. Pat Docherty was supposed to be fighting Joe Aitken of Paisley but Docherty couldn't make it – so Lynch was drafted in as a "sub". I thought Aitken would be too experienced for Benny but I was proved wrong. Again in 1932 I was through at the Music Hall in Edinburgh on a Harold Bownas Promotion – I was seconding George "Ginger" McLeod and Lynch pole-axed him.

B.D.: Why was he so good overall in your opinion?

J.A.: He had great physical strength – great lung capcity. He also had an unusually thick neck which meant he could absorb hard punches. He was put on the floor by Tommy Pardoe but got up and stopped him. Lynch could also Kayo an opponent with a single blow.

B.D.: Whom did you rate most highly, Lynch or his successor, as a world champion Scottish "fly"?

J.A.: Jackie Paterson was definitely the harder puncher but Lynch was ahead in moral courage – when the going got really tough. Lynch also had a greater variety of punches. But again Paterson was the hardest hitter, pound for pound, that Scotland had ever produced.

B.D.: What did you put that fact down to?

J.A.: As a young man Paterson worked as a butcher – making mince through the machine developed the digital tendons in his wrist. The digital tendons are the most vital part of a boxer's body when he throws a hook – and how Paterson could hook! Paterson's manager Pat Collins also worked hard for Paterson.

B.D.: When did you first see Paterson?

J.A.: I first saw him as an amateur but I always felt that with his punching power the smaller gloves of the professional game would have suited him better – and so it proved.

B.D.: What about the fight with Kane in 1943 for the world title?

J.A.: Both Paterson and Peter Kane were at RAF Padgate where they gave an exhibition. Kane boxed so much better in this bout that he clearly had no qualms about putting his title on the line at Hampden Park. But don't forget Kane had to lose weight – this weakened the Lancashire boy. If the fight had been over the bantam weight at eight stones six pounds I would have taken Kane to beat Paterson every time – Kane had a better variety of punches than Paterson.

B.D.: Paterson's life ended tragically too – like Benny Lynch's. Were you surprised?

J.A.: I was sorry the way he went. But he never had much money sense – gambling, that kind of thing.

B.D.: You helped your father with British welterweight champion Jake Kilrain from Bellshill. How did he come under your father's management?

J.A.: My father came across Harry Owens – that was Kilrain's real name – in 1929 at an amateur competition. He was only 15 years old but he weighed a well distributed nine stones. He was at the competition because he wanted to get even with someone he didn't like – he beat him too in a way that obviously impressed my father.

B.D.: When did Kilrain turn professional?

J.A.: In 1931 when he was 17. He came from a poor family who were living by then in Baillieston. He fought his early fights for 21 shillings and sixpence (*£1.07*) – that was £1 for the fight and 1/6d for his fare. I was delegated to train him and second him so I helped him develop a strong body punch. But you know he really had his best days as a lightweight? *(nine stones six pounds)*.

B.D.: What makes you say that?

J.A.: In 1933 when he was only 19 years old he chinned Tommy Spiers of Alloa, the Scottish champion. He whacked Stevie Nolan, the Southern Area champion. Then he went over to Belfast and beat a great Irish scrapper called Billy Gilmour. Johnny Cuthbert, the British champion, was so afraid of losing his title in 1933 at the Liverpool Stadium that he made Kilrain come in overweight – just as well he did because Jake outpointed him!

B.D.: The Liverpool fight crowd have a great reputation. How was he received down there?

J.A.: Kilrain was an all-action fighter. They loved him down there. If he had stayed at lightweight he could have been one of the best in the world.

B.D.: What was he like as an individual?

J.A.: Jake was a man of contradictions. In the ring, especially just before a fight, he was incredibly calm. I remember my father saying that just before an important contest commenced "Kilrain sat like an old man in his corner" – meaning he was as calm as an old man relaxing. But outside the ring – oh he was a bad-tempered guy! The worst thing that happened to him was when he split his thumb and was out of the game for 15 months.

B.D.: What happened then?

J.A.: He got in league with an Aberdeen "bookie" who gave him a job. They were a real fast crowd. He neglected training but eventually he came back.

B.D.: What did you rate his best performance?

J.A.: That was his fight at Shawfield Park when he took the British welterweight title from Dave McCleave *(2 June 1936)*. I was in his corner that night. McCleave was taller than Jake and had a longer reach and brilliant left jab – so my father instructed Kilrain to slow him up. Every time he jabbed Kilrain answered with a body punch – body punching causes "overhang".

B.D.: What is that?

J.A.: Eventually the boxer bends farther and nearer to his opponent as his body aches more from the punches. Kilrain fractured McCleave's breastbone – he hit him so hard. He was inspired that night. He eventually kayoed McCleave with a body punch in the eighth round.

B.D.: If I can backtrack to Paterson – I believe he was partially responsible for you training two American world champions in the Dalmarnock gym?

J.A.: That's right. I "entertained" Dado Marino from Hawaii and his manager "Sad Sam Ichinose" in July 1947. (*Dado Marino was the first grandfather to win a world title when he outpointed England's Terry Allen for the world flyweight title. His fight with Paterson did not materialise because the latter was overweight.*) They were here to fight Jackie Paterson for his world title. They were both delightful gentlemen. So was the world bantam champion Manuel Ortiz – he was a Mexican-American from California. He outpointed Paterson but lost the title eventually to the South African Vic Toweel. Manuel Ortiz was the best bantamweight boxer I ever saw.

B.D.: Even better than your world bantamweight John Caldwell?

J.A.: Even better than him! Ortiz's stance – the all-important position of his hands and feet – was outstanding. He beat Paterson well. In fact Norman Hurst, who was a very famous boxing writer for Kemsley newspapers, called Paterson that night "a game coward" – he was more interested in simply lasting the distance than he was in winning. But to return to Dado Marino, both he and Manuel Ortiz were exemplary trainers in the Dalmarnock gym – beautiful fighters to handle.

B.D.: Do you have any amusing experiences from your days in the ring?

J.A.: Several spring to mind. I remember on one occasion when I was seconding in a boxing booth in Coatbridge – the fight was between two locals, Isaac McGowan of Coatbridge and Jim Christie from Carnbroe – the referee was also acting as the MC and to impress everyone he did his announcing in a "high pan" accent – very posh he was. Well, during the actual contest he collided with one of the boxers and he suddenly blurted out in a local accent you could cut with a knife, "Fer Christ's sake gie's a bit order!"

B.D.: When did you take bantamweight Billy Rafferty under your wing?

J.A.: After the Second World War I had a quiet spell when I wasn't involved too much with pro's. But then in the 1950s I started to come back again. Billy Rafferty came to me himself – asked me to take him on. There was no contract – we just shook hands. I told him that he could leave me anytime he pleased – he never did, even though attempts were made to poach him away. I didn't really fancy fight managing – I despised the "meal ticket" approach too many managers I saw in the game had at that time.

B.D.: What were Billy's strengths?

J.A.: Billy trained like a Trojan. As a result he had great lung capacity. He was durable – when you hit him it was like hitting a revolving door, he just kept coming back at you. He was a rough diamond, Billy, but I taught him to disguise his faults. But above all else Billy beat better opponents than himself with speed.

B.D.: Can you give me an example?

J.A.: Sure! He fought Len Reece of Wales in a final eliminator for the British bantamweight title. I overheard Reece's handlers, Wally Leslie and Frank Duffet, telling Reece not to worry about Billy's speed as he could never keep it up – but he did and he won on points!

B.D.: What titles did Billy win?

J.A.: Surprisingly, none! He had a lot of bad luck, mind you. Like the time he went to Belfast to fight Freddie Gilroy. (*Freddie Gilroy became British and Empire champion. This Irish hotshot effectively ended the career of Peter Keenan in 1958. He was one of Britain's outstanding post-war bantamweights even if his world title aspirations foundered on the rock of French North African hardiness – he could never overcome Alphonse Halimi the world kingpin.*) Billy had to postpone the fight for two weeks as he had damaged a ligament in his foot. I wanted Billy to have a month to recuperate but George Connell, the Belfast promoter, was adamant he couldn't agree to this. Besides Billy really needed the money at that point – so despite his training being broken we went ahead.

B.D.: What was the outcome of all this?

J.A.: Billy was stopped on a cut eye – yet Gilroy was cut worse than Rafferty and he was tiring. But the referee gave the benefit of the doubt to the Irishman.

B.D.: Do you think he could have beaten Gilroy under normal circumstances?

J.A.: Well, judge for yourself! The great Mexican bantam Ignacio Pina beat Gilroy – and Rafferty defeated Pina at Manchester.

B.D.: What about Pina?

J.A.: Pina was not your average Mexican bantamweight. They tend to be short stocky characters – he was tall for a bantam and thin. He had a long reach. He had defeated Gilroy, remember – but there is a story behind this fight. Rafferty came to me, said Mickey Duff had offered him £750 to fight Pina. Billy wanted my advice. I said to him, "For £750 – not on your life!" I told Billy to tell Duff that he wanted £1,000 minimum to go in with Pina – and just for devilment I said, "We want our travel expenses as well". I thought this might provoke a response – and I wasn't wrong. Duff sent us our travel expenses all right – two third class railway tickets! After Billy had beaten Pina at Bellevue Stadium *(Manchester)*, Duff came up to me in the ring and said, "Aitchison, you're a great little trainer and a c**t as well!" I took that as a compliment coming from him.

B.D.: What did you rate as Billy Rafferty's best performance?

J.A.: That was the night in Paisley when he defeated the American bantamweight Dwight Hawkins. Hawkins was the fourth best bantam in the world at the time according to *Ring* magazine. Billy outpointed him well – he really was impressive.

B.D.: What was Rafferty like to handle?

J.A.: Billy was a dream – no temperamental problems. He was addicted to the two most essential things in a boxer's training if they want to succeed – roadwork and sparring. We are still very good friends. I encouraged him to apply for his referee's licence and I will regard that my mission is accomplished when he is awarded his star "A" class licence which will let him handle world title fights. It is no more than he deserves.

B.D.: Johnny Caldwell was the world champion bantamweight you handled. What do you recall of that era?

J.A.: Ironically enough, John Caldwell was a devout Roman Catholic from Belfast. I had been boxing instructor to the Royal Ulster Constabulary between 1936 and 1939. Yet we got on famously together. Indeed, when a rift developed between Caldwell's manager Docherty and myself, Caldwell was counselled by a Roman Catholic priest in Belfast to go back to me.

B.D.: How did you rate Caldwell in comparison to the other fighters that you handled?

J.A.: John Caldwell didn't realise just how good he really was. He had outstanding ability and he was an excellent trainer. Sometimes he thought I drove him too hard. I remember when he was going to fight Frankie Jones of Plean I brought in top sparring partners – I even brought Ken Buchanan, who was then an amateur, through for him. I was driving Caldwell to build up pace. During one of these sessions Caldwell screamed at me, "Can't you count the time – I want to feel like fighting, not dying!"

B.D.: But it paid off?

J.A.: Obviously. He became the world bantam champion. (*He was recognised as such by Britain, the British Empire and Europe. The USA, South America and Japan recognised the Brazilian, Eder Jofre.*) His manager was Sam Docherty who had promoted most of Peter Keenan's big fights at Firhill Park.

B.D.: What was Caldwell's best performance?

J.A.: He had a few. He slaughtered young Martin of Spain who had annihilated the British and European flyweight champion the Welshman Dai Dower. I put that particular victory down to the good sparring he had with Billy Rafferty and

Derry Treanor. But his best performance was his first fight with Alphonse Halimi the world champion – he was conditioned to the minute then.

B.D.: What instructions did you give him on how to tackle Halimi?

J.A.: I didn't have a fight plan at first – I didn't know enough about Halimi at that stage. But Caldwell was in great form anyway.

B.D.: You mentioned some kind of "rift" earlier. What was that all about?

J.A.: Caldwell's manager Sammy Docherty asked Billy Rafferty to go to Brazil and fight Eder Jofre – Jofre was one of the classiest bantams ever. I knew Billy simply wasn't in shape to take on such a task. Billy asked me if he should go – I said a firm "No!" Billy then refused Docherty's offer. Consequently I lost Caldwell because of this. That was when he consulted the priest. Overall I always felt Johnny Caldwell never fully realised his potential.

B.D.: If I may backtrack again, you were appointed trainer to the Scottish Olympic team at the 1948 Olympics in London? (*It will be recalled that the other great Scots trainer Charles Cotter had trained the Scottish contingent in the 1908 London Olympics.*)

J.A.: Yes.

B.D.: Any outstanding memories of that?

J.A.: Mainly my dealings with Peter Keenan. I liked Peter a lot – we are still friends – but in 1948 young mister Keenan was a very headstrong character. I think he resented me at first but I put him in his place – and I will never forget the funny face he pulled that day. It still amuses me now to think of it. But Peter was one of the best boxers Scotland has ever produced.

B.D.: Sir Iain Colquhoun of Luss employed you as a private boxing coach. How did that happen?

J.A.: Well, as you know Sir Iain was one of the leading figures in the fight game until his death in 1948. I received a letter requesting that I take his son Torquil Colquhoun and teach him to box. I agreed. Torquil was home from Eton. He had been an enthusiastic fencer at Eton but he had a fencer's rather than a boxer's stance. I liked the boy – he was game and enthusiastic although he could never have been a champion boxer. (*Torquil Colquhoun died tragically young, aged 21, in a mountaineering accident.*)

B.D.: Who in your opinion was the greatest fighter you have ever seen?

J.A.: Sugar Ray Leonard, without a doubt. As I always said, "You don't build a ship from the top deck down" – the feet and movement are the basis of fistic ability. Leonard had it all. He was also the best technically – he was even better than Benny Lynch at cutting off an opponent in the ring and that is saying something. However technique is not everything – temperament is as important as technique. Ken Buchanan had a super fighting temperament. That is why he could take such a good punch – he was always so relaxed in the ring, as was John Caldwell.

B.D.: To sum up then, what would your ideal Scottish fighter be like? What qualities would he embody?

J.A.: My ideal Scottish fighter would have:

(a) The cover and hook of Tancy Lee.
(b) The varied infighting of Jim Higgins.
(c) The agility of Mick McAdam (*Airdrie boxer prominent in the 1920s*).
(d) The stamina of Elky Clark.
(e) The poise of Jim Cater (*great Scottish amateur boxer of the 1920s*).
(f) The speed and right uppercut of "Hamilton" Johnny Brown.
(g) The "one-two" (left to head, right to body in quick combination) of Tommy Milligan.
(h) The quarter turn of Jim Cameron.
(i) "The up and over" of Johnny McMillan (*up-and-over – slip left lead-body punch and hook over extended arm in quick combination*).
(j) The left hook of Benny Lynch.
(k) The right hand body punch of Jake Kilrain.
(l) The aggression of Johnny McGrory.
(m) The looping right of Jackie Paterson.
(n) The generalship of Peter Keenan.
(o) The courage of Billy Rafferty.
(p) The temperament of Ken Buchanan.

B.D.: Joe Aitchison, thank you.

EPILOGUE

As Joe Aitchison dealt at some length with the career of Elky Clark we think it is of interest to readers to read who Clark himself thought was his most difficult opponent. The following is reproduced from the official fight programme of the Peter Keenan v. Danny O'Sullivan British bantam title contest which took place on Wednesday, 9 May 1951 at Firhill Stadium. Elky Clark was then working as boxing critic of the *Daily Record.*

Elky Clark, Former European Flyweight Champion and Boxing Critic for the *Scottish Daily Record* details below whom he considers was

HIS TOUGHEST OPPONENT EVER

CONTINENTAL fighters have always maintained a high standard of physical fitness and an aptitude to be able to take all the punishment that an opponent can hand out. Two fights in my career which stand out most prominently, were my contests against that tough, capable little fly-weight, Francois Morrachini of France.

Both fights were 20 rounds apiece and, while I won both on points, I consider they were the most gruelling, dramatic efforts I ever went through.

In the first contest we battered away, and it was give and take till the final bell. I was declared the winner but it was hectic and I could hardly eat for about a week after it. How Morrachini felt I don't know.

The following day the promoter, Mr. Harry Jacobs, was insistent for a return. At that time I was European fly-weight champion and he wanted me to meet the Frenchman with the title at stake. I was, however, not interested in such a contest as he was one of those tough French fighters who had to be nearly half killed before he would take a full count.

The promoter offered me a large sum and tried to sweeten things up by giving me a Jack Solomons cigar, but I wasn't biting. I asked double the amount. He thought I was kidding but it was no joke. I didn't care if I ever saw Morrachini again.

After a long argument he finally agreed to my terms and we met three months later at the same venue. Tommy Milligan also defended his European middleweight title against Ted Moore, Plymouth, on the same bill.

My first fight with the French boy was hard enough but the second was worse. I floored him in the first round for a count of 9 and thought to myself that I could finish him within the scheduled 20 rounds distance, but the wish was the father of the thought. Morrachini was still there at the end of the last session as strong as he had started.

I hit Morrachini with everthing bar the pail but it took no effect.

He just stood and stared at me – white froth coming from his nose and mouth, then he would come back fighting as strongly as ever.

It was hopeless trying to knock him out so finally I decided to box him.

But Morrachini did not last long in the game after this fight. The continual pummelling received in our fights had softened him up for future opponents. I understand the Frenchman was killed in a cafe brawl in France a few years later, when he tried to save a friend in a fight. While I am not sure how he met his end, I can testify that he was one of the toughest cleanest fighters that ever stepped into the ring.

SUGAR RAY
Sweet n' Sour In Scotland

One of the benefits of the modern television video recorder is that it permits boxing fans to witness fistic greats of yesteryear, to see an excellence that was formerly privy only to those fortunate enough to afford an 8mm or 16mm film projector.

In this connection one whose boxing greatness has repeatedly illuminated my television screen via video is "Sugar" Ray Robinson. I defy anyone to show me a more perfectly executed left hook than the one the brilliant negro landed on the jaw of Utah's Gene Fullmer on 2 May 1957. And have you ever watched more devastating combinations than those thrown by the "Sugar" man at Jake Lamotta on 14 February 1951 when he won the world middleweight title for the first of five times?

The brilliant ringcraft of Robinson is highlighted in the video film of Robinson v. Carmen Basilio II when "Sugar" Ray "talks" to the referee to clarify some "point" – when all he in fact is doing is purchasing a "breather" for his ageing legs and lungs!

Among the ten most electrifying kayos must be counted the one achieved by Robinson over Carl "Bobo" Olson on 9 December 1955 – a win that returned to him the world middleweight crown he had relinquished two years before to pursue a song-and-dance act in nightclubs.

It is no mere coincidence that Scottish fistic *congnoscenti* such as Bobby Neil and Dick McTaggart rate "Sugar" Ray as the greatest boxer who ever lived. This American, born Walker Smith in Detroit, USA, had it all, fistically speaking.

One of Walker Smith's great heroes was "The Brown Bomber", Joe Louis. The youthful middleweight genius used to carry the great heavyweight's bag on occasion from the Motor City Gym where Louis trained for a time. This was the start of a friendship that would see them make a mutual stand against racism in a southern army camp in 1944 – a stand that resulted in their fellow negroes being admitted to ringside for the first time.

By the time this incident took place Walker Smith had permanently borrowed the name of "Ray Robinson" from another youth. The "Sugar" tag came when someone described an early ring performance as being "as sweet as sugar". As "Sugar" Ray Robinson he ran up a fantastic pro' record. From 1940 onwards when his pro' career began he won the world welterweight title once – against Tommy Bell in 1946 – and the middleweight crown a record FIVE times. He failed to lift the world light-heavyweight crown in June 1952 when heat, rather than his opponent, Italian-American Joey Maxim, forced him into a state of collapse in the 13th round.

Incidentally, although it was certainly not his intention at the time, the "Sugar" man struck another blow against white racism by this defeat. Slavery – the very institution that had brought Walker Smith and his ancestors to the USA – was based on a belief that Africans could toil in the sub-tropical cotton and tobacco fields much better than whites could. That this is a fallacy is evident in the negro Robinson collapsing with heat-induced dehydration whilst his white foe Maxim still even had enough juice left to do an energetic victory jig at the end of the contest!

In 1951, at the peak of his powers, he came to Britain and created a sensation in rationing-constrained England by his entourage and lifestyle, which resembled that of a Renaissance prince. In addition to the normal trainer and manager, he was accompanied by a personal hairdresser, a dwarf and a male friend who rejoiced in the unlikely name of JUNE Smith! This flamboyance extended to his choice of cars. A large salmon pink Cadillac was his pride and joy during the peak years.

Yet Robinson never pretended that his boxing prowess in the ring made him omnipotent outside of it. He had such a fear of elevators (lifts) that on one occasion he walked up 20 floors by the stairs to keep an appointment. Another phobia he admitted to was a total aversion for the body hair of white opponents! In his biography *Sugar Ray* he recounted how he had cringed every time a particularly hairy specimen – the Italian-American Joey Rindone, whom he stopped – had clinched with him, rubbing his chest hair against Robinson's smooth black skin. So this genius had a human face as well. There was nothing Olympian or remote about him.

However, when he came to Scotland in August 1964 much had changed since those prime time days. The flamboyant lifestyle had been curbed by Uncle Sam's taxmen grabbing back-taxes; the retinue of soap opera cast proportions had been pensioned off to the obscurity from whence he had plucked it.

It was not simply his financial muscle which had constricted since the halcyon days of the early Fifties. His legendary skills were finding it increasingly difficult to resist the rusts of time. Proof of this lay in the quality of some of his most recent opponents and the places in the USA where he met them.

His last port of call before his jet touched down at Prestwick had been Omaha, Nebraska. Now, the Dundee district of Omaha had given the world two internationally famous film stars in Marlon Brando and Henry Fonda but in boxing terms Omaha was to Madison Square Garden what Tristan da Cunha is to the Kremlin in terms of political clout. There – in Omaha – Robinson had fought one Art Hernandez, thus giving the latter his one and only ring distinction. Hernandez had drawn with "Robbie".

However, as promoter Peter Keenan can readily testify the "Sugar Man" and his longtime manager George "The Emperor" Gainsford were anything but cheap to entice to Scotland. Keenan had to pay £23 per day (about £200 at today's values) to keep them in a manner to which they had now become accustomed. All told, Peter Keenan reckoned the six-man Robinson team cost him £500 a week, (roughly equivalent to a building labourer's ANNUAL wage in 1964) for their suite in the McDonald Hotel, Giffnock. Why, one might ask, had the Anderston man, now Scotland's number one fight promoter, gone to such expense?

Keenan was fighting hard – not just to bring big-time boxing to Paisley Ice Rink and the Kelvin Hall, but to keep it alive, because it is a matter of record that by the mid-Sixties big-time Scottish professional boxing was beginning to lose the mass appeal it had enjoyed for the 40-odd years since Nat Dresner introduced it in the early Twenties. The reasons for this are complex and outwith the scope of this chapter but suffice to say that this decline would continue until the pro' fight game had all but disappeared in Scotland by 1972 – all this despite Peter Keenan's commendable efforts to halt the rot by importing living legends like Robinson.

That decline, however, was in the future. The whole Scottish press and electronic media corps were well represented on Friday, 15 August 1964 when the man the whole world agreed was the greatest ever flew into Scotland. This, though, was no courtesy call or Roman holiday for Robinson. There was a serious mission to be accomplished. Peter Keenan had signed the "Sugar Man" to fight current British middleweight champion Mick Leahy at Paisley Ice Rink over ten rounds.

Leahy was born in 1935 in the Republic of Ireland – a fact that might have disqualified him from ever contesting a British boxing title which the regulations stipulated was only open to British subjects. Leahy circumvented this potential hazard to his boxing ambitions by becoming a naturalised British subject. This was good news for him but ultimately bad news for George Aldridge whom he stopped inside a round at Nottingham in May 1963 to lift the British title and the Lonsdale belt. In October of the same year Leahy was outpointed over 15 close rounds by Gomeo Brennan of the Bahamas in London for the British Empire title.

The Irishman had several creditable results in his record. He had drawn with Canada's Wilfie Greaves who had drawn with the then world champion Dick Tiger. That he had a tough chin is evident in the fact that he was only ever kayoed once and that in the early part of his career. A year after his Paisley meeting with Robinson, Leahy would take Italian Olympic champion and future world professional middleweight champion Nino Benevenuti to a decision. Surprisingly though, at the time of his meeting with the "Sugar Man" most ringside pundits tended to dismiss the Irishman as an unworthy opponent. This assessment was based more on memory than actual reality as the *Daily Record*'s Dick Currie cautioned: "Around nine o'clock tonight... many fans will expect to watch the dynamic Robinson of thirteen years ago... nobody can withstand the march of time...".

Shortly after his arrival in Glasgow "Sugar" Ray gave an exhibition of punching the punchball and shadow boxing to an appreciative audience in Peter Keenan's gym in the basement of the latter's Charing Cross home. This venue was but a stone's throw from the St Andrew's Halls where exactly 20 years and five weeks previously "Sugar" Ray's hero and friend Joe Louis had entertained a wartime Glasgow crowd. Robinson had more time to spread himself around than his old heavyweight chum. He duly visited the Parochial Hall in Burbank where young Walter McGowan was training.

The "Burbank Boy Wonder" was acutally training to fight a stablemate of Robinson's – Natalio Jiminez of the Dominican Republic. Walter McGowan told me, "Robinson was a gentleman – a fabulous guy!" He recalled the skipping and gym routines he did with the fabled American.

There may have been those who scoffed at the idea of this sleek black aristocrat of the ring condescending to train in a place like the Parochial Hall in Burbank. Burbank, California, which is situated at the centre of the glitzy American film industry – sure! But Burbank, Lanarkshire? Those who thought thus simply demonstrated their profound ignorance of Scottish and American boxing history. Forty years before, in 1924, American Olympic light-heavyweight champion Eddie Egan had trodden the streets of Burbank when he was an honoured guest at the 21st birthday celebrations (which lasted a whole week) of his university and boxing boon companion, the future Duke of Hamilton. Eddie Egan had gone on to become chairman of the all-powerful New York State Athletic Commission which controlled a goodly portion of the American pro' boxing world. Egan and Robinson knew each other of old from various dealings they had had back in the days when Robinson was world welter kingpin. So there were strong historical ties between Burbank and New York – despite what the ignorant scoffers might have thought.

It is axiomatic in boxing that whilst the legs go first with a veteran boxer his punch will always remain as a potent reminder of his past glories. There was evidence of this on the eighth day of Robinson's Scottish tour during a sparring session in the Burbank Parochial Hall. Robinson's sparring partner was an ex-Empire Games middleweight called Milo Colhoun. During the second heat of their sparring bout the young Jamaican caught Robinson with two hard punches. At first Robinson seemed to ignore this youthful impertinence but in the final minute of the ultimate round "Sugar" Ray cut loose with an exhibition of the kind of heavy artillery that had pulverised many a past foe. A left hook and right cross catapulted Colhoun into the ropes. Questioned about the incident later, Robinson acknowledged that he had put Colhoun under severe pressure but claimed he had exercised compassion by not finishing the Jamaican off.

There were other critics of Peter Keenan's initiative who feared that Robinson may have come to just go through the motions in his bout with Leahy in exchange for a quite substantial number of quick bucks. There were some precedents for this. On 2 October 1956 former American heavyweight great, Ezzard Charles, had stepped into a London ring and produced an absolute stinker of a performance against Welshman Dick Richardson. Glasgow referee Frank Wilson had disqualified the former "Cincinnati Flash" for giving a passionate embrace to his British opponent that continued for the whole of the five minutes the "contest" had lasted. Charles had been at the same fag-end of an otherwise illustrious career that

Robinson was now (in 1964). Almost as though to allay these fears Robinson told assembled press men: "I just can't let this Scottish crowd down . . . I will be battling with all I know – like it was for the world title."

Another aspect of the Robinson v. Leahy contest that intrigued many was that the Irishman was managed by George Middleton. Middleton had been in Randolph Turpin's corner on that blissful evening in London on 10 July 1951 when the "Leamington Licker" had taken Robinson's only recently acquired world middleweight title on points. Turpin's 64-day rule as world kingpin sent post-war Britain into an orgy of clebration – a celebration all the more piquant because the English boxer's victory had been totally unexpected.

Middleton stated that he considered it a great honour that his fighter (Leahy) should share a ring with the "Sugar Man". Sweet sentiments that were to give way to somewhat more sour feelings after the bout. The sweetness lasted all the way up to the weigh-in on the morning of Thursday, 3 September 1964. That day was the 25th anniversary of the Second World War and when Robinson stepped on the scales it seemed as though a miniature version of that epic conflict was about to erupt. The "Sugar Man" weighed 11 stones ten-and-a-half pounds – three-and-a-half pounds over the poundage stipulated in the pre-fight contract.

George Middleton angrily insisted that Robinson come in at the agreed weight or there would be no fight. Robinson and George Gainsford denied that there had been any weight stipulation at all but this was contradicted by promoter Peter Keenan who referred them to the contract they had signed. In the end Robinson did some stiff jogging around Kelvingrove Park and paid a £50 forfeit to ensure the bout went ahead.

The contest itself was highly controversial and Welsh referee Ike Powell, who was involved in several ring controversies involving Bobby Neil and later Walter McGowan, found himself in hot water again, at least with Robinson's manager George "The Emperor" Gainsford.

The consensus of opinion of those at ringside was that Robinson deserved the decision by dint of his superior ring skills over the undoubted strength of Leahy. Peter Keenan told me, "Robinson definitely won it in my book . . . ".

Leahy fought in his typical no-frills style where aggression was substituted for any lack in the boxing skills department. All the flashes of fistic brilliance came, as expected, from Robinson but Ike Powell clearly thought that one or two flashes of brilliance do not a completed round make and gave the edge to the more industrious Irishman.

One ringside observer who was decidedly unhappy – apart from Robinson's manager – was George Middleton. The Midlands-based manager announced he was going to sue Robinson and his pilot Gainsford for "causing inconvenience". Gainsford for his part lodged an official complaint about Ike Powell's decision with the Scottish Area Council and the British Board of Boxing Control. The atmosphere was decidedly sour in contrast to all the earlier sweetness that had been prevalent wherever Robinson went.

Nevertheless, that the sour taste of the aftermath did not endure is evident in the recollections of all those I spoke to in connection with this chapter. John "Cowboy" McCormack who sparred with Sugar Ray, albeit briefly, was immensely impressed by his qualities outwith the ring. Peter Keenan, despite his contractual dispute, was equally impressed by Robinson. So all in all it had been a memorable episode in Scottish boxing history.

POSTSCRIPT

Ironically Leahy's career would end the following year – the same year, 1965, as Robinson called it a day. He never won another contest after beating Robinson in Paisley. That fight had been the high noon of his career. Five weeks after leaving Paisley Leahy lost to Hungarian Lazlo Papp in Vienna over 15 rounds for the European title. By mid-December he had lost his British title on points to Wally Swift in Nottingham.

Robinson fared little better in the ring. Shortly after the Leahy defeat he went to London and stopped Nigerian Johnny Angel inside the distance. The following year he fought his last contest, in which he was outpointed by Irish-American Joey Archer.

On Thursday, 10 December 1965, in an emotional and packed Madison Square Garden Robinson took his final bow and was chaired around the ring by four of the men whom he had engaged in gaining his record five world middleweight titles – Carmen Basilio, Randy Turpin, "Bobo" Olson and Gene Fullmer. The affair was made all the more poignant by the fact that one of the four – Randy Turpin – would commit suicide just six months later.

As for Peter Keenan, whose initiative in bringing the "Sugar Man" to Scotland must be commended, he battled on to keep professional boxing alive in Scotland. Initially, his efforts were to be in vain. By June 1966 there was only one licensed manager operating in Scotland – Keenan himself. In the same year only two amateur clubs ran shows in Glasgow. Scottish boxing had reached its nadir in domestic terms. But Peter Keenan was there when the revival began in earnest in April 1979 when the Anderston man, in association with Mickey Duff presented the Jim Watt v. Alfredo Pitalua world title fight. This marked the beginning of a Scottish fistic renaissance that has endured to this day.

CHIC CALDERWOOD of Craigneuk
1812 Without the Overture

There are some men for whose lives misfortune displays an affection so stubborn that it makes the devotion of that faithful canine, Greyfriars Bobby, seem fickle by comparison.

In soccer such a man was Scotsman Allan Brown who, in 1953 played a large part in guiding Blackpool to their first and only FA Cup final success. Brown, a classy inside-forward, had been the main architect of Blackpool's victory in the sixth round against Arsenal but he broke his leg in the process. One can only speculate that the pain in his mind must have exceeded the pain in his leg as he witnessed his team-mates collecting winning medals.

In lawn tennis the Australian Ken Rosewall could never play well enough in the numerous Wimbledon finals in which he appeared to discourage his number one camp follower – misfortune – from being persistently infatuated with him.

Scottish boxing in the 1950s and 1960s had a similar unfortunate in "Chic" Calderwood. If the year 1812 was not a good one for fighting men – Napoleon suffered his first major reverse in Russia – it at least offered the compensation of inspiring that great Russian composer Tchaikovsky to write his memorable *1812 Overture.* There was ultimately no such compensation in life for this unlucky light-heavyweight from Craigneuk in Lanarkshire who perished in a car crash at the comparatively youthful age of 29 in 1966.

Calderwood's life was truly a case of 1812 without the overture. Yet there were times when it seemed that celebration rather than commiseration would be the outstanding hallmark of his career. Perhaps the greatest irony of all is that Calderwood lived his life less like so many Scottish boxing champions have done – behaving like thoroughbreds in the Derby of personal disaster. The bottle and TB killed Lynch; greyhound racing sank Paterson; gambling left Calderwood's opponent John "Cowboy" McCormack a poorer man than he should have been.

In 1983 I interviewed Tommy Gilmour Junior in the Dundee studios of Radio Tay. Young Tommy's father – Tommy Gilmour Senior, "The Star Maker" – had managed Calderwood. Gilmour the younger told me, "Chic was an extremely quiet guy. You could be in a room at a social gathering and never realise he was there."

Calderwood's main passions outside the ring were fast cars, slow horses and women. But his misfortune was that he was smitten with a disease that generations of Scots have come to identify with the international soccer field – inconsistency. His ring performances were either as scintillating as Archie Gemmell's goal

Chic Calderwood. The young lad is today better known as Tommy Gilmour Junior – leading fight promoter.

against Holland in 1978 or spectacles on a par with two pub teams playing on the morning after Hogmanay.

Yet like so many who embrace the much tougher pro' game his amateur career was studded with success – as a middleweight. Between 1955 and 1956 Chic Calderwood won three amateur titles in a fashion that made him the recipient of several offers to enter the ranks of the professionals.

In 1957 the two most outstanding promoters and managers in Scotland were Tommy Gilmour Senior and Samuel Docherty. Calderwood elected to be managed by Gilmour, "The Star Maker". The latter had guided Peter Keenan to a world title fight and he also knew the game inside out. It was the start of a career of triumph and frustration; of real achievement riddled with the smallpox of tragedy.

Chic Calderwood was born in the mining village of Craigneuk, Lanarkshire, on Friday, 9 January 1937. Calderwood's father had performed as a pro' fighter under the pseudonym of Kid Farlow. Despite his industrial heritage, the young Chic revealed a preference for rural life – a trait that was to reach fruition in his stated aim to become a farmer once he forsook the highly urbanised sport of professional boxing. Even as a young man Chic Calderood liked to roam around the many rural corners of Lanarkshire. He also loved horses and animals of the four-legged kind generally. Indeed, it was not until the rather late age of 16 that he embraced the distinctly less pastoral hobby of stalking his fellow bipeds in the ring with mayhem on his mind.

To the outside world Calderwood often displayed as much emotion as a horse quietly grazing in a field, yet he was articulate and expressive through music, playing the accordian and trumpet to a fairly high standard. Yet the peasant qualities of dourness and solidity clung to his image in and out of the ring.

Though Chic may have been late in starting his fistic career he was certainly in earnest. His initial season as a vested warrior saw him capture the Scottish Western District youth title at ten stones. In 1955 the Scottish Senior middleweight title became his. Twelve months later not only was his SABA title retained but the Western District "middles" crown was added to his growing list of amateur honours. Calderwood never did manage to become a national (ABA) title-holder, being a beaten semi-finalist at Wembley on two occasions. He did however avenge one of these semi-final setbacks as an amateur once he joined the punch-for-pay ranks. In 1956 Ron Redrup outpointed Calderwood in the ABA semi-finals, only to pay severely for this dent in the Craigneuk clouter's record by being stopped in the 11th round when he disputed the Scotsman's British professional light-heavy-weight crown at Blackpool in 1963.

The year 1957 saw the young Lanarkshire light-heavy make his debut in the pro' ranks. His opponent from Middlesborough at Falkirk Ice Rink was Jimmy Teasdale. He knocked the Englishman out inside two rounds. His next three opponents were stopped also inside the distance so it had been an auspicious start for the young Lanarkshire boxer who still worked as a surface worker at Kingshill No. 1 Colliery.

The coming of 1958 also saw Calderwood dispose of his first real "name" opponent, a tough and experienced "scouse" called Billy Ellaway who was dismissed in six rounds. What gave an extra edge to this performance was that it took place at Johnny Best's Liverpool Stadium – renowned as the "Graveyard of Champions". Not only did contender Calderwood not "die" there but the classic stiff left jabbing and right crosses employed against Ellaway resurrected memories of some of the great fighters of yesteryear who had graced the Merseyside ring.

However, the most significant fight thus far in his budding career was his next one, on Wednesday, 29 October 1958, when he entered the Kelvin Hall ring to dispute the Scottish light-heavyweight title. Even in the late 1950s it was highly unusual for a young boxer with a dozen fights under his belt to obtain an Area title bout (Scottish titles were/are classified as "Area titles"). It is a measure of the

Craigneuk fighter's ability that he was nominated to fight for such a title so soon in his career.

The fight is unique in that it was the only Scottish title fight to feature two opponents who worked in the same coalmine. Calderwood's opponent Dave Mooney was an underground worker at Kingshill No. 1 where Chic worked as a surface worker. Managed by Harry Wales, Mooney was a powerful slugger who loved to come inside and hook head and body.

In boxing the best tactics to counter a come-forward hooker are to jab powerfully and keep the slugger on his back foot, thus denying him the necessary leverage to toss his own bombs. This is precisely what Calderwood did to perfection, jabbing and crossing Mooney into submission inside five rounds. When the end was signalled by referee Eugene Henderson, Mooney was drowning under a deluge of the Craigneuk fighter's hooks. Mooney's badly puffed left eye also gave eloquent testimony to Calderwood's punching power.

If 1958 had been a good year 1959 was to prove even better. Not only was the Lanarkshire light-heavy to prolong his impressive unbeaten run but he was to establish a common bond with the then world champion of his division, the legendary Archie Moore, by kayoing Empire cruiserweight Yolande Pompey of Trinidad. True, the Pompey whom Calderwood defeated was not the same man who had given Archie Moore severe problems for the first six rounds of their world title fight, on 5 June 1956 in London, before being stopped in the tenth. Nor was the Trinidadian confronting Calderwood the same tiger who had kayoed former world champion Randolph Turpin, but he still had considerably more experience than his younger adversary. His punching power was also an acknowledged feature of his armoury. All these factors counted for naught, though, as Pompey was knocked out by a peach of a left hook from the Craigneuk clouter.

This and seven other victories over the likes of Ron Redrup (who had beaten him as an amateur) and Canadian Burke Emery did not go unsung in the corridors of boxing power, particularly in Glasgow where Peter Keenan was just as excited as any punter at the prospect of someone who had previously been outwith the ken of Scottish fight fans – a genuine light-heavyweight of potential world class.

Calderwood's manager Tommy Gilmour enlisted Peter Keenan's support in convincing the British Board of Boxing Control to recognise his forthcoming battle on 9 December with Warwick's Jack Whittaker at Paisley Ice Rink as being an eliminator for the British title recently made vacant by the retirement of Randolph Turpin. When the BBBC conferred this status on the bout they also propelled young Calderwood on to the threshold of Scottish sporting immortality – if he won he would be the first ever Scot to fight for this title at British level.

Yet strangley enough the Calderwood style was not universally admired despite its ability to translate endeavour into victory. Joe Aitchison told me, "Calderwood was always a bit too mechanical for my liking." These sentiments were echoed by English boxing expert Peter Wilson who, whilst applauding one of the Craigneuk man's greatest successes – his points victory over top American Sonny Ray – could write: "...but there is still an enormous amount of amateur about the

Craigneuk boy, for he never puts his punches together in combinations."

Someone who was exceedingly grateful about the latter fact was Warwick's Jack Whittaker who was "mechanically" disassembled by the power-packed jabs of Calderwood who forced him to retire in round seven. History had been made and immortality beckoned the 22-year-old Scots boxer closer to its bosom. Barring the gate was a rather ferocious Londoner called Arthur Howard – "The Islington Tiger". The date fixed, 28 January 1960, ensured that for two people at least 1960 could be one of the happiest or saddest years of their lives. The British light-heavyweight title and a much coveted Lonsdale belt guaranteed that.

Arthur Howard, "The Islington Tiger", was as tough as his nickname suggested. His style was based on durability, outgaming and outlasting opponents who had exhausted themselves battering away at this human rock of a man. Howard had fought for the British light-heavyweight title in 1957 when the reigning champion Randolph Turpin had outpointed him over 15 rounds. True, this was a Turpin far removed from the sleek destroyer who had outpointed "Sugar" Ray Robinson in 1951 but it speaks volumes for Howard's toughness that he was able to stand up to the "Leamington Licker" for 15 hard rounds.

Durability was uppermost in the Islington boxer's mind when he told the press that he was training for a 20 round fight. He also forecast that his Scottish foe would have the best of the first four rounds but from then on it would be his fight. This was not mere bravado – Howard had never been knocked out as a professional fighter or stopped.

On this occasion Howard proved to be something of a fortune teller for Calderwood did indeed establish his mastery within the first five rounds, though not in a manner approved by the tough Islington brawler. The first three stanzas were relatively quiet but from the fourth Calderwood started to ram home the left jab through the Londoner's hooks and swings. Right hooks were also drilled into Howard's stomach once he had been put off balance by the jabs thudding into his face and head. Soon Howard's left eye was shut tight. Nevertheless "The Islington Tiger" kept plugging away for another eight rounds, shipping punishment until, mercifully, referee Ike Powell called a halt at the end of the 13th round.

For the first time in Scottish boxing history a native son of Caledonia had the Lonsdale championship belt for the light-heavyweight division fixed around his waist. It was a unique and never-to-be-equalled feat – one that nothing and nobody could take away from the Craigneuk fighter.

Yet Bitch Fortune was lurking in the alleyways of the near future, waiting to add her own unwanted and cheerless kiss to those of the delighted Calderwood family and fans in the ring.

Another spectator who was impressed by Calderwood's performance, for different reasons, was Mickey Duff, then an upwardly mobile young manager and matchmaker. Duff had been commissioned by world champion Archie Moore's manager Willie Ketchum to "spy" on the young Scottish light-heavy and report back on his potential danger to the American negro's tenancy of the championship. In September 1959 Ketchum had also promised Calderwood's manager Tommy Gilmour, that if his charge won his next two fights he could fight Moore. So impressed was Duff by the Howard performance that he sent a cable informing Ketchum that he thought Calderwood was capable of giving any light-heavy problems.

Heady stuff, but as we have already indicated, Bitch Fortune was poised to turn this victorious brew of events into the bitter vinegar of disappointment.

There was no hint of trouble at first. Calderwood signed to meet the American Donnie Fleeman – who would be one of young Cassius Clay's first victims when he turned pro' – in March 1960. Whilst sparring for the Fleeman bout Chic broke the bone of his left thumb, thus losing the chance to establish himself further in international boxing circles.

Nonetheless, even if he could not fight, a broken thumb did not prevent negotiation and already Tommy Gilmour was canvassing for his man to be granted a crack at the vacant Empire light-heavyweight title. Once upon a time a newly established British champion could have regarded an Empire title scrap with the same inevitability that makes Monday follow Sunday but two quite separate countries – South Africa and Tonga – had developed a monopoly-like grip on this particular crown. Mike Holt of South Africa and Tonga's Johnny Halafihi had already fought and drawn twice for the Empire title and Holt's mentor Mike Klisser was so in love with the idea of his man winning it that he seemed to think he had some copyright in staging the deciding bout. This is evident by his action in trying to stop Peter Keenan from promoting a contest in Firhill Stadium between the Craigneuk man and the Tongan. Klisser even raised an unsuccessful action in Edinburgh's court of session to stop the contest taking place.

The problem arose when former world "middles" king, Carl "Bobo" Olson, defeated Holt, putting him out of the game for three months. Klisser thought that Holt, having never been beaten in his quest for the title, should not now be swept aside because of injury. This line of reasoning was rejected by all including the court of session who threw out the South African's plea for a restraining injunction.

Then a member of the Calderwood family inadvertently upset the Craigneuk clouter's peace of mind, or rather the British Board of Boxing Control did. Despite the dour, phlegmatic image he projected to strangers Chic Calderwood had a close, caring and warm family life. Especially close to the new British champion was his uncle, Willie Calderwood, who acted as a coach, trainer and counsellor to his fighting nephew. The problem was that the BBBC had a "no relatives in the corner" ruling and Calderwood wanted his Uncle Willie to be with him in his corner for the Halafihi fight. Despite protests by the Craigneuk man's management the Board remained adamant. When Chic entered the Firhill Park ring on the night of 9 June 1960 he did so without benefit of Uncle Willie's counsel.

What of the Scottish and British title-holder's Tongan opponent?

Johnny Halafihi was as devoted to rugby as he was to boxing. His younger brother Nan indeed played rugby league for Hull Kingston Rovers and Johnny was trained by Hull's team trainer Roy Francis. That Halafihi was no mug is evident in the two draws he had gained fighting South African Mike Holt. Yet Halafihi had a stamina problem. Strong in the early rounds of a fight, he tended to fade if the contest went beyond four rounds. Neither was the Tongan a classic stand-up boxer. He liked to come on inside and haul and maul. Attrition rather than artistry was his game plan once the gong signalled the start of combat.

With the benefit of hindsight one can say that Halafihi was a tailor-made opponent for the Scottish champion. A stiff classic left jab inside hooks or swings is the most potent antidote to a haul-and-maul type fighter like the Tongan. Yet the fight was in fact anything but easy for the Craigneuk champion. The Tongan established an early lead and even managed to deck Calderwood briefly – an affront to Craigneuk Chic's dignity that was repaid with interest in the tenth round when Calderwood dumped Halafihi with a sizzling right cross.

Eventually Calderwood's jab, which had some of the properties associated with a plastic surgeon's scalpel, began to alter the handsome Tongan's features. The end came for Halafihi just eight seconds before the close of the 12th round when referee Billy Jones stopped the contest to examine Halafihi's badly cut left eyelid. In addition to this injury, Calderwood's slashing jabs had inflicted three cuts between the brow and eyelid of the Tongan scrapper.

It was another Calderwood first – the first Scottish British light-heavy Empire title-holder.

Further evidence that 1960 was going to be the Austerlitz year for this Scottish ring Napoleon was not long in arriving. It came in two months, in fact, when Peter Keenan applied pressure on the BBBC for that body to recognise Calderwood's upcoming battle with world-rated American Willie Pastrano as a final eliminator for Archie Moore's world title.

Pastrano was managed by the famous Dundee brothers, Italian-Americans who had inherited the Scottish names from two Italo-American fighters of the 1920s called Vince and Johnny Dundee. The latter pair had in turn been given their Scottish labels by a Dundonian called Scotty Menteith, who emigrated to the USA and became one of America's greatest fight managers. Peter Keenan who entertained both the brothers Dundee – Angelo and Chris – when Pastrano arrived in Scotland told me, "They were both great guys. I liked them both a lot – very easy to deal with too".

The world title fight proposition was not the only inducement for Calderwood to do well against Pastrano. "Cowboy" McCormack's manager, Al Philips, was also British agent for the current European light-heavies monarch, the German Erich Schoeppner. Philips offered "Tam" Gilmour, Calderwood's manager, £4,000 to fight the German in October 1960 – should he be victorious over Pastrano. Gilmour rejected the £4,000 as being inadequate but such matters were academic at this stage. First there was Pastrano.

Willie Pastrano belonged, like Joe Frazier, to the "gluttony" school of world boxing champions. The "gluttony" school of fighters are men whose motives for taking up the hardest game are that, far from being victims of childhood malnutrition, they are so positively overnourished that they literally have vitamins dripping from their ear lobes. Such men make a nonsense of the much peddled "hungry fighter" theory. (Other noted *alumni* of the "gluttony school" are Don Cockell and "Buster" Mathis. Roberto Duran is also a self-confessed glutton whose weight used to shoot up alarmingly between bouts.)

Like Frazier almost a decade later, Pastrano was driven to the boxing gym initially only as a means of losing the weight that made his childhood peers tease him and call him "Fat Willie". Once he got there however he discovered he had a natural boxing talent – a talent that was encouraged by Angelo Dundee. Indeed Willie Pastrano was the prototype, stylistically speaking, of Muhammad Ali, whom Dundee would handle later on in the Sixties. The Pastrano style of "stick and move" was simply Ali's much more celebrated "float like a butterfly and sting like a bee". For "blood and thunder" merchants "Willie the Wisp" may have been not their particular cup of tea but it brought results to the Louisiana-based fighter.

In British rings alone Pastrano won more than he lost. He defeated Dick Richardson, Brian London, Joe Bygraves and Terry Downes. Against the latter on 30 November 1964 he also proved he could punch if need be, as he stopped Downes in the 11th round whilst trailing badly on points. (He lost in a return against Brian London in London in 1958; he also lost to Joe Erskine on points.)

In world terms Pastrano became global champion on 1 June 1963 when he controversially outpointed reigning light-heavy kingpin Harold Johnson. This was nearly three years after he met Calderwood so the Louisiana dancing master who confronted Calderwood was far from being an over-the-hill fighter – indeed he was at his peak, which merely underscores the merit of the Craigneuk boxer's subsequent performance.

Pastrano was also something of a "character" outside the ring. Bitter Calderwood foe John "Cowboy" McCormack sparred with "Willie the Wisp". His verdict? "Pastrano was a beautiful boxer – hard to pin down and hit – and a great guy to boot." One of the Louisiana man's habits was positively unique in ring annals. He wore his then wife's wedding ring suspended from his boxing boot laces. So whatever he may have lacked in ring ferocity he more than compensated for by his colourful character and personality.

The contest took place at the now familiar Calderwood stomping ground of Paisley Ice Rink on the 16 September 1960. The Scottish press were frankly pessimistic about Calderwood's chances against "Willie the Wisp". This assessment was based on the fact that Pastrano had met a better class of opponent than his Scottish foe; the American had only lost seven fights out of a career total that included about three times the bouts that Calderwood had fought.

On the other hand the Scottish Napoleon of the light-heavies was undefeated and had never been knocked out – a fact which was reflected in the world ratings where Chic was rated number three to Pastrano's number four.

The real problem from an objectively technical viewpoint was that Calderwood was a renowned jabber but Pastrano was an even more renowned exponent of this punch, which is the key that unlocks the door to the armoury of more devastating blows such as the hook. With the benefit of hindsight one can say the Craigneuk man appeared to be in the unenviable position of someone trying to outdance Fred Astaire, for Pastrano was a ring dancing master the like of whom was never equalled until another Angelo Dundee protégé, Muhammad Ali, burst on the scene.

Pastrano had an added incentive to beat Calderwood. His manager's brother Chris Dundee, the Miami-based promoter, had promised him a world title shot against Archie Moore in December should he beat the "Craigneuk clouter".

The run-up to this fight displayed promoter Peter Keenan's flair and enterprise. A theme close to Keenan's heart was the need for the pro' and amateur games to have closer links. To encourage this Peter Keenan offered free fight tickets to the first 20 amateur boxers who attended the official weigh-in!

Once Welsh referee Ike Powell signalled the start of combat it became increasingly evident that the pessimists seemed to have assessed the outcome correctly. In the battle of the left jabs Pastrano emerged as the master for the first seven rounds of this ten-round contest. The American's left was like a rapier, slashing an inch-long gash in one of Calderwood's eyebrows. From then on until the fateful seventh round the American made this inviting injury his main target.

Inexplicably, Pastrano chose to allow Calderwood to lead from the start of the seventh, thus giving the heavily punished Scots fighter an opportunity to put leverage into his jabs – a leverage previously impossible due to Chic being kept on his back foot by the American. As a result rounds seven through to nine saw Calderwood rampant – like some fistic Prometheus suddenly unchained by the lassitude of Pastrano.

This transformation worried the American light-heavy's manager, Angelo Dundee, who shouted furiously at his errant charge, "Let's go boy!" These rather prosaic words had a febrilator-like effect on this dilatory dancing master from Louisiana. In the tenth and final round Pastrano blasted his way back with a brilliant array of text book punches. This dazzling exhibition convinced his manager Angelo Dundee and many members of the press and public at ringside that the result was a foregone conclusion for "Willie the Wisp".

On the other hand there were those who were equally convinced that they had just witnessed Chic Calderwood's finest hour thus far as a boxer. In this connection he had proved that he could take the best an exceptionally gifted American could dish out and even exact some retribution on his own account. Welsh referee Ike Powell had clearly been more impressed by the Craigneuk man's performance for it was to his corner he walked to indicate that the Scotsman had won a famous victory.

One who does not accept that this was the Craigneuk clouter's best ever performance was his trainer and chief second, Duncan Jowett. Duncan has now been involved in boxing in various capacities for nigh on 46 years. He came into the Calderwood camp in 1960 as trainer and second but in fact he became closer than anyone to knowing Calderwood – although "Dunky", as he is universally known, told me, "Even I didn't get to know Chic all THAT closely. He was a man of moods you see..."; Dunky continued, "They say the Pastrano performance was his greatest but I disagree – that was his fight against Johnny Persol".

That Calderwood's victory had repercussions far beyond Paisley Ice Rink soon became evident from two sources: the buzz of transatlantic communication between the USA and Scotland and the serious talks that took place in Glasgow between Peter Keenan and Chic's manager Tommy Gilmour on how best to bring the Craigneuk man into world title contention. With regard to the former, Miami promoter Chris Dundee contacted top Scottish boxing journalist Dick Currie with a proposal to have Calderwood box Pastrano in Miami. Another correspondent from the Home of the Brave and Land of the Free was top American booking agent and *Ring* editor Jersey Jones, who informed Peter Keenan that Madison Square Garden matchmaker Teddy Brenner was enthusiastic about featuring Calderwood at the New York fistic mecca in November against Pastrano in a rubber match.

Manager Gilmour vetoed any talk of a return match with Pastrano but continued to talk world title strategy with Keenan. The Anderston-born promoter in turn vetoed talk of having the Moore v. Calderwood world title bash in Scotland. This decision was based on Keenan's realistic assessment of the commercial realities of the professional fight game as it stood then in 1960, a judgment that was vindicated in due course by the demands of the reigning world light-heavyweight champion "Ancient Archie Moore", who would demand not a princely sum, nor even a kingly one, but a mega-monarchical £60,000 plus training expenses to come to Scotland.

There is little doubt in my mind that Moore knew Calderwood would have forced him painfully to abdicate his light-heavyweight throne and this explains his exorbitant demands. This is an impression confirmed by "Dunky" Jowett who told me, "Chic fought a German called Rolf Peters at Paisley Ice Rink...he outclassed this guy while Moore was sitting at ringside. As we were leaving the arena Moore looked at Chic, shook hands and said with a big smile, 'Chic you're too young and I'm too old'."

They never did meet. There were other reasons for the American champion's reticence apart from age. Just before the Pastrano fight Moore had had to call off a title defence with the German Erich Schoeppner in Montreal, Canada, because of weight problems.

Peter Keenan was confidentially informed by a top American fight figure that Moore had no intention of ever fighting Craigneuk's light-heavy Napoleon.

However combat, not speculation, is the fuel that propels a contender up the ratings and a British Guyanan called Joey Armstrong was next in line for the unenviable task of trying to halt Calderwood's triumphal train of progress. Dunky Jowett recalls: "Armstrong was nothing special in my opinion but this fight demonstrated Calderwood's ability to learn and execute new punches. When I first took him under my wing he had a virtually non-existent left hook. I changed that. He used the left hook that night. The result was Armstrong had to be rescued by the referee."

Another to feel the venom of the Craigneuk fighter's left hook was an unfortunate German with film-star type blond looks called Rolf Peters. This contest at Paisley, as I have mentioned, had none other than Archie Moore sitting at ringside behind a pair of dark glasses – courtesy of a black eye at the hands of Guilio Rinaldi, an Italian who would figure greatly in the Calderwood story at a future date. In the meantime the American saw his touted Scottish foe outclass and hammer Peters mercilessly into submission until a compassionate Edinburgh referee, Eugene Henderson, stopped the slaughter in round four. "Dunky" Jowett's legacy – the left hook – softened the German up for a right hand finisher.

Moore showed what a skilled diplomat he was by feeding "disinformation" to the British press-men at ringside when he told them, "I would like to defend my title against Chic. He has great potential."

On 1 November 1960 Chic Calderwood established another of those firsts which make him unique in the annals of Scottish ring history. He became the first ever Scottish light-heavyweight to be given a number one world rating. But there was to be little time to bask in any reflected glory – not with a formidable Chicago negro called Sonny Ray to fight in three weeks' time.

Sonny Ray's world rating had slipped somewhat from fourth in September 1959 to 12th by the time he met Calderwood on Tuesday, 22 November 1960, at Wembley, but he was still a formidable fighter as events were to prove. The contest was another example of an all-too-common event in Chic Calderwood's life – Bitch Fortune offering her fickle but illusory favours behind a seductive negligee of triumph. Despite Calderwood winning at least eight of the ten rounds contested disaster struck in the fifth round. Ray for once planted a savage hook on Calderwood's nose, causing it to haemorrhage alarmingly. "Dunky" Jowett, who was in the Scots boxer's corner, recalls, "By round seven Chic had lost at least four pints of blood...he swallowed a lot of it too which obviously affected his performance."

Yet still the Lanarkshire man managed to punish Ray with his famed left jab and "Dunky" Jowett's special – the left hook off the jab. There were never any doubts once the final bell rang. But his was a Pyrrhic victory although there was no hint of it at first.

"Dunky" Jowett recounts: "I was unhappy about the injury and asked him repeatedly if there was anything more seriously wrong with his nose. He just shrugged but I persisted until he promised he would go straight to the local "Law Hospital" in Lanarkshire. Well, he did but Chic was a man of so few words that he incredibly didn't even bother to tell the doctor there that he was a professional boxer! This affected the doctor's diagnosis – he was told to go home and not to blow his nose." In fact the Calderwood nose was broken in two places – a not uncommon boxing injury, it is true, but few fractured noses cost their victims as many thousands of pounds as this one which had a catastrophic short term effect at least on the world-rated Lanarkshire light-heavyweight. Sonny Ray was at least gracious in defeat, opining that Chic would certainly defeat Archie Moore should they meet, but against this smidgeon of balm for the Calderwood ego had to be set the fact that the injury kayoed a European title bout with the German Erich Schoeppner in January 1961. It also blew apart influential English promoter Harry Levene's plan to put Calderwood in with a top-rated American. There was talk too of a fight with the National Boxing Association's "champion", Harold Johnson of Philadelphia. Yet so often did Calderwood have the carrot of a world title fight dangled before him that inwardly he must have experienced a degree of disbelief akin to that of those prisoners at Buchenwald who could see the legend "Work Makes You Free" displayed above the gate of that infamous death factory.

If the close of 1960 had not augured well for the Craigneuk Napoleon of the light-heavyweight division then 1961 was to prove a real Waterloo of a year. Chic's nemesis, however, was not to be an Irish peer like the Duke of Wellington but a sleek American called Von Clay. This ring tiger's name might have suggested a German pottery salesman but the only pots he ever peddled were shots at his opponent's head and body.

I can well remember watching the contest on television and being struck by the positive menace this large shaven-headed negro exuded as he stood in his corner waiting for the opening bell. Clay was no stand-up boxer like his more famous namesake, Cassius, who would soon make his debut as a freshman pro' back in the USA. Von Clay was the type of opponent according to "Dunky" Jowett whom "Calderwood loathed. The Yank fought out of a crouch. This type of opponent always created problems for a stand-up jabber like Chic." Added to this in round one Von Clay planted a solid punch on the Craigneuk battler's still tender nose, creating twin problems with breathing and incessant bleeding.

Again, the best tactic for a crouching hooker like the American negro when faced by a classic left jabber like the Scot is to draw the left hand lead and hook "over and under" once the lead has been slipped. This the American did, decking Calderwood in the fourth round. But it would be a gross distortion of the fight to suggest that the Scots boxer was the recipient of a one-sided hammering. On the contrary, despite the constant blood dripping from his nose he smote the American with his potent left jab and hook of the jab once he had resolved the initial problem of the crouch.

"Dunky" Jowett opines, "I am not and never have been one for screaming about verdicts but I genuinely thought Calderwood was worth a draw, especially for his performance later on in the fight. You should have seen Clay's banged up features after the fight – swollen and bumpy from the jab." Nevertheless, the proud unbeaten record had gone, the referee clearly placing due emphasis in the scoring on the two trips Calderwood had taken to the canvas during the fight.

However moody and introspective Calderwood was – and he was as famed for being those things as he was for his fighting ability – self-pity and inactivity were two "luxuries" his management did not permit him to sample.

After a break from boxing he restored his winning ways in 1961 by an inside distance win over former ABA English star Dave Rent. Then he drew with Jim Cooper, twin brother of British heavyweight champion Henry. "Dunky" Jowett recalls, "The real story behind the Cooper fight was that by this stage Chic was mucking about with his training and skipping sessions at the gym. Before he had always trained well – a bit moody and surly, sure – but with Jim Cooper he hadn't trained properly for two weeks before the fight." This was evident in his lacklustre showing. Though normally a slow starter, he never revealed anything like the form of which he was capable.

Nevertheless the Cooper fight did unravel one interesting facet of the normally uncommunicative Craigneuk man's personality – his absolute conviction that should he ever get Jim Cooper's more illustrious brother in the ring he would beat him! Calderwood told his trainer and *confidant* "Dunky" Jowett this many times. There are those who, recalling Chic's disastrous heavyweight excursion against American Freddie Mack (when Calderwood ignored Jowett's orders and fought weighing a stone heavier than he should have), will scoff at this idea but apparently Calderwood based his own assessment on their styles. Henry Cooper's style, he claimed, was tailor-made for himself. What is not generally known is that at the time of Chic's death in November 1963 negotiations were being made to match Calderwood and Henry Cooper, although the press at the time were more preoccupied with a reported fight with "Young" John McCormack the budding Irish star light-heavy.

However, to return to 1961, after the Cooper fight manager "Tam" Gilmour was determined to restore his fistic Napoleon to global contention. After due consideration he lighted upon a stroke so daring that there were some who wondered if he was not having a brainstorm. He contracted for the Craigneuk fighter to meet the formidable Henry Hank on his own home ground of Detroit, Michigan. Even viewed from the safe distance of the 26 years that have elapsed since the bout took place this decision smacks of the Emperor Napoleon agreeing to switch the venue of Waterloo from just outside Brussels to the playing fields of Eton.

Hank's career has been discussed in a previous chapter on John "Cowboy" McCormack, so suffice to say he really was one of the great American fighters of the Sixties – which makes Calderwood's performance of taking him the distance to a hotly disputed decision all the more creditable. Dunky Jowett's feelings on the verdict? "Definitely a home-town decision. Big Chic gave as good as he got – a draw would have been a fairer result." Many at ringside agreed.

So it was back to Scotland to rest and then defend his British title against old foe, the Bristolian Stan Cullis who in boxing terms was nothing like as illustrious as the famous English soccer centre-half of that name. This pugilistic Stan Cullis was a hard, no-frills fighter who was clearly out of his depth although he did emulate the footballing Cullis by "stopping" a great deal of shots – unfortunately with his jaw rather than his instep – on that evening of 12 February 1962 in London's National Sporting Club. By the fourth round Cullis was kayoed and Calderwood had added another coveted notch to his Lonsdale belt.

This victory was also symptomatic of another persistent trend throughout Chic Calderwood's career. He was truly a Napoleon-like figure at domestic level beating all comers. Indeed with only one exception he never lost a contest to a British-based fighter. Even that one solitary domestic defeat – against "Cowboy"

McCormack – was on a cut eye and he was otherwise not in serious trouble when the stoppage came.

A less happy trend in this undoubtedly talented Scottish light-heavy's life was his treatment over world title fights. In this department he was an unfortunate victim of the Ken Rosewall/Allan Brown perpetual frustration syndrome. What makes his failure doubly galling in this department was that he was not aided by the one body who should have backed him to the hilt – especially after the Pastrano victory.

When Pastrano came as world champion to Britain in November 1964 to defend his world light-heavyweight crown at Bellevue, Manchester, it was not the British champion – Chic Calderwood – who faced him as it should have been. It was Terry Downes, who was given this shot purely on the strength of having beaten three mediocre light-heavies and having the right connections. To add insult to injury this fight took place on St Andrew's Day – 30 November 1964.

"Tam" Gilmour protested loud and long but to no avail. When Calderwood's chance finally did come to dispute the world crown he was, in "Dunky" Jowett's words, "three years too late". This fight took place in San Juan, Puerto Rico, in 1965 against old "Cowboy" McCormack Olympic opponent, Jose "Chequi" Torres. Torres knocked Calderwood out with clinical efficiency in round two but as we shall see later the latter's enthusiasm for the game had gone on the wane before then.

After his February 1962 victory over Stan Cullis, Chic continued his winning ways against old Tongan foe Johnny Halafihi in a rematch for the Empire crown at Newcastle. The Tongan certainly did better this time, lasting the full 15 round distance, but the result was the same – Calderwood's gloved fist was raised in victory at the final bell.

The really exciting news, though, had broken in the Calderwood camp a month or so previous to this bout. The European Boxing Union had grown tired of the posturing and prevarication of their champion Erich Schoeppner, whose agent Al Philips had teased "Tam" Gilmour two years before with an inadequate purse offer. Consequently, in May 1962 they vacated the European light-heavyweight title and nominated the Craigneuk battler and Italian Guilio Rinaldi to fight it out for the vacant crown. The fight was fixed for 28 September in Rome.

The bare facts of the record book inform us that Chic was outpointed by the Italian but "Dunky" Jowett tells the real story from the vantage point of Calderwood's corner: "This was the fight that in my mind proved Big Chic had guts when the chips were really down. At the end of the fourth round he told me, 'Dunky my right hand's injured. I cannae use it.' So I tell him, 'Use your jab only then – you're winning!' At the end of the seventh Chic comes back and says, 'The left is hurt as well.' 'Tam' and I decide we better pull him out but he went mental. 'Naw! Naw! Let me fight on. I'm still good enough for this guy.' So we did."

Certainly Calderwood appeared to have won. He had decked the Italian in the first round and punished him throughout the remainder of the fight with the famed left jab and hook off the jab. "Dunky" Jowett recalled, "I thought it was a formality – until I saw the Spanish referee make the sign of the cross and walk over to Rinaldi's corner. Then I knew we had been done." The normally partisan Roman fans showed their displeasure at the decision by bombarding the ring with bread and fruit. Even many of them thought Calderwood had been robbed.

For Chic Calderwood 1963 was to emerge as a real 1812 year. A year that must have made him reflect that life is a rose rooted in dung. The year started pleasantly enough with the prospect of revenge and the opportunity to become the first Scotsman ever to win a Lord Lonsdale light-heavyweight belt outright.

The revenge factor was provided by his opponent on that penultimate day of July 1983 in Blackpool – Ron Redrup, who had gained a victory over the Craigneuk Champion whilst an amateur. But in truth Calderwood had blossomed as a professional whilst Redrup had barely bloomed in the paid game.

"Dunky" Jowett remembers this fight for reasons other than the Lonsdale belt triumph. "This fight was the one where everything I had taught him about the hook came to fruition. He used it in a devastating fashion that night, even though I had seen him perform better overall in other fights." The cumulative effect of this heavy punching was seen in round 11 by which time Redrup's corner retired him due to a lacerated eye and swollen head.

Once again it seemed that Chic Calderwood's star was rising, that is, until a veteran American negro called Eddie Cotton from Seattle, Washington, came to Paisley Ice Rink to spoil the party.

Cotton had fought everyone who was anybody in the world light-heavyweight division and was still regarded as a respectable opponent for the Craigneuk champion. More than prestige, however, was at stake in this one. Dunky Jowett recalls, "We had three fights lined up in the USA but after the decision against Calderwood we had to shelve our plans. The decision was highly controversial – I don't condone such behaviour, but a half bottle of whisky was even launched at the referee from ringside."

Soon misfortunes seemed to be queuing up to grasp Calderwood's hand.

Gustave "Bubi" Scholz was one of Germany's best post-war boxers, a clever southpaw who counter-punched beautifully. An orthodox lead-first jabber like Calderwood is every southpaw counter-puncher's prayer. So it proved with the Craigneuk boxer. Calderwood lost on points but in view of what was to come perhaps he actually pined to be back in the ring with Scholz.

That Chic Calderwood displayed a total lack of judgment in associating with some pretty nefarious characters outside of boxing cannot be doubted, especially in view of what happened at the end of 1963. Suffice to say that he paid for this lack of judgment in full. He was imprisoned, and under Regulation 15 Paragraph 5B which states, "Misconduct shall mean conduct detrimental to the interests of boxing or the public. . ." he was stripped of his titles. Titles he had never lost in the ring.

This was Waterloo and the Retreat from Moscow wrapped into one for the Scottish Napoleon of light-heavies.

Jail sentences have never been a bar to progress in boxing. This is as true in

Britain as in the USA where several great world champions such as Rocky Graziano did time. As recently as June 1979 a former convict called Paul Sykes disputed the British heavyweight championship with John L. Gardner. By 1964, having tholed his assize, Calderwood was back in fight circulation thanks to Peter Keenan who never was one to kick a man when he was down.

The comeback fight took place in the Kelvin Hall, Glasgow, on 28 May 1964. Calderwood's chosen opponent was a Jamaican sparring partner of the then Cassius Clay called Allan Harmon, who was reckoned to be able to provide a stiff test for the comebacking Craigneuker. Manager "Tam" Gilmour was quoted as saying that this was Big Chic's last chance to make it in the big time. By that criterion Calderwood should have retired there and then for his performance was anything but vintage.

Harmon, despite his credentials, turned out to be a very moderate opponent. Calderwood toiled and was hesitant, even untypically letting the Jamaican off the hook in round three when he had softened him up for the kill with a series of jolting jabs. These punches cut Harmon's eye, providing his corner with an exit visa from what they clearly regarded as being a lost cause. The end came suddenly when his seconds indicated that the Jamaican could not continue. It was an unsatisfactory ending to a dreich spectacle which had been characterised by slow hand-clapping by a crowd who could clearly remember better days as far as the Scottish fighter was concerned.

Never ones to participate in orgies of post-fight despair the Calderwood management team decided to send Chic to Wales before his next scheduled fight in Porthcawl against Freddie Cross. Welsh-born Cross had the distinction of having beaten Terry Downes on a cut eye decision; he had also fought as a middleweight against top-class British "middles" Martin Hansen, Phil Edwards, Alex Buxton and George Aldridge. As a light-heavy Cross would become number two in the British ratings.

Calderwood's sojourn in Wales training hard agreed with him because he produced one of his best performances against the Welshman. That Wednesday, 29 July 1964, saw Chic jab Cross' head so often that the latter looked at times like a dropsical woodpecker. Only in the first two rounds did Cross look the part because then he employed a crouch – something that induced in Calderwood a perplexity that a Chilean called Arturo Godoy provoked in Joe Louis by adopting the same tactics a quarter of a century before.

Things changed in the third. A stunning combination of rights and lefts opened a cut on Cross' eyelid. In round five the left hook off the jab nearly ended matters but Cross was nothing if not game and he miraculously went the distance. Nobody quibbled in Porthcawl's Coney Beach Arena when referee Joe Morgan raised the Scots fighter's hand in token of triumph. Many of the Welsh fans stood and cheered for they had seen classic jabbing at its very best.

This indeed was another trend in Calderwood's career. He reserved some of his best performances for opponents from the principality of Wales. Even in his twilight days his last great performance was against a Welshman – Derek Richards in 1966.

Richards was a protégé of Wally Leslie who had steered Welsh milkman Dick Richardson to a European heavyweight championship in 1960. According to "Dunky" Jowett, "Leslie was forecasting that Coventry-based Richards would practise all kinds of mayhem on Calderwood once he got him in the ring." Well, mayhem there certainly was that evening of 24 January 1966 but it was poor Richards who was the recipient of some devastating Calderwood hooks that ended his interest in matters within the first two rounds.

One wonders if a desire to avenge national honour was one of the motives behind Welsh screen tough guy Stanley Baker's offer of £1,000 sidestakes if Calderwood would meet Stepney light-heavy John Henricson with his title at stake. They never did meet. (A Calderwood did fight Henricson – Tom Calderwood, Chic's brother.)

To return to 1964, in recognition of the superb form displayed in the Freddie Cross contest Chic Calderwood found himself nominated to fight again for the titles he had lost through folly rather than fighting.

His foe on Armistice Day 1964 was a Hampshire boxer called Bob Nicolson whom he met at the now familiar Paisley Ice Rink. "Dunky" Jowett reminisced: "I thought Bob Nicolson was easily one of the nicest guys I have ever met. He was such a nice guy that for the first time in my life I actually felt sorry for a Calderwood opponent. I knew Nicolson would lose. . . and so he did."

Yet the Farnborough man did not disgrace himself up to the seventh round when Calderwood produced some fierce right hand punching which twice decked Nicolson. The bell spared the Hampshire boxer but his corner had seen enough and had retired him. Thus a year that had commenced in the most miserable of circumstances ended amid a fanfare of success. Calderwood was much too phlegmatic to display much euphoria, which was just as well in view of the happenings in 1965.

If ever a year encapsulated the life and times of Chic Calderwood it was 1965, a year of inconsistency with a capital "I", when he produced arguably his worst performance, and one in which many knowledgeable critics including "Dunky" Jowett consider to be his best – against top-rated American Johnny Persol.

The Craigneuk man's performance which reminded those who witnessed it of all the boxing "B" movies they had ever seen, took place on Tuesday, 12 January 1965, in the Royal Albert Hall on a Mike Barrett promotion. The Calderwood opponent was a Mississippi electrician called Otha Brown whose main recommendation was that he was managed by Angelo Dundee. Ironically, the official programme pen picture writer stated: "Brown turned pro' without benefit of one amateur bout" – a fact that was evident in the boring fare he and Calderwood served up.

Mike Barrett, the English promoter, had spent a goodly portion of the Second World War living in Greenock as an evacuee. Greenock was the birthplace of the pirate Captain Kidd and no doubt Mike would have liked Calderwood and Brown to have walked the plank after the dross they had provided for his patrons. Thankfully for the peace of mind of Greenock Morton supporter Mike Barrett,

Henry Cooper was topping the bill and produced a great performance in stopping New Yorker Dick Wipperman in five.

Surprisingly, there was little inkling of Calderwood's bad form in training. On the contrary, during his London training stint, according to "Dunky" Jowett, Calderwood twice decked the blond bomber Billy Walker – then at his peak. In sparring with Chic you never knew what was going to happen – which on reflection makes me conclude that handling Calderwood must have been tantamount to being fed a diet of club sandwiches alternatively layered with caviare and cockroaches. ("Dunky" Jowett will probably disagree with this statement but even he admitted it was no easy job dealing with the Craigneuk clouter's moods.)

The caviare performance of his career was undoubtedly his outstanding points decision over world-rated American Johnny Persol. Persol, a negro who was being handled by the legendary Gil Clancy who had steered Emile Griffith to a world championship, came to the Solihull Ring with an unbeaten record of 15 fights. He was on a build-up, with his future as heir apparent to the world light-heavyweight crown being openly discussed in American boxing magazines.

Although it is unlikely that Chic Calderwood knew or cared much about American history perhaps the best way to describe his performance on 5 May 1965 would be to say from the eighth round onwards the Craigneuk man acted as though he were General Sherman and Persol was the state of Georgia, as he laid waste to the Brooklyn negro's features with sharp left hand work.

Yet for the first three rounds the American prospered, if only because he used the old Calderwood "bogey" tactic of fighting in a crouch and winging hooks at his Scottish rival. However, for a world-rated fighter he tended to slap too much rather than punch cleanly. This drew a warning for incorrect hitting from referee Austin O'Connor in the third round.

By the tenth and final round, Persol, his face resembling a street map of Atlanta, circa 1865, knew he had met his master. Nevertheless, some 14 months later Persol would tell readers of *Boxing Illustrated* that "the SPLIT DECISION" he lost to Chic Calderwood was "so bad even the newspapers said so". It is a measure of Calderwood's punches that poor Johnny Persol thought that referee Austin O'Connor was really two people for one cannot possibly have a split decision in a British ring where only the referee scores!

After the Persol victory there wasn't much to cheer about in the life of Chic Calderwood, although his demise was as unexpected as it was horrible and so terribly ironic on that Sunday of 13 November 1966.

Speed had always been a Calderwood passion. Immediately after the British title win over Arthur Howard, manager "Tam" Gilmour had sharply vetoed Chic's declared aim of purchasing a sports car. Yet when the end came he was driving a Mini. Again, this was no speed-crazy Jack Johnson taunting death just once too often by wheelspinning around a series of hairpin bends in North Carolina; this was no Salvador Sanchez foolhardily swerving to overtake right into the path of a lorry in Texas. Chic Calderwood was doing zero m.p.h. when he died.

"Dunky" Jowett explains it thus: "He drove up to a severe humpback bridge at Braidwood (*Lanarkshire*). It was one of those bridges where cars had to give way. Chic was sitting waiting for his turn to pass when a big, heavy Austin Cambridge car driven by a young guy and three of his mates charged onto the bridge. Their speed meant that when they hit the crest of the hump their wheels froze and they dived straight into Chic. The impact drove his car back yards away into a bus shelter."

Thus perished Chic Calderwood who truly was a Napoleon, at least of the British light-heavyweights. He only lost once to a British fighter as a pro' and then on a cut eye.

First Scotsman to win the British and Empire title at his weight, first to win a Lonsdale belt at light-heavyweight. These are lasting achievements that can never be equalled because they are unique. But equally Bitch Fortune's fickle infatuation with him and his own lack of judgment ensured that his personal life would ultimately resemble 1812 without the overture.

ALEX MORRISON – Boxing Promoter

Throughout my travels in pursuit of transforming this book from blurred concept to concrete reality I encountered impressive human qualitites in such abundance that a palate more world-weary than mine might have become jaded. In those I interviewed impressiveness of character was as commonplace as beautiful thighs at a "Miss World" contest. Nevertheless – promoter Alex Morrison – is by any criterion an ultra-impressive man.

Although now 50 years of age, his physique still commands that attention and respect that his ring opponents learned to accord him when he became, at 44, the oldest man in Scottish amateur boxing history to win a Scottish super-heavyweight boxing title. Again, any man who can overcome a serious drinking problem – a problem so bad that it cost him eight years of his life in various prisons for drink-related offences – and then build a road haulage business with 15 vehicles and a goodly number of employees can hardly be regarded as Joe Average. Add to this his ownership of one of the best gyms and stable of boxers in Scotland and the tag "self-made man" would appear to be tailor-made for this transplanted Highlander who has called Glasgow home for the last 35 years.

I have used the words "appear to be" advisedly. For accompanying Alex during our interview at Edinburgh's Royal Scot Hotel was his wife of 28 years, Ann. Ann Morrison is not only a most attractive lady but I sensed in her an inner strength which undoubtedly helped her keep together the Morrison family of two sons and three daughters during the hard times. Even now this strength quietly but firmly underpins Alex's present success as a manager, promoter and transport magnate.

But for me the most impressive thing about this Gallowgate-based promoter is not his expensive personal jewellery, nor is it his even more expensive limousine or the Sydney Street gym which evokes in me happy memories. No, it is his rough-hewn integrity that impresses me most.

There are those who will sneer at the word "integrity" being applied to a man who has "done time", a man who is a boxing promoter – a species who have the souls of piranha fish and the rapacity of a battalion of Vikings, or so the fable goes. Such simpletons forget that 2,000 years ago a Holy Land hooker called Mary Magdalen demonstrated that integrity and caring for other people was not the personal monopoly of so-called "respectable" society.

If this strikes the reader as some sort of special pleading it is not. The best and most eloquent advocate Alex Morrison has are his present deeds, particularly in connection with the help and support he has given to a reformed heroin addict called Bobby McDermott.

Alex Morrison needs no special pleading. His accomplishments speak for themselves.

B.D.: Alex, where were you born?

A.M.: I was born near Dunvegan Castle on the Isle of Skye.

B.D.: Was your father a boxer?

A.M.: No, my father was a self-employed joiner. He never boxed. I didn't really become involved in boxing until I came down to Glasgow when I was 15 years old.

B.D.: What did you work at when you first arrived in Glasgow?

A.M.: I worked as an engineering apprentice in John Brown's shipyard. I was eventually sacked because I wouldn't attend day release classes. Then I did a variety of jobs.

B.D.: Where did boxing come into this?

A.M.: I went to the National Amateur Boxing Club in Glasgow's Oxford Street – it was there that I met and was influenced by the great Jim Maharg. (*Jim Maharg was until his recent death in December 1987 one of the most respected and revered figures in Scottish boxing. For many years a ring whip, he was in the 1930s one of the best flyweights ever produced by Scotland. A fitness fanatic, he was still sparring in his late sixties. Maharg employed Benny Lynch as a sparring partner. He treasured the receipt which proved this and was very proud of it.*) Jim took me in hand. He stood no nonsense – no swearing or smoking was allowed. He taught discipline. I drifted away from boxing – but that is why I called the amateur club I founded and still support "The Maharg ABC", to show my respect for him. He was a marvellous wee guy.

B.D.: Have you any favourite stories about wee Jim?

A.M.: Yes. After the decision in the Scottish welterweight title battle between my fighter Dave Douglas and Gary Jacobs last year (*1987*) I was furious when the decision went against Douglas. I was expressing my anger in no uncertain terms when wee Jim – who had a stutter – said, "A-A-Alex-c-c-count-tae-t-ten!" I turned angrily to him and said, "YOU count to ten!" To which Jim replied, "T-t-that w-w-would take me aw' day!" Well, I killed myself laughing at this pawky reply! It totally defused my anger. But that was typical of Jim. He was always calm and dignified – yet strangely enough I think he eventually came to look up to me.

B.D.: Because he knew all about your past problems – the drink, prison etc. – and how you had overcome them. Tell me about this phase of your life. Did it teach you any valuable lessons with regard to your boxing career or business career?

A.M.: I had a severe drinking problem. I was jailed for drink related offences – driving, fighting with the police, stuff like that. I did the bulk of my sentences in the "Bar-L" (*Barlinnie Prison, Glasgow*). I did learn quite a lot there. Let me give you two examples. Every prisoner was entitled to one piece of fresh fruit per day. The "screws" put this at the end of the hall on a big table then you went forward to get yours – the strong guys took more than one piece, the weak none. No matter what the theory was, that's how it happened. It was the same at recreation time. Twelve newspapers were put on a table – you had to fight to make sure you were one of the 12 who got the newspaper. It is the same in business and boxing – you have to fight to get what you want. Another thing I learned came from me being an unofficial block leader. I learned how to compromise with authority if necessary. If I didn't keep the "bampots" in my block in order the prison officers

Alex Morrison – brains for business – brawn for boxing.

would do things like switch the cell lights off early and hassle us all generally. So I learned to negotiate, make deals.

B.D.: Whom do you find the harder to deal with as a businessman or promoter – business managers or boxing managers?

A.M.: Boxing managers are tougher than managers in business.

B.D.: Why?

A.M.: The manager in a business I deal with normally has principles – some of the fight managers have none.

B.D.: Can you give me an example?

A.M.: There are English fight managers who run and live off stables of losers – guys who have won 15 fights and lost 70. No hopers – bodies who are hired because they are guaranteed to lose and make the local fighter look good.

B.D.: But surely if you as a manager and fight promoter wanted to boost one of your own boys, wouldn't you hire one of these "rent-a-loser" boxers?

A.M.: I am not denying I would look for moderate opposition for a young guy just starting out as a pro', but I have some principles. You are doing your boy no favours feeding him hopeless opponents. Besides, I would and have ditched fighters who were quite prepared to take money and lose a contest not because they were crooked but because they were "yellow" – like a fighter I had. He was winning on points when on returning to the corner he tells me, "Alex, my hand is gone." I knew this was a lie, so I said, "You're not quitting – no way!" The referee came over and asked if anything was wrong. He had noticed us arguing. I told the ref, "If he goes down disqualify him for not trying!" The ref nodded and I sent him out for the next round. Funny thing was he got better and better as the fight went on but each time he came back to the corner he would say huffily, "This is DEFINITELY my last round." He won the decision!

B.D.: Did he fight again?

A.M.: He was back again in the ring the following Thursday! But then I have had a guy so petrified he broke out in skin rashes. That's what I admire about bantam Bobby "Sherbo" McDermott. I tried him out once just to see what he was made of – I said to him during a fight, "If you throw this one you could make some money." He didn't know I was just testing him. He told me to "**** off!" and went on fighting. I knew he was for real then. But ring cowards – they do exist!

B.D.: Who are the bravest boys you have handled?

A.M.: "Sherbo" McDermott, Dave "Gypsy" Douglas and a brave bantam called Donny Hood are those that spring to mind. Dave McCabe too. But to go back to one of your earlier points I have on more than one occasion rejected opponents for my boys because they were so bad. Incidentally that is one of the things I don't like about Terry Lawless. Terry has a caring image for his fighters and that's true, he does look after them – but too well! In my opinion he doesn't care much about some of the poor opponents he puts up against his boys.

B.D.: Didn't you get current British contender Joe Kelly from Terry Lawless?

A.M.: Yes. I paid Lawless £500 for his contract.

B.D.: Let's talk about money, Alex. You are a promoter and a manager. Legend has it that all promoters/managers are leeches who bleed the boxers dry. What do you say to that?

A.M.: I will give you some figures and then you be the judge. A boxer in Britain will normally be paid £200 gross for a six two-minute round fight. If he sells tickets to friends and fans with any other promoter he may be lucky to get ten per cent of ticket sales on top of his £200. With me a six-round fighter gets £200 plus 50 per cent of ALL income from ticket sales that he has generated. I have had fighters pull £1,000 a fight with this system.

B.D.: But does that mean you don't employ fighters who don't have a personal following?

A.M.: Of course not! Take light-welterweight Dave McCabe of Gartcosh. Dave himself admits, "Nobody likes me!" He also says, "All my enemies buy tickets to see me get beaten!" So yes, I employ boxers without a personal following, although if they have one it means they earn more. I offer the same terms to other fighters. Dave "Gypsy" Douglas v. Garry Jacobs cost me £5,000 so nobody gets "ripped-off" by me. On the contrary, if a lad comes off the street in answer to my advertisement in the *Boxing News* I will kit him out – cost £100 minimum. I will pay for his pre-fight medical – normal cost £20. I will also pay his skull X-ray – £12 – and pay for his licence at £10. So right away I have paid £142 that other managers would expect a boxer to pay.

B.D.: Have you had much response to your 'ad' in *Boxing News*?

A.M.: Yes, but the best guy I found from this source was an Irish boxer – really good but he became homesick so he quit. I lost a lot of money that I had invested in him in order to make him a pro'.

B.D.: What about "freebies" Alex?

A.M.: I am a great believer in what the late Harry Levene had up in his office – a notice which said: "If your friends won't pay to see you nobody else will." That was Harry's attitude to "comps" and that is mine.

B.D.: In your opinion who is the most impressive British promoter you have met?

A.M.: Without a doubt Barney Eastwood – or "Bee-Jay" as he is called.

B.D.: Why?

A.M.: You'll understand why when I tell you this. I received a phone call from Barney at short notice. "Alex," he says, "I need a boy at featherweight right away for my bill in Belfast." So I agreed. Barney lifted young Craig Windsor of Blantyre and myself by private executive jet from Glasgow Airport to Belfast. We arrived at Belfast and were conveyed by Mercedes to a luxury five-star hotel. After the fight young Craig couldn't believe it – Barney paid £600 to him, three times the normal fee for a six by two minutes contest. Then we were flown back by executive jet to Glasgow and taken home by hired Mercedes. There is one other thing that impressed me – "Bee-Jay" was universally liked by all the ordinary people we met, waiters, taxi drivers. Barney and I hope to continue our association. My fighter Joe Kelly could fight Barney's fighter Dave McAuley.

B.D.: On that score, what ambitions do you have? If Kelly wins a British title could you promote a European title fight in Glasgow?

A.M.: I would love to but it costs £50,000 to stage a European title bout nowadays. I couldn't do it. Without the television money I couldn't look at it. The TV boys in Scotland will network boxing but they would rather televise hours of curling than a domestic boxing tournament – I know because I tried. Take the Paul Downie v. Dave Savage Scottish junior lightweight title scrap – a great fight but the TV boys didn't want to know.

B.D.: What about the family? Do they help with the boxing? Do you help, Ann?

Ann Morrison: I suppose I do. I wash all the boxers' gear – help out which way I can.

A.M.: My daughter Catherine tried recently to become the first female promoter in Scottish boxing history. She wasn't successful in her application – but she will try again.

B.D.: Don't you think there could be a clash of interests in being a manager and promoter combined?

A.M.: There are dangers, yes! But this is something I am working on. As you know I support the "Maharg Amateur Boxing Club" – Arthur Melrose looks after the club. But I am hoping that Arthur will be granted a pro' manager's licence then I will concentrate exclusively on promoting.

B.D.: What are your thoughts on the amateur game, Alex?

A.M.: The "amateurs" are more professional than we are! Let me give you an example. An amateur show was organised in the Masonic Hall in Drumchapel. Twelve bouts took place, each having a corner (red or blue) sponsored at between £20-£50 per corner – so that is, say 24 times £50 in sponsorship taken in. £1,200 – no boxers to pay, minimal officials' expenses. Add the admission charges money and you are talking about a sum equal if not better than what I net sometimes in my professional shows in the "Plaza" Ballroom in Glasgow! Again there are some top-class "amateurs" who won't fight on an amateur bill for under £100 fee.

B.D.: What is your own outstanding memory of your amateur days as a super-heavyweight.?

A.M.: Being asked to virtually pay to represent my country!

B.D.: How did that happen?

A.M.: I was over in Copenhagen to box for Scotland v. Denmark. In Denmark the police are the licensing authority for amateur boxing. The Danish police have a rule that nobody over a certain age can box – when they found out I was over 40 they banned me. Next thing I know some SABA officials asked me to repay my air fare to Denmark as I was a businessman! I declined. I thought it was incredible!

B.D.: I know you do a lot of charitable work for the Clipton School for the Mentally Handicapped and you would rather not publicly discuss your good works, but tell me at least about Bobby "Sherbo" McDermott whom I know you have treated like a son.

A.M.: "Sherbo" comes from Possilpark. He was a heroin addict but was reformed by the time I took him on as a fighter. "Sherbo" finds it hard to break away from his early environment.

B.D.: You mean like the American adage, "You can take the man out of the ghetto but you can't take the ghetto out of the man"?

A.M.: Something like that. I will give you an example. I took "Sherbo" over to Paris to fight. We were booked into a top grade Parisian five-star hotel. Late the first night, when I woke up I noticed a shadowy form sitting in a bedside chair. It was "Sherbo". Now you have refereed "Sherbo", Brian – you know how tough he is in there. Fearless! I asked him, "What's up?" He replied, "Ah cannae sleep. I dinnae like being in a room by myself – am no' used tae it." You see "Sherbo" had always been used to sleeping four or five to a room.

B.D.: The papers reported a rift between "Sherbo" and yourself when he seemed to collapse on the Barry McGuigan v. Pedroza undercard at Queen's Park Rangers ground. What was the story there?

A.M.: In fact we discovered that "Sherbo" has a blood sugar problem called hyperglycemia. You see he doesn't eat properly – "pot noodles", beans are his stable diet. Sometimes he eats nothing. I put "Sherbo" in a nice new flat, banked £1,000 of his purse money, even put him through driving lessons – but it didn't last. He drifted back to Possilpark. Yet Ann and I have an enormous affection for Bobby. You can't help liking him – he has a marvellous sense of humour.

B.D.: Can you illustrate your last point?

A.M.: There was a charity boxing show which was graced by the Lord Provost of Glasgow. At the end of the show I was squiring the Provost to his Rolls Royce chauffeur-driven car when "Sherbo" whizzes past us and jumps into the back seat. He then asked the Lord Provost, "Say Jim, gie's a lift to Possilpark!" The Lord Provost loved the joke. Again ex-Lord Provost David Hodge loves "Sherbo" – they get on tremendously well. One day "Sherbo" said to him, "Davie, come up and see me in Possil but dinnae bring that chain ye wear or you'll get mugged!" He was referring to the chain that ex-Provosts are entitled to wear on certain occasions.

B.D.: What about your trainer, Willie Connolly? How did you first employ him?

A.M.: Willie does a tremendous job. He has a great way with the boys. I met Willie in the amateurs some years back.

B.D.: Tommy Gilmour and yourself are now Scotland's leading boxing promoters but you don't compete really. Any particular reason?

A.M.: It would be pointless competing – there simply isn't a big enough demand for pro' boxing in Scotland to merit cut-throat competition. Besides, Tommy and I get along well together – we don't want to compete against each other. The problem is, in my opinion there isn't any working class left in the old sense – everybody's middle-class now so boxing more and more becomes a dinner jacket and dinner affair.

B.D.: Yet you gave up your dinner shows recently at the Hospitality Inn with the Whitbread Sporting Club. Why?

A.M.: I became disillusioned by certain factors behind the scenes. Don't misunderstand me, I could clear £1,000 profit a week on some of these shows – not bad for a night's work, eh? But no! Certain people got up my nose – especially by their patronising attitude to boxers, an attitude I hate. So I quit. But I could go back. Some things would·have to be different though.

B.D.: Finally, Alex what about future expansion plans?

A.M.: I am going to put shows on in Kilmarnock in Ayrshire. Ayrshire used to be a great boxing place. I have an Ayrshire lad called Joe Mullen who can sell tickets so that's my next port of call.

B.D.: Alex and Ann Morrison, thank you.

MCTAGGART MBE
Boxing's Esperanto for Excellence

You just know there is something unique about a boxer who, 23 years after throwing his last competitive punch is the subject of a half-hour documentary on Russian television. Particularly when that boxer is Scottish and the only Briton to be so honoured in the entire history of the USSR. This singular honour, bestowed only in 1988 in recognition of the fact that he was in Leningrad with a Scottish boxing team was but another accolade in the glorious career of Dick McTaggart MBE – Scotland and Britain's greatest ever vested warrior.

Unfortunately, just as the stone-deaf Beethoven never ever heard his great Ninth Symphony, *so Dundee's Dick McTaggart was fast asleep in his Leningrad hotel room, unaware that his exploits were being lauded nationwide from Tashkent to Tomsk. Despite frantic efforts to rouse him by a colleage the former Olympic lightweight champion rose from his slumbers only in time to see the credits rolling over a montage sequence of his contests.*

Yet in the late 1950s and 1960s when those slim McTaggart legs encased in the ubiquitous white boots appeared on television, eyes wearied by a hard day's toil in the factory or office would re-focus sharply with anticipation at the prospect of a feast of fistic skills which the blond crew-cutted Dundee southpaw rarely failed to provide.

Further proof that the name of this quiet son of the Dundee tenements became the Esperanto word for boxing excellence was furnished during our interview at his comfortable Glasgow home. Dick showed me a large article from a Jersey newspaper which appeared in the 1970s. McTaggart and his Kent-born wife Doreen had taken their four daughters for a quiet holiday to this Channel Island resort but within hours of landing Dick was besieged by local journalists who only left them in peace once he conceded them an interview.

On examining the Dundonian boxer's record one can perhaps fully understand why throughout Europe, the Commonwealth and the Americas this incredibly gifted Scottish south-paw is so universally acknowledged as a synonym for ring brilliance. In 634 fights he only tasted defeat 24 times. In the Olympics he won gold at Melbourne in 1956 plus the Val Barker Trophy for boxing excellence. Bronze was gained four years later in Rome. In 1958 he was British Empire champion at Cardiff. He was European champion in Yugoslavia in 1961. In addition he was British ABA champion in 1956, 1961, 1963 and 1965 and Scottish champion seven times between 1957 and 1965. Strangely enough he was Olympic champion BEFORE he ever became Scottish champion! In the year that he won European gold in Belgrade in 1961 he was not even Scottish champion, having quit boxing earlier that year.

These are but two paradoxes in a career replete with them. As McTaggart himself makes clear in the interview below if Europe provided him with triumphs it also furnished him with frustrations. In 1957 dreams of European glory in Prague were abruptly terminated when fellow Scot and future pro', Johnny Kidd of Aberdeen, knocked McTaggart cold inside a round.

Then, when the Russian southpaw Karoskin outpointed the Dundonian in Lucerne in 1959 a major Scottish newspaper seriously raised the question of Dundee Dick's retiral on the grounds that he was "washed up". This judgement was based not only on the Lucerne setback but on his loss earlier in that year of his British ABA title to domestic arch-rival Johnny Cooke of Bootle.

Typically, this superb ring individualist answered the knockers by triumph in the ring rather than tirades outside of it. With the pessimists' jibes still ringing in his ears he went straight to Hamilton Town Hall and defeated old foe Jim Lynch of Glasgow Transport. This show was promoted by Joe Gans, father of old McTaggart friend and amateur colleague Walter McGowan.

What makes these 1959 utterances about the need to retire all the more absurd is that in the same week he was given an extremely tasty offer to turn professional, an offer he rejected.

Further European defeats – against German Gunter Meir in Moscow in 1963 and against Austrian Rupert Koenig in Berlin – merely made him cherish his solitary European championship victory all the more.

Another paradox lay in the McTaggart relationship with the Royal Air Force. If ever proof was required that a young man could serve in the armed services without being squeezed dry of the peculiar juices of individualism then Dick McTaggart is it. Far from limiting his individuality, the six years he spent in Air Force blue positively enhanced it. Indeed the twin trademarks of crew-cut and white boots were little excursions into uniqueness provoked by his highly regulated service life at RAF Halton near Aylesbury. The RAF connection also provided McTaggart – who was Allied Forces champion in 1956 – with another unique distinction. He must surely be the only NATO soldier to be lionised on television in the spiritual home of the Warsaw Pact!

That Scotland's greatest ever amateur boxer acknowledged his debt to the Royal Air Force can be gleaned from the fact that when Corporal McTaggart was paraded around Dens Park, home of Dundee FC, on 15 December 1956, with Val Barker trophy in hand, the pick-up truck which bore him to this hero's welcome by 20,000 fellow Dundonians bore the Royal Air Force badge on the rear.

The RAF also provided the opportunity for the Olympic champion to garner even more distinction. He was Imperial Services champion for three consecutive years – in 1954, 1955 – 6, and again in 1958, as well as RAF champion throughout those years.

Nevertheless, whilst the RAF may have reinforced the discipline he had acquired from a commitment to boxing extending back to childhood, service life did not make him overly respectful of authority, as an incident which grabbed the sporting headlines in 1960 proves. During that year the brilliant Dundee southpaw was stopped on a cut eye before his hometown crowd by Londoner Freddie King. As the interview below makes abundantly clear, age has not mellowed to any extent the bitterness Dick feels about King's tactics or the actions of the Perth referee who he still feels failed to protect him on this occasion.

The upshot of McTaggart's angry declaration that the Perth referee would never again handle one of his contests, was an appearance before senior officials of the Scottish Amateur Boxing Association to explain himself. It is something of a measure of Dick McTaggart's popularity

Why Dick McTaggart can't get Londoner Freddie King out of his mind.

that subsequent to the King bout the referee involved was barracked at the Scottish Amateur Championships every time he stepped into the St Andrew's Halls (Glasgow) ring.

As a former referee I cannot pretend to condone this conduct or indeed the Dundonian's statement that he would select his own officials. But on the other hand, having seen two photographs from the McTaggart scrapbook that clearly confirm that King made McTaggart's groin a repeated target, I can sympathise with the Olympic lightweight champion's aggravation at those breaches of ring etiquette being apparently ignored.

However, such incidents were but minor irritants in a career whose achievements clearly confirm the judgement that his talent was of such an order to justify the description of him as a "Michaelangelo amongst the housepainters". The McTaggart style was based on an economy of effort that made many of his contests look like a fistic duet between a boxer slowly warming up and one who fought as though every round was his last. Complementing this laid-back style was a talent for evasion that, had the average debtor possessed it, would have induced mass nervous breakdowns amongst the most case-hardened sheriff officers.

Today Dick McTaggart is happily married with four daughters and resides permanently in Glasgow's southside. He is the Scottish Amateur Boxing Association's official team coach on a part-time basis, a post he combines happily with working at the Hillingdon factory of the Rolls Royce company. Even in his daily toil the McTaggart name is associated with the ultimate in class.

The interview which follows took place in April 1988.

B.D.: Dick, where and when did it all start?

D.McT.: I was encouraged to take up boxing by my uncle Danny Cunningham who fought in a famous boxing booth in Dundee called Stewart's. My uncle Willie White also encouraged me by paying my boxing club fees. I took up the game when I was about eleven.

B.D.: When did you win your first title?

D.McT.: In 1946 I won the Midland Area junior flyweight title by beating my brother Archie.

B.D.: You defeated your own brother?

D.McT.: Aye, I defeated my other brother Peter as well in 1952. He was an ex-Navy champion!

B.D.: Which club did you start with? Who were your trainers?

D.McT: I started off with the "Hawkhill" Club. George Kidd, who was a famous professional all-in wrestler, trained there too. My handlers in those days were Jim and Alex Thomas but it was Frankie Quinn at the "Dundee ABC" in Dudhope Castle who really brought me on. Frankie didn't drink or smoke and he taught me self-discipline. I needed somebody like Frankie – I liked to enjoy myself.

B.D.: How else did Frank Quinn develop you as a boxer?

D.McT: He helped me develop a good right hook. Remember too that I wasn't a natural southpaw as some people seem to think. I was able to fight orthodox but I preferred southpaw and Frankie didn't try to change me.

Why Dick McTaggart can't get Londoner Freddie King out of his mind.

B.D.: The thing I remember particularly about your 1950s TV appearances – apart from your ring performances – were your white boxing boots. Everyone in those days wore black boots.

D.McT.: Yes. I more or less was the first to wear them. Being in the RAF I wore uniform every day, so the boots and my crew-cut hairstyle were a reaction against the sameness of my uniform.

B.D.: I have the impression that your six-year RAF stint helped your boxing career a great deal?

D.McT.: Definitely. I was lucky that I spent six years in the same place – RAF Halton near Aylesbury. The facilities were good and "Chiefy" Roy who was in charge of the RAF boxing team made sure we had good sparring.

B.D.: What about coaching in the RAF?

D.McT.: There wasn't any – didn't need it. I was fighting a better class of opponent half the time in the services than the average boxing club member in "civvy street" was. That kept me on my toes.

B.D.: You won the Olympic gold medal at lightweight in Melbourne, 1956. Was that your greatest achievement?

D.McT.: No way! My European gold medal in Belgrade in 1961 when I beat the Yugoslav Peter Benedek was my greatest achievement, greater in my mind than Melbourne.

B.D.: That will surprise many – it surprises me. But why?

D.McT.: I had done it all by then EXCEPT win a European gold. I was beginning to think I'd never do it.

B.D.: Let's go back to Melbourne. What are your memories of that?

D.McT.: My opponent in the final – a German called Harry Kurschat – was enormously tough. I decked him twice in the first round. I just kept punching and punching him but he kept coming back for more.

B.D.: You won by unanimous decision?

D.McT.: I won every single one of my Melbourne contests by unanimous decision, that's why I was awarded the "Val Barker trophy". I mean, how many times in amateur boxing do you get three unanimous decisions on the trot in the same tournament?

B.D.: In the 1950s and 1960s which did you regard as the top amateur boxing country?

D.McT.: Without a doubt, Russia! Kakoskin who beat me in Switzerland was especially good. Funny thing though, he is now a "bigwig" in Russia – a Master of Sport. He was responsible for having Russian TV put on a half-hour documentary about my life when I was over in Leningrad two months ago. Funny thing is I missed seeing it – I was sleeping in my hotel room when Gordon Hendry, the SABA referee, came charging in and said, "You're on TV! They're doing your life!" Well, we switched on just in time to see the credits rolling!

B.D.: What do you think was your worst amateur defeat?

D.McT.:That's easy – Dave Charnley stopped me inside a round in 1953 (*Dave Charnley went on to miss winning the world professional lightweight title by a whisker in 1961*

Dick McTaggart displays the Val Barker trophy for best Olympic stylist in 1956. On his left is fellow gold medallist Terry Spinks.

when he was outpointed by Joe Brown of Texas.) Charnley was dynamite, but mind you I was only 18 years old. I wanted a return but he turned pro'. Charnley was a southpaw and I hated fighting other southpaws. It was the same in Lucerne – that Russian Kakoskin. He beat me in the "Europeans" – he was a southpaw.

B.D.: Speaking of Dave Charnley turning pro', I have discussed you, Dick, many times with other boxing people and most have expressed the view that McTaggart would not have made it as a pro'. What do you say to that?

D.McT.: Then you and your mates were talking rubbish! I could have made it as a pro' all right. I haven't the slightest doubt about that!

B.D.: Why didn't you then?

D.McT.: Firstly because of these (*removing his spectacles*), it runs in the McTaggart family – bad eyesight. I never would have passed the pro' game medical, I think. Then there is the fact that I didn't like the pro' game. If a manager is going to invest £5,000 in you he is going to want his pound of flesh in return. Look, when I was unemployed and broke, living in a tenement in Dundee at Erskine Street a pro' manager dumped £500 in notes on my kitchen table and said, "Sign". I told him to go away! My daughters tell me now, "Dad, think of the money we could have had today!" Now do you think pro' managers would have kept on pestering me if I couldn't have made it as a pro'? Even Peter Keenan – who is one of my sporting heroes – had a go at trying to make me go pro', but I told him "No" as well.

B.D.: Which Scottish opponents do you rate most highly?

D.McT.: Jimmy Gibson of the Woodside Club (*Dunfermline*). I fought and beat him seven times and Jimmy Lynch of the Glasgow Transport Club – I fought and beat him seven times, although strangely enough in our most vital fight – in 1961 – I thought he was a clear winner but the judges voted for me, thank goodness! But if I had lost then he – not I – would have been sent to Belgrade and I would not have won my European gold medal.

B. D.: Your greatest achievement?

D.McT: Right, as I said before it meant more to me than Melbourne in 1956. Don't forget in early 1961 I had chucked the game – I was cheesed off with boxing – so I didn't compete in the Scottish championships. Jimmy Lynch and I had to have a "fight-off" to decide who went to Belgrade. Lynch "won" but the judges gave it to me. As I have said already I'm glad they did!

B.D.: Why did you rate Gibson and Lynch so highly?

D.McT: Both of these guys were really clever. It was always a battle of brains as well as fists in the ring with them.

B.D.: Which opponent did you respect least?

D.McT: Freddie King of London – he stopped me on a cut eye.

B.D.: Why?

D.McT.: Look. I will show you the photographs and you be the judge. (*Bringing a large photo album, he indicates a picture depicting King butting him in the groin – also punching him there.*) I protested to the ref. He didn't help much.

B.D.: And landed yourself on the mat for post-contest comments?

Dick McTaggart arrives home in Dundee in December 1956 with Val Barker trophy in hand.

D.McT.: Yes, but that was a storm in a tea-cup – nothing much happened then.

B.D.: Your greatest English rival was Johnny Cooke of Bootle. Do you know he "blamed" you for making him turn pro'? (*As a pro' Cooke held the British and Empire welterweight title from February 1967 until January 1968 when he was outpointed by Ralph Charles.*)

D.McT.: No! When did he say that?

B.D.: In 1970. He told English journalists that when you killed off his chances in 1960 of going to the Rome Olympics by beating him on a questionable decision he was so fed up that he went pro'. He also said that although you won your six contests by four wins to his two that it should have been 3 – 3.

D.McT.: I don't agree with that! But he was a tough opponent okay!

B.D.: I watched your scraps on TV. They always looked hard. What was it about Cooke that made him so tough?

D.McT.: Cooke was hard – awkward – but very clever with it, clever at holding, working inside. He beat me the first two times we met but I mastered his style eventually. But I have to say towards the end I found fighting Cooke boring.

B.D.: Overall, which of your opponents impressed you most?

D.McT.: Oh! The Pole, Pazdior. He beat me in Rome, although funnily enough I thought I boxed better against him than I did against Kurschat in Melbourne! I lost on a majority 3 – 2 decision. Pazdior beat me three times though. He was a gentleman. He is now in a wheelchair, poor guy! Parkinson's disease.

B.D.: Any other memorable fights?

D.McT.: Yes. In Perth in 1963 I boxed the ears off a Ghanaian named Clement Quarte for the gold medal. The Ghanaian was awarded the decision and he fainted with shock! He was out for ten minutes!

B.D.:Looking at the other home countries, whom did you rate as your best opponents from Wales and Ireland?

D.McT.: The toughest Welshman I ever met was another southpaw called Malcolm Collins. He was an awkward customer, yet I thought I had done enough to win. It was an RAF versus Wales show – two Welsh judges and one RAF. Guess what? The Welsh voted for Collins, so I lost!

B.D.: And Irish?

D.McT.: Oh, without a doubt Freddie Tiedt. He was a tough little customer. He turned pro' but I really was impressed by him – clever, tough. You knew you had been in a contest with him!

B.D.: Who was the greatest amateur boxer you ever saw?

D.McT.: Muhammad Ali – without doubt. I saw him in the final against that brilliant Pole, Pietryzkowski. Don't forget how good the Pole was. (*The Polish boxer boxed in Scotland against Alf Barker of Dunfermline the year before he fought Ali.*) But Ali was, well, what can you say?

B.D.: I know that years back you said that "Sugar Ray" Robinson was your all-time pro' favourite. Does that still hold?

D.McT.: Yes. He was the greatest pro'.

B.D.: What about Scottish pro' fighters? Whom did you rate most highly?

D.McT.: I never saw Lynch, but Peter Keenan I have always admired. He was a real fighter – a hard man, great performer. I also liked Walter McGowan and Ken Buchanan. I saw Ken Buchanan and Jim Watt fighting. Ken won okay, I thought. Jim Watt is a good guy too.

B.D.: You are now Scottish National Coach. What do you emphasise in training?

D.McT.: The traditional things. I am not strict for strictness sake. I insist that they are fit and come in at the right weight. But I am strict when I have to be.

B.D.: Do you encourage weights in training?

D.McT.: Not a lot. We use some. I had a case recently of a boxer who was winning by a mile in the second round when suddenly he said, "It's those weights – I can't go on." He had run out of stamina. So weights are used in moderation – in circuit training.

B.D.: What do you think is the biggest difference between the amateur game today and in your day?

D.McT.: It is more restricted today. In my day district championships would have run from two p.m. to two a.m. Now you have people getting walkovers into the British championships. In Kenny Buchanan or Walter McGowan's day they had to fight three or four contests before they got to a final. Again, there was more money in the amateur game in my heyday. Remember, I was known as the most televised sportsman in Britain in the 1950s and 1960s. The amateur game received £50,000 a year – a huge sum in those days, from television fees.

B.D.: Which country's amateur boxers impressed you least?

D.McT.: You will be surprised no doubt to learn the USA! I fought six Yanks but none of them impressed me. Take the Great Britain side that beat the USA 10 – 0 in December 1961. The guy I beat, Cesar Marcus, was one of the poorest amateurs I ever fought.

B.D.: Would you say anything is better today?

D.McT.: Yes, I had too many contests. They don't fight so often now. I think that's a good thing. They won't burn out so quickly nowadays.

B.D.: Dick McTaggart, thank you!

How Good was BENNY LYNCH?

To many in Scotland and indeed Great Britain a question such as "How good was Benny Lynch?" might be considered as being on the same scale of absurdity as, "Can Kenny Dalglish kick a football?" Wasn't Lynch as much a genius in the ring as Dalglish was deadly in the penalty box?

Unfortunately, patriotism renders all assessments whether they be of genius, stupidity or earthquakes as relative. What passes for a mere seismic hiccup in Tokyo would be a serious earth tremor in Scotland. In certain parts of Germany there are still old men who would seriously have you believe that 30 April 1945 – the day Adolf Hitler died – was the blackest day in human history since the Crucifixion. To an Argentinian fight fan of the 1950s exclamations of awe that Benny Lynch of Glasgow packed cruiser-like hitting power into a five-foot-three-inch frame would have been shrugged aside on the grounds that the South American country's own great flyweight world champion – Pascual Perez – displayed equally fearsome punching power packed into an even tinier four-foot-eleven-inch frame. In this connection it is significant that the foreign-dominated WBC list Lynch as the sixth greatest flyweight of all time below Perez, who is rated third. Jimmy Wilde of Wales is rated number one. On the other hand the father of all boxing rating systems, the late Nat Fleischer, rated Lynch five places above Perez whom he listed as tenth. Again Fleischer rated Wilde as number one flyweight of all time.

Such confusion as to the real quality of the flyweight genius from the Gorbals is remarkably absent in Britain. A positively dazzling galaxy of Britain's finest boxing writers are unanimous that Benny Lynch was (a) Scotland's greatest ever boxer, and (b) a better all-round boxer and puncher than the Welsh flyweight known as "The Ghost with a Hammer in His Hand". Gilbert Odd, Frank Butler, Denzil Batchelor, John Burrowes and Harry Mullan collectively represent a depth of knowledge of boxing and what constitutes fistic quality that is second to none.

My own contribution to the debate on the question, "How good was Benny Lynch?" is based on long discussions I had with two men who fought him in the ring; discussions which arose from firm personal friendships that I established with them in my dual capacity as Radio Tay boxing correspondent and boxing referee.

I first interviewed Freddie Tennant in December 1982 in the North Isla Street studios of Radio Tay in Dundee. I subsequently visited Freddie at his home in the Ardler district of the northern jute city on several occasions. Our conversation invariably came round to Fred's four battles with Benny Lynch. Those who knew

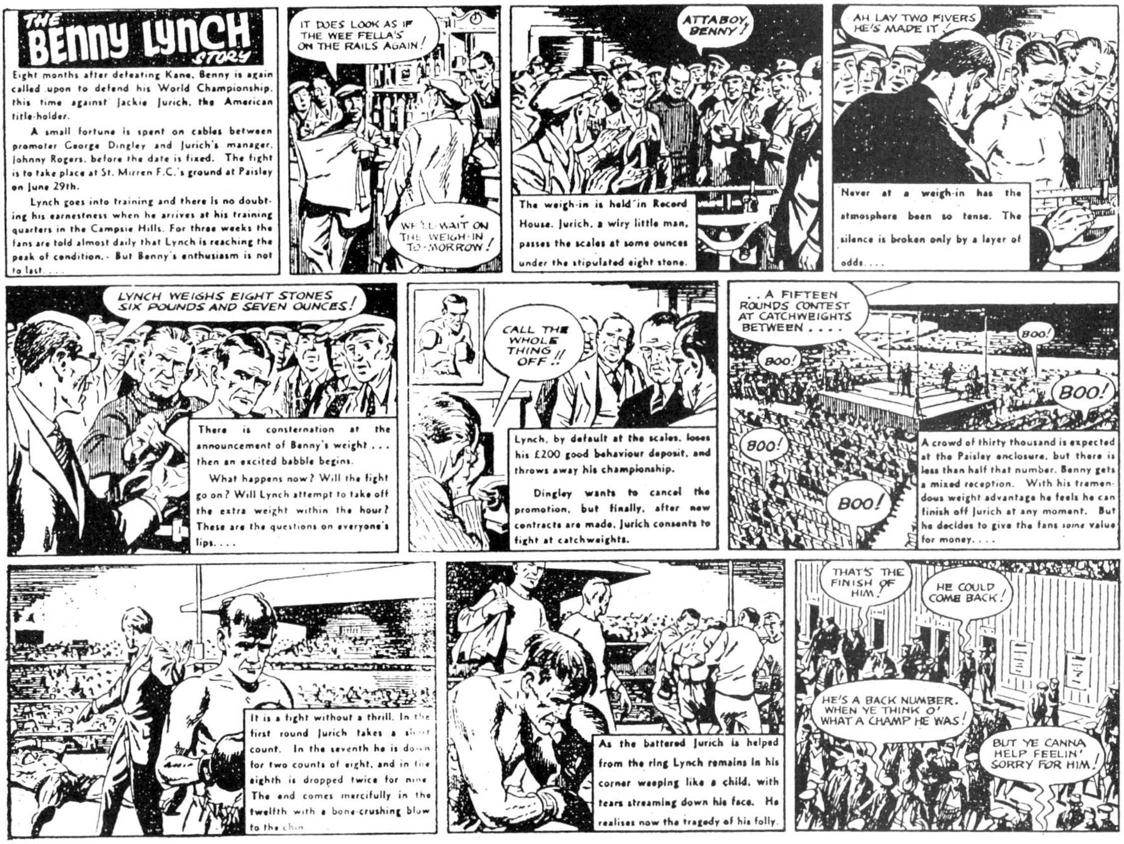

The Sunday Mail *captured well the downfall of Benny Lynch in this 1960's picture story.*

Fred as well as, or even better than I did, will confirm that his favourite word for expressing approval was "fantastic". In his conversations with me the former Scottish flyweight champion from Dundee used this sign of approval with the same frequency as he had thrown jabs at the object of our mutual admiration.

Freddie told me: "The first time I met Benny (*on Friday, 8 July 1932, in the Ring Stadium, Glasgow*) he was just another opponent to me. I had no fear. I came out throwing punches and so did he. In the early rounds I found him easy to jab – I kept mixing my jabs up to his head and body. Well, in the middle of the fight I thought I had been hit wae' a shotgun. I never saw it comin'. . . my corner man told me it was a hook. So I found myself on the canvas – but I got up and won the fight on points." Fred continued: "A few months later (*Monday, 17 October 1932 at The Pavilion, Leith*) we met again. This time I was wary of that hook so I danced and ducked. Maybe I was just too wary because he got the decision – I think it could have gone either way.''

The contest with Lynch that Fred remembered most was the draw he fought with the Gorbals flyweight genius at Bridgeton's Premierland Stadium in Glasgow on 23 December 1932. Fred opined: ''The crowd shouted themselves hoarse that night. What a scrap. I knew better than to hang my chin out this time – I still remembered our first scrap.''

Fred's memories proved accurate when I checked them out against a report in the *Dundee Courier and Advertiser* for 24 December 1932. The Dundee newspaper reported: ''In one of the hottest and fastest bouts ever witnessed in Premierland, Glasgow, Fred Tennant, Dundee, and Benny Lynch, Glasgow, fought ten rounds to a drawn decision last night. The crowd was repeatedly on their feet at the exciting exchanges. Lynch was a terrific battler at close range and whilst he held the supremacy in this branch, Tennant counterbalanced it with most effective punching at long range.'' The report concluded by observing: ''Tennant was as usual a veritable box of tricks. His ducking and evading of his opponent's fierce swings could only be described as brilliant.''

Fred was convinced that he won on that occasion and he stressed to me that what had contributed so much to his success (apart from his good condition) was that he was able to learn from his previous meetings with Lynch. Those who didn't suffered catastrophically because one of the factors that made the wee Gorbals battler a genius in the ring was an ability to profit from previous mistakes – both his own and those of his opponents.

One who suffered grievously for this incapacity to learn the correct lessons from a prior meeting with Benny Lynch was Jackie Brown of Manchester. It was an incapacity that of course contributed to the Gorbals boxer becoming Scotland's first-ever world boxing champion when he blasted the Manchester man out in four minutes and 42 seconds to take the crown. Brown had been warned after his 4 March 1935 draw with Lynch in Glasgow, by his manager Harry Fleming, ''You will be stopped by Lynch in two rounds if you try and mix it with him next time.'' He did try and he paid the penalty. Moss Deyong, who refereed this contest stated that it was savage smashes to the liver that began the downfall of Brown. (It is surely one of the most superb ironies of boxing history that Lynch, an alcoholic, should win his world crown by wreaking havoc with his fists on his opponent's liver – the very organ that would contribute so much to his own downfall.)

In their previous meeting in March Lynch had sussed out Brown's susceptibility to body punches but for reasons of boxing politics had not capitalised on it in order to lull the Mancunian into a false sense of security. In addition, Jim Maharg told me that he advised Lynch that Brown's body was his weak spot, a judgement based on the fact that Maharg was twice disqualified (and fined) for hitting the Mancunian in the body.

This of course raises the question, ''How good was Jackie Brown?'' The failure of his name to appear in any transatlantic polls of flyweight greats might suggest that Brown was a poor world title-holder. Nothing could be further from the truth.

Dundee's Freddie Tennant
who once defeated Benny Lynch.

When Brown outpointed the Frenchman Valentin Angelmann over 15 rounds, former world bantam champion Joe Bowker told Jimmy Wilde, "If this kid had been around in your day you would have starved."

Brown not only shared Lynch's Irish ancestry he was also a natural ring genius with the same talent for self-destruction outwith the ropes that his nemesis from Glasgow possessed. He spent three months in prison the year before his 1935 world title joust with Lynch for biting a man's ear in a brawl. A week before his massacre at the hands of the Gorbals genius Brown had gone on the "ran-dan" as a result of which he was at one point a full half stone outside the championship limit. Such events were to become a familiar part of the Lynch scenario too. But it was the

Lynch punch above all else that destroyed Brown, allied to the latter's inability to learn as Lynch had learned from their previous meeting.

Freddie Tennant emphasised this when we came to discuss his fourth and final fight with Lynch which took place on Friday, 5 May 1933. The location was again Jim Gilmour's Premierland Stadium in Bridgeton. "I learned each time from Lynch but he learned even better. I knew something was afoot when he didn't come tearing in like before. I kept waiting for him to make his move. It wasn't till later I realised he was letting me waste energy. Then towards the fight's end the 'fun' started. He caught me with the left hook, then piled on left and rights as I staggered against the ropes. Then he would batter my ribs. I don't remember much about the last two rounds except that I was glad when the bell rang." The *Dundee Courier and Advertiser* of Saturday, 6 May 1933 also stressed that "There was little in it up to the eighth session when Lynch opened up."

Benny Lynch was the master of the full repertoire of boxing punches but as Freddie Tennant noted his hooks had an especially marked destructive quality. This was particularly true in the days when the spirit of Lynch's genius was still relatively undiluted by alcoholic dissipation, as we can glean from a contest that took place on Thursday, 13 December 1934, at the Edinburgh National Sporting Club. The wee man from the Gorbals was faced with an Aberdonian then resident in London called Sandy McEwan.

Although he could have no inkling that he was doing so, the Edinburgh *Evening News* journalist who covered this contest bestowed on posterity a graphic picture of the Lynch genius at its most pristine. The journalist reported: "It was a stirring bout, the contrast in styles being an outstanding feature. While Lynch was at the top of his form there was no doubt that the unorthodox style of the sturdily built Aberdonian had the champ guessing at times. Where the title-holder shone was in his splendid footwork. McEwan was inclined to swing wildly, particularly with left hooks. A PUNCH THAT LYNCH MADE GOOD USE OF BUT MORE IN A MASTERLY FASION (*Emphasis mine. B.B.D.*). At certain periods the science of the Glasgow boy was revealed in a marked degree, his jabbing and clipping with his left hand being accomplished in his best style while he hooked to advantage in nearly every round of the contest. There was never a dull moment throughout and the ninth round was a particularly thrilling affair . . . The boys, toe to toe swopped punches, until Lynch launched a furious double-handed attack." What makes the future flyweight kingpin's performance even more noteworthy was that it was achieved with a staved right hand, an injury sustained in the early rounds of the contest.

It was the left hook that paved the way for victory over arguably his most dangerous rival, Peter Kane of Lancashire. The referee that historic evening of 13 October 1937 at Shawfield Park was the late W. Barrington Dalby who called it the "greatest fight I ever refereed". Although he decked Kane with a right in the opening round, Dalby (who had the unsurpassed view of the action enjoyed by all third men in the ring) made it clear that it was left hooks that did to Kane what 41 other opponents had previously failed to do – pave the way for the kayo that came in round 13 even though the final blows were a left to the stomach and a right to the jaw.

Yet mastery of the conventional punches alone was not simply the essence of the Lynch genius. Employing the unorthodox to devastating effect has always been one of the hallmarks of ring greatness. Muhammad Ali and "Rope-a-Dope" Kid McCoy and his "corkscrew" punch, a forerunner of the modern hook, are but two examples of this. Thus it was that Scotland's first world champion confirmed his genius in the eyes of Scotland's greatest boxing referee this century – Eugene Henderson. Mr Henderson had refereed Lynch before stepping into the ring of the Edinburgh National Sporting Club on the evening of Thursday, 29 November 1934, but he admits he was not overly impressed – that is until the bell rang for this contest. In the opposite corner to the Glasgow flyweight maestro was former ABA (1930–31) flyweight champion from Wales, Johnny Griffiths.

The textbooks tell the orthodox fighter "Never lead with your right" and it is generally sound advice – that is except when Lynch employed it as a lightning feint to raise the opponent's left hand, thus exposing the body for a following left hook. This is exactly what the Gorbals maestro did to Griffiths. As the Edinburgh *Evening News* of Friday, 30 November 1934 recorded it: "Griffiths made the first advance of the fight but was quickly repulsed, Lynch driving his man to the ropes with a fast two-handed body attack.... ...Then a right hand lead by Lynch caused Griffiths to raise his guard and the champion, quick to take his chance jumped in and smashed home a left to the solar plexus. Griffiths crumpled to the floor holding his stomach and failed to rise before beating the count...".

What electrified Eugene Henderson was that several years before this incident he and another top-class Scottish flyweight, Johnny Hill, had perfected a similar move, only after long tortuous hours in the gym. But Lynch had executed the manoeuvre purely on instinct – the kind of inspired instinct commonly called genius.

The ferocity of Lynch's punching is a point of common agreement amongst those who have felt compelled to assess it, or as in the case of Freddie Tennant and Jim Maharg, those who have experienced it directly. Where disagreement arises is as to its relative destructive power. Moss Deyong who refereed the world championship triumph against Manchester's Jackie Brown put it at welterweight force, Frank Butler at featherweight proportions. Barrington Dalby thought that Lynch's punch would have been decisive against Jimmy Wilde, a viewpoint with which I am inclined to agree, for if Wilde was "The Ghost with a Hammer in His Hand" then Lynch was "The Jock with Jeopardy in his Dukes".

It is this factor that makes me opine that Lynch would have mastered Miguel Canto, the Mexican whom the WBC rate two places above him in their all-time great flyweights. On paper Canto's record 15 defences of his WBC flyweight title against Lynch's three would suggest the Mexican should be a runaway winner in the greatness stakes but this is to oversimplify. Of Canto's 15 defences, 14 went the full distance of 15 rounds. With no punch to speak of, the Mexican against Lynch would have been akin to someone hunting a tiger with a feather duster.

Jim Maharg knew Benny Lynch better than most. He employed Lynch as a sparring partner and was already himself an established champion by the time Lynch began to grab the headlines. Jim told me: "Lynch was as good as they said he was. He could do it all – although I think he picked up his body punching from his time with me." (Maharg was a noted body puncher. He won the right to fight Jackie Brown for his British title by beating Brown's fellow Mancunian Fred Bebbington with left hooks to the body.)

So in world terms only Pascual Perez of those rated above him would have had sufficient punching power and skill to trouble Lynch. Nat Fleischer's rating of Frankie Genaro above Lynch I find frankly incredible. Genaro was knocked out inside a minute in Paris by Emile Pladner. Lynch only suffered the indignity of a kayo once in over one hundred fights – against Aurel Toma, in his last contest, fought at a time when his reflexes were pickled in alcohol. Genaro was also kayoed inside two rounds by Victor Young Perez. At his prime the Lynch power of punch allied to Genaro's susceptible chin would have done for this American former Olympic champion.

Similarly Fidel La Barba certainly defeated Scotland's Elky Clark in a world title fight but I think it would have been a very different result had the American been facing Lynch. La Barba scored only 15 kayos in 72 pro' fights, which scarcely suggests the weight of punch to trouble seriously a peak Lynch. On the other hand La Barba was never knocked out. La Barba v. Lynch would have been an intriguing match but I should still have favoured Lynch to win.

So how good was Benny Lynch? The question is best answered by harking back to a point made earlier. Nobody obtains a better view of a contest than a referee. Three top-class referees who handled the Gorbals flyweight king – Deyong, Dalby and Henderson – were unanimous in praising him, expressing their admiration in the ultimate accolade of "genius". That is how good Benny Lynch was. He was a genius with an equal proportion of greatness and gunpowder in his gloves.

Buchanan and Son
Jawing at the Woodside

Undefeated British lightweight champion, 1968 – 1971, undefeated European champion, 1974 – 75, world lightweight champion, 1970 – 1972 – this litany of high achievement is certainly impressive but it does not reveal the most outstanding fact of all: the Scot who earned these distinctions is regarded worldwide as one of the greatest fighters to step into a ring. That man is Ken Buchanan MBE.

Buchanan's fan club ranges from two doctors of my acquaintance in Montgomery, Alabama, to the entire British and American press corps. (Even the late and great Peter Wilson, whilst expressing a keen personal dislike for Ken, admired his outstanding technical virtuosity in the ring.)

The British press voted him the best British fighter to emerge since 1945 in a poll conducted in 1975. The American scribblers presented prestigious awards never bestowed on any British fighter before or since.

My own knowledge of Ken Buchanan is somewhat unique in the sense that of the scores of writers to put pen to paper about Scotland's world champion I am the only one who can honestly claim to have shared a ring and crossed gloves with him, not once for a publicity stunt as the American writer George Plimpton did with world lightheavyweight champion Archie Moore, but three times a week between January and June 1962 at the Sparta ABC's McDonald Road premises in Edinburgh.

Lest any gullible soul feel moved to recommend me retrospectively for some award for valour it should be stated that my task was eased by the fact that this was not the Ken Buchanan who poleaxed British title contender Brian Hudson with a superb right hand punch in 57 seconds of the fifth round in their 1970 title joust. No, the 16-year-old boy I faced on a Monday, Wednesday and Thursday was certainly a talented and promising amateur, but he was an apprentice joiner and I was an apprentice baker. This future world champion and MBE lived in an identical prefab in Edinburgh's Mountcastle to the one I inhabited in Gilmerton. So, initially at least, the awe factor that is so important in boxing was conspicuous by its absence. However, whatever social equality that existed between us soon began to disappear inside the ropes in a peculiarly pernicious (from my point of view) fashion, while a different, more painful, inequality began to assert itself instead. Nevertheless, whilst attempting to mug fresh air is a very frustrating exercise, I was at least spared the fate of so many of the future lightweight king's foes who were made to look foolish before multitudes.

The audience of my weekly martyrdom normally consisted of club personnel such as ABA welterweight champion Jimmy Malcolm, Mick Raeburn (another welterweight whom I particularly enjoyed boxing), Bobby Campbell, a 14-year-old heavyweight, and a clever bantam called Alex Gilroy, plus trainers George Shaw and Cecil "Bobby" Horne. The latter's contribution to the fistic development of Ken Buchanan is freely acknowledged by Ken's father Tommy. He told me, "Bobby Horne was the best coach Ken ever had in the amateurs... he taught him a lot...". This is a fact I can readily endorse as I clearly recall Bobby Horne standing in the middle of the Sparta ring, jab pads on hands, showing the future world lightweight champion the intricacies of combination punching during those evenings of more than a quarter of a century ago.

Our comradeship, born in mutual sweat and my discomfort, has endured the years. In 1979 Ken Buchanan sponsored my application for a referee's licence. A telephone call in January 1986 brought him to the Kirkcaldy amateur show that I was promoting for the "Lang Toun's" Boys' Club, thus boosting the "gate" considerably.

The interview which follows took place in the Woodside Hotel, Musselburgh – the town which is the birthplace of Hugh Roddin who thrilled the grandparents of many of those same New Yorkers who were so often enraptured by Ken Buchanan in Madison Square Garden. This hotel overlooks the same Musselburgh race course where another famed boxing Scot, Eugene Henderson, had trained as a young man. The setting, therefore, was steeped in the very boxing history that Ken Buchanan helped to create. I interviewed Ken and father Tommy – Buchanan and Son – there in April 1988.

B.D.: Tommy, did you ever box yourself?

T.B.: Never competitively. My cousin, Mungo Bird, was quite a useful pro' in the 1930s. He boxed in Stewart's Booth in Jane Street, but I was a member of the Lonsdale Club – that was next to the old tram depot at Shrubhill. But an accident to my wrist stopped me boxing.

B.D.: What happened to your wrist?

T.B.: I was trying to get into Tynecastle Park to see a football match and one of the gatemen shut a gate to stop the crowd surge. Unfortunately my arm was pushed forward by the impetus of the crowd and my wrist was severely cut. That prevented me from boxing. But I was a regular at the Jane Street booth (*Benny Lynch boxed there in the early 1930s*).

B.D.: Any favourite memories of the venue?

T.B.: Yes. There was a great character there – a middleweight called "Beef" Robinson. He was not very skilful but he was game and he could hit well. Well, one evening he was hit by a peach of a left hook and he crashed face first on to the canvas – spark out! So peaceful did Robinson look in the middle of the ring that the crowd chanted, "A blanket for Beef – let 'im sleep!" The Jane Street booth had a great atmosphere... I can remember George McKenzie there too – he was British featherweight champion in the 1920s.

B.D.: When did you first really conclude that Ken was a bit "special", Tommy?

T.B.: When he was about 12 years old – also during the series of bouts, four, he had with Billy Appleby (*Billy Appleby of the Buccleuch ABC who was one of the fighting Appleby clan who won honours at district and national level*). When he was 12 I told Ken that boxing was about avoiding punishment while punishing the other guy. He never forgot that – it was the basis of his style.

Ken Buchanan: That's right. That's exactly what I am trying to teach one of the boys I am handling at the moment – Sean Heron. Don't lead with your face but your fist! He's a good learner too.

B.D.: Is he the only boxer you are managing at the moment, Ken?

K.B.: No, I have two others – the boy Galloway and Owney Smith – I try to teach them to box, not just fight.

B.D.: What about promoting, Ken?

K.B.: No, it just doesn't appeal to me. There is too much hassle on that side of the game. I would much rather train and manage fighters.

B.D.: If I may turn to you, Tommy, what do you think was Ken's best performance as an amateur?

T.B.: Against the Italian Gioncento Silvero. He lost that night on a hotly disputed decision but he jabbed the Italian silly.

B.D.: Ken?

K.B.: Yes, I would agree with that. The Italian was good though too – kept coming forward all the time.

B.D.: Any amusing stories from the amateur days?

T.B.: Yes. I always remember Ken was fighting for Scotland in Glasgow. His late mother was a big fan, as you know. During a pause in the action Ken's mum shouted out, "Use your left, Ken!" It rang round the stadium clear as a bell. As quick as a flash a voice retorted with a thick Glasgow accent, "That's right, Kenny – dae as yer Mammy tells ye!" The crowd roared with laughter and I even noticed Ken, who was normally so intense inside the ropes, smiling then.

B.D.: Why didn't you go pro' with a Scottish manager, Ken?

K.B.: My dad and I actually flew down to London to chat to Bobby Neil about signing up with him. I was quite keen at first to sign up. Bobby made a lot of the fact that he was an "ex-Sparta" Club member, that kind of thing.

T.B.: Yes Ken was actually keener than I was to go with Bobby.

B.D.: Why didn't you sign then with Neil?

K.B.: From my angle everything was okay until we reached the airport in London. Then as Bobby Neil and I were exchanging pleasantries before we parted he said, "Just one thing, Ken – if you sign with me you'll have to change your style, but that shouldn't be any problem." Well, it was a problem. There was no way I was going to change my style – I never was a "charge forward" fighter and never could be. So it was that that decided me against going with Bobby Neil.

B.D.: You worked Ken's corner when he was a pro', Tommy. There are those who say relatives in the corner are bad news – I'm thinking of Mike Rossman who lost his WBA world light-heavyweight title to Victor Galindez because he and his father fell out in the corner during the fight.

T.B.: No! I insisted on playing second fiddle to Eddie Thomas. Eddie Thomas was a great corner man – efficient, cool and good at assessing an opponent's strengths – none better. There is no way I would interfere with Eddie as a corner man.

K.B.: I would back my Dad there – great corner man Eddie. Best I ever had.

B.D.: So what was the cause of the rift with Thomas?

T.B.: Eddie was not as good a manager as he was a seond. Take the fight with Donato Paduano in Madison Square Garden (*in 1970*). (*Donato Paduano was described by* Boxing News *in 1970 as "the most exciting prospect in the North American continent", a judgement based on victories over Frenchman Marcel Cerdan Jnr and old Dick McTaggart opponent Johnny Cooke. A natural welterweight, Paduano was as famed for his precision left hand jabbing as Ken Buchanan was*). Teddy Brenner, the Madison Square Garden matchmaker, Eddie Thomas and I were standing in the lift going up to the Madison Square Garden when Brenner said, "By the way, Tommy, there will be a few pounds difference between your boy and Paduano." I asked Brenner, "What do you mean by a few pounds?" All the time I was watching Eddie Thomas out of the corner of my eye. He was the manager – he should have spoken up – but he said nothing. Well it turned out that Ken was spotting Paduano nearly a stone by the time they entered the ring.

B.D.: Yet Ken produced one of his best ever performances. He jabbed Paduano silly. The odds, I recall, were heavily in his favour.

T.B.: Nobody gave Ken a chance in Madison Square Garden but I still think Eddie was taking too big a risk spotting that weight.

K.B.: Paduano was made to fight my fight. He kept coming forward which suited me just fine.

T.B.: You should have heard the American fans raving about Ken's performance after the bout!

B.D.: Paduano was a boxer but you outboxed him, just as you did with Morris Cullen of Shotton (*for the British title in 1968*). I must admit when the Cullen match was announced I thought it might be a stinker of a fight because you were both so similar in style – Cullen and yourself were classic left jabbers.

K.B.: Yes, but our strategy was to beat him to the punch. We agreed before the fight that to beat him I would have to land my jab first. That's what I did throughout the fight – softened him up before putting him away in round eleven.

B.D.: Did he say anything after the fight?

K.B.: Not a word.

T.B.: I went down to Cullen's dressing-room to thank him for a sporting contest but he didn't even look at me or acknowledge my presence, so I left.

B.D.: Turning to your fight with Jim Watt in January 1973 at the St Andrew's Sporting Club, do you regard that as one of your sweetest victories?

K.B.: Not really. I thought it was a "crap" fight. Jim Watt was not 100 per cent confident that night. Every time I hit him with a half-decent shot he hung on. I think his manager Jim Murray did him no favours. I mean I think Murray's pre-fight talk put Jim under a lot of pressure.

T.B.: I also think that certain statements Watt has made recently in English papers that he was only "an apprentice" when he fought Ken are nonsense. He was an experienced pro' when he fought Ken.

B.D.: Nevertheless, certain respected English scribes questioned the appointment of an Edinburgh referee for this contest?

T.B.: Yes, but George Smith was doing us no favours. Ken won okay. Besides I thought George Smith might have cautioned Watt a couple of times for his inside work in the clinches.

B.D.: If I may backtrack to Eddie Thomas, what was the real story of the rupture between Ken and Eddie? Was it simply money?

T.B.: No, there was a misunderstanding. It was a shame really. Eddie heard that I had applied for a licence to manage. Actually it was to handle my other son – Alan – but Eddie jumped to the conclusion that I was trying to take over. I wasn't. So that's what finally brought about the split. But I still feel that if Eddie could have negotiated as well as he handled Ken's corner during fights then there would have been no problem.

B.D.: Let's turn to Roberto Duran to whom Ken lost his world lightweight title in 1972 at Madison Square Garden. Do you think you were ahead at any stage of the fight?

K.B.: No way! He was ahead okay but it was the way I lost.

B.D.: You mean you felt Johnny Lo Bianco offered you no protection in there?

T.B.: I can answer that one. Most people have seen the blatant low blow that ended the fight but few people realise that Duran kneed, actually kneed, Ken in the groin! A Panamanian fan at ringside on seeing this came up to me in the corner and apologised for his countryman's behaviour.

B.D.: I have watched this fight on film several times and I feel it was – even allowing for Duran – a below par performance by yourself. Was there any particular background worry? Were you worried about fighting Duran in particular?

K.B.: No. To me at that stage Duran was just a guy I was ordered to fight by the WBA but my preparation could have been better.

T.B.: Yes. We made a mistake in allowing ourselves to be handled in America by Gil Glancy. I wanted Joe Dimaria who had handled Ken previously so well over there. Joe Dimaria also provided an excellent sparring partner in Edwin Viruet – he later fought Duran twice. In fact Viruet was good for Ken (*laughing*). He used to torment Ken in the ring and put him on edge for the fight.

B.D.: How did he torment you?

K.B.: The little so-and-so was slippery. He used to try to take the mickey out of me.

T.B.: We couldn't get Edwin Viruet. You see the system over there worked against us. Gil Glancy provided us with two sparring partners – one was a virtual novice, the other a pro' with only three fights. That level of sparring talent couldn't possibly extend or prepare Ken. Glancy had these boys on contract. It was the New York boxing "close" season so he had to pay them a retainer – so by employing them with Ken we were paying their wages, not him. So whose interests was he representing?

B.D.: To return to Johnny Lo Bianco, he handled your fight with the Korean, Changil Kim. You had no complaints with him as a referee then?

K.B.: That's because I stopped the Korean early in the fight inside the distance.

B.D.: Was Roberto Duran your toughest opponent?

K.B.: No. Ishmael Laguna was the best boxer I ever fought as a pro'. He was classier than Duran. (*During their September 1970 world title fight won by Buchanan on points Laguna so badly lacerated his Scottish foe's left eye that Buchanan had to have surgery by a top Harley Street specialist.*)

T.B.: Laguna actually came to us after the Duran fight and told us he couldn't believe that Roberto had beaten Ken. Duran had twice been a sparring partner for Laguna. Laguna thought Ken would win when he heard they were matched.

B.D.: Who hit you hardest as a pro', Ken? Duran or Laguna?

K.B.: Neither of them. The hardest punch I ever took was in London from a guy called Ivan Whiter. He was a welterweight and how he could hit. He caught me once and, oh, how I felt that punch!

B.D.: To go back to Duran, Ken, you said he employed dirty tactics. Did you ever deliberately foul an opponent?

K.B.: Only once – the Mexican-American Chu Chu Malave butted me, so I said, "Right you bastard, two can play that game." I butted open a gash above one of his eyes. Then I stopped him. I have no regrets – he deserved it.

B.D.: Did you ever receive offers to fight as world champion in Scotland?

T.B.: There was talk. Jack Solomons talked about it but it never came to anything.

B.D.: You stopped Carlos Ortiz, a former world lightweight champion, in Madison Square Garden. How did you rate him?

K.B.: I gained no satisfaction from fighting him. The guy had been a good champion in the early 1960s (*Ortiz beat among others Dave Charnley of England and the legendary American, Joe "Old Bones" Brown*) but he was way over the hill when I met him. I don't remember that fight with any affection.

B.D.: What do you think of some of the rule changes that the WBC and others have introduced since your heyday. I'm thinking of 12 round world title fights?

K.B.: I don't think 12 round fights make that much of a difference. Most of the damage done in fights occurs in the first six rounds when both of you are still fresh. After that you both tend to get tired – it limits your efficiency.

B.D.: Apart from handling fighters what do you do now, Ken?

K.B.: I now sell insurance and live in Portobello. I am quite happy.

B.D.: Kenny and Tommy Buchanan, thank you!

POSTSCRIPT

Ken Buchanan's talent was unique enough to make him Scotland's greatest fistic champion. He fought a better class of opponent than Paterson, Watt and McGowan and perhaps Lynch, although that is open to question as I have never seen Small Montana in action in the ring.

Based on personal experience and interviews with those who knew them Lynch, Watt and McGowan certainly had more sparkling personalities than the Edinburgh world lightweight king but the last two named were highly perishable commodities when transposed to a foreign field, whilst Buchanan, like a top-grade malt whisky, held his own in any foreign environment no matter how distant he was from his native shores. In the twilight of his career he lost in places like Denmark and Japan to Charlie Nash and Guts Ishiimatu but the fact remains these were post-peak performances. He was and remains one of the most accomplished British fighters to fight in foreign rings.

His ring style was in some respects a metaphor for his own personality, elusive and tough, and the soaring singularity of his talent was matched by an equally singleminded determination that nobody, but nobody, knew better than Kenny Buchanan what was good for him.

At Scottish domestic level it was his supreme misfortune to attain his most piquant bouquet at a time when professional boxing in Scotland had all but died. When he first arrived back in Scotland in September 1970 after winning the world title the delirium with which Edinburgh football fans had applauded Hearts winning the Scottish Cup 14 years before was conspicuous by its absence.

Yet if he was unique he was also heir to another older Scottish fistic tradition – taking the "Big Apple" by storm. As we have seen earlier in this book Hugh Roddin and Alex Lafferty of Airdrie both won acclaim in New York. There they gained a celebrity that had eluded them in their native land – just like Ken Buchanan 60 years later.

JACK JOHNSON – Dundee Freemason

What did Tommy Burns, Stanley Ketchel, Jim Jeffries and Lodge Forfar and Kincardineshire of The Order of International Freemasons have in common? The answer is that at various points in their personal histories each of them had the misfortune to tangle with a negro from Galveston, Texas, called Arthur "John" Johnson, the first negro heavyweight world champion, universally known as "Jack" Johnson.

Over the years this highly intelligent and well-educated son of an illiterate Texas woodcutter has consistently come top in polls of greatest heavyweight champions of all time. Even allowing for the poor technical quality of early films his knockouts of Ketchel and Jeffries reveal a very impressive performer indeed, and although the claims of respective heavyweight champions to "all-time great" status remain largely a matter of opinion and personal taste, on two distinct points of Johnson's career there can be no argument. Largely self-taught, he was enormously well educated and fluent in several languages. He also treated with sovereign and justifiable contempt the white racism of his era. He broke the sexual taboo that prohibited white women and negro men from cohabiting and he drove expensive cars at a time when they were even more of a status symbol than they are today – and at a time when many a southern negro was lynched for simply complaining about the draughts in his tar paper shack. Johnson had a weakness for other kinds of white status symbols too, the more exclusive the better.

One can understand then why becoming a Freemason should appeal to the Galveston boxer. Johnson fancied himself as patriotic an American as the next man and had not every American president since and including George Washington been a member of the secret and exclusive brotherhood of Freemasonry? Not only would posterity remember Arthur John Johnson as the first negro heavyweight champion but also as a fraternal soulmate of Abraham Lincoln and others who had been "on the square".

Jack Johnson's opportunity to join the brotherhood came in October 1911, some 15 months after he had left racial bigots such as Jack London, the famous writer, biting their living room carpets with impotent rage at his sound thrashing of ex-champion Jim Jeffries at Reno, Nevada. The world champ was far away from the blistering heat and bigotry of the Nevada desert in Newcastle-upon-Tyne. He was fulfilling a theatrical engagement when he met a member of the cast who just happened to be a member of Lodge Forfar and Kincardine. Johnson told his fellow music hall performer that he had always wanted to be a Freemason, but was particularly keen as he was now married to a woman whose father was a Masonic bigwig back in the United States with no less than 32 degrees of Freemasonry to his name.

Despite its name and location in Dundee the Forfar and Kincardine Lodge was, by a strange irony, founded in Newcastle-on-Tyne on 1 August 1808 by officers of the Forfar and Kincardine Militia Regiment who were stationed in the Tyneside town at the time. A cable northwards to the lodge from Johnson's theatrical sponsor brought a cordial invitation to the American world champion to be inducted into the first degree of Freemasonry at the Meadow Street Hall of Lodge Forfar and Kincardine. Thus on the morning of 13 October 1911 Johnson and his wife sped northwards by train to the Tayside jute city.

Originally the lodge had intended to initiate the world champ at noon but Johnson threw them into disarray by cabling in advance that the arrangement would have to be brought forward two hours to enable him to complete his contractual obligations to the Newcastle music hall which was employing him. The senior brethren of the lodge then had to send messengers throughout the city of Dundee by taxi to inform the remaining brethren of the change of plan. The partial success of this measure was to leave those same senior brethren with a nose as metaphorically bloodied as that of Jim Jeffries after his bout with Johnson.

Johnson arrived quietly and proceeded to the Royal Hotel, where he left his wife, before travelling by taxi with his music hall sponsor to the Masonic Hall in Meadow Street. In contrast to what was to follow there were few people in Meadow Street when he entered the lodge. He was duly initiated.

On conclusion of the ceremony the world heavyweight champion made a speech which was reported verbatim by a lodge member who was also a journalist with the *Dundee Advertiser* newspaper. This scribe reported Johnson as saying: "Well, Master, I want to speak to you and all the boys from the bottom of ma heart. I'm real pleased and proud to be heah and to become a Mason under the auspices of such a fine lodge and such a splendid band of brothers. Sure it has been one of the great ambitions of my life to become a Mason and this is the proudest day of my existence. Mrs Johnson's father is a big Mason across the pond. He holds 32 degrees. Some day I will do the same (Applause). My wife will be real glad to know I am a Mason at last. . . (bowing low to the assembled brethren) God bless each an' every one of you from the bottom of my heart. . . ."

Although not always noted for his sincerity (in later years strapped for cash he peddled a bogus story about taking a dive in Havana, Cuba, when he lost his title to Jess Willard), on this occasion Johnson was apparently touched by the obvious lack of racism of the Forfar and Kincardine brethren. His feelings were to be enhanced by the tumultuous welcome he received from the townsfolk of Dundee. They had finally got wind of his presence in the city and now crowded him all the way to the Royal Hotel. Even at the railway station canny Dundonians knocked over luggage-laden barrows in their eagerness to shake the champion's hand. How favourably he must have compared the behaviour of this crowd – which included at least one Dundee town councillor – with the vicious racist mob which had surrounded the ring that scorching hot day of 4 July 1910 in Reno, Nevada.

Before he left Johnson spoke to the assembled newsmen in the Royal Hotel. He told them: "This is my first visit to Scotland and it won't be my last. . . I know thousands of Scotsmen all over the world and they're the very best fellas going. I'm coming back to Scotland with my stable of motor cars in January when I hope to appear at the King's Theatre. . . ."

With more than a touch of naivety, if not irony, Johnson asked the pressmen if there were any hills in Scotland! One Dundee journalist recommended "The Devil's Elbow", "Rest-and-be-Thankful" and "Trinafour" – all gradients of such severity as to make one speculate if this *bona fide* Dundee newshound was not the Grand Wizard of the Ku Klux Klan in disguise!

Yet as Arthur Johnson left Lodge Forfar and Kincardine on the shoulders of four of his new-found brethren he had as little inkling as they did that he had in fact brought shame and humilitation to those Dundonians who were trying to restore this sorely abused Texan negro's faith – a little at least – in the Caucasion race.

The actions of those such as the Right Worshipful Master of Lodge Forfar and Kincardine on this day were to cause eyebrows to raise and questions to be asked by Grand Lodge Committee members in Edinburgh. Not on questions of race – Freemasonry is totally opposed to such nonsense – but on procedural grounds. As a result the Right Worshipful Master and three past Worshipful Masters were called to the Grand Committee in Edinburgh to account for their conduct of affairs. The result of the enquiry was graphically described in the *Dundee Advertiser* of Saturday, 20 April 1912: "Jack Johnson the champion pugilist of the world was recently admitted to the company of Dundee Freemasons by Lodge Forfar and Kincardine of the craft. But objection having been taken his initiation was declared null and void by Grand Lodge of Scotland. Now a further drastic step is announced. . . . The suspension of all Masonic privileges to Forfar and Kincardine – and the suspension also for three years of three past Worshipful Masters and the Right Worshipful Master. . . ."

It was a sad and divisive postscript to a gesture meant to enhance brotherhood. It is likely that Johnson saw these events (quite wrongly in this case) as just another ploy by the white power structure to get him – only three weeks before his initiation into Lodge Forfar and Kincardine, future Dundee MP and then British Home Secretary Winston Churchill had bowed to pressure and banned Johnson's proposed fight with Bombardier Billy Wells the British Champion.

He never did come back to test his driving skills on "The Devil's Elbow" or "Trinafour". Perhaps the sense of humiliation imposed on him by the Grand Lodge in Edinburgh was a potent factor here. Whatever the reason a bizarre little chapter of Scottish sporting history had been created out of a conversation in a Newcastle theatre dressing-room and the desire of Dundonians to honour a boxing great in the spirit of Robert Burns:

> *That man for man the world owr'*
> *Shall brithers be for aw that.*

JIM WATT MBE – Scottish Boxing's Affable Alchemist

There is in English literature a famous short story by Somerset Maugham entitled *The Verger*. In this tale a verger (church officer) at a fashionable London church is truly content with his lot in life but is sacked because of the snobbery of the congregation. Desolate with grief, the verger seeks comfort in cigarettes but discovers that there is no tobacconists's shop for miles around the church. Armed with his savings and determination to console himself for the grievous disappointment of being unable to continue as a verger, our hero opens a tobacconist's shop near the church which has dispensed with him. A shop that blossoms from a single unit into a chain. This chain in turn makes the erstwhile verger a very successful and wealthy man indeed.

A fairy tale? Yes! Until one analyses the success of James Watt MBE, Scotland's fourth and most successful – in every sense of the word – world boxing champion. Maugham's tale of *The Verger* is like a parable of Jim Watt's own life and boxing career. The blond Glasgow southpaw, like the verger, had an uncanny knack of transforming the dross of disappointment into the pure gold of personal triumph – a knack that might have made the alchemists of old, had they possessed it, acceptable in the academies of legitimate science.

In this connection the savage winter of 1962 – 1963 made most of us who can recall it vividly, shiver in misery. The misery was doubled by the almost total annihilation of football fixtures, yet it was this same Arctic interlude that froze forever in time Jim Watt, potential footballer, and gave us Jim Watt, freshman fighter. The disappointment at being unable to play football propelled the Possilpark youth into becoming a member of James Murray's Cardowan Amateur Boxing Club and thus taking the first steps that would culminate in world lightweight championship victory in 1979.

Again, a disappointing failure by Mickey Duff to get Scottish television backing led to Watt having to defend his European lightweight title against Perico Fernandez in Spain – landing Watt with the "problem" of a £12,000 purse (his largest up to that point). In addition this "inconvenience" was to give Watt one of several boxing "firsts". Jim Watt of Scotland on retaining his title against Perico Fernandez of Spain became the very first British fighter to win a European title on Spanish soil. Even the great Ken Buchanan failed in his Hispanic excursion against Miguel Velasquez in 1970.

Further proof that this fair-haired Glasgow boxer had a verger-like inability to appreciate his own real talents and the direction his life should take can be gleaned from a statement he made to the then editor of *Boxing News*, Graham Houston, in August 1970. He told Houston that he did "not particularly like watching boxing". This from a man who today is rightly praised for his professionalism as a television fight commentator in tandem with Reg Gutteridge!

In 1968, Watt as newly crowned ABA lightweight champion caused many eyebrows to raise when he turned down the traditional privilege of an ABA champion to represent Britain in the Mexico Olympics – a decision prompted by Watt's belief that he could not win a gold medal and therefore he would not settle for second best. Yet the old alchemy was at work. The dross-laden memories invoked by the level of criticism that resulted from his refusal to participate in the 1968 Olympics were transformed to gold by another Olympics – the 1980 Moscow Games – as Reg Gutteridge explains: "I had known Jim Watt as a boxer before 1980... but we weren't mates or anything like that. However, during the 1980 Olympics I was doing ringside commentaries on the boxing in the Russian capital and Jim Watt had been invited to do a studio back-up in Britain... It was during this broadcast that I said to myself, 'Hang on there! This guy Watt is a natural for this.' It was an impression that was confirmed a couple of weeks later when I received a letter from the chairman of Tyne-Tees Television congratulating us on our teamwork. He was amazed to learn that Jim had been thousands of miles away in a British studio whilst I was in Moscow. The Tyne-Tees chap thought we were side by side. We just clicked – that's all!"

Thus the Glasgow southpaw, who was so little known during his early fight career that manager James Murray was forced to adopt the desperate expedient of handing out free photographs, became a kenspeckle figure in millions of households. It was another example of this fistic alchemist's ability to transform adversity into accomplishment.

Yet in Jim Watt's success lies a profound irony – not that irony is anything new in the fight game. (Max Schemling, trumpeted by the Nazis as a classic example of Aryan manhood had a Jewish manager – Joe Jacobs.) Watt, the proud Glaswegian, the Scotsman whose deep national pride made him conclude his 15 round points win over American Howard Davis in Ibrox Park by singing *Flower of Scotland* – a song that is the very negation of everything English – is perhaps one of the finest examples in support of Doctor Samuel Johnson's statement that: "The noblest prospect a Scotsman ever sees is the High Road to England." For it was in Romford, Essex, not Ruchill, that Watt found his fistic saviour in the person of Terry Lawless. The legendary English trainer more than anyone else played Lincoln to Watt's Ulysses Sinclair Grant.

It was the sassenach Lawless who transformed the Glasgow boxer from a basically defensive fighter into the tiger who kept ruthlessly punching Sean O'Grady when the latter turned to complain to the referee about an alleged butt.

It was Lawless with his contacts who turned Watt from a man exhilarated to receive £4,200 for his losing championship scrap with Ken Buchanan in 1973 into the recipient of 20 times as much for comprehensively outboxing Howard Davis.

Again it was the shrewd opportunism of Lawless that enabled him to persuade fellow Englishman Mickey Duff, against his better judgement, to offer the size of purse necessary to bring Jim Watt's European title defence against Spaniard Antonio Guinaldo to Glasgow. Even when this crucial contest was endangered by a serious back injury Watt was saved by two sassenachs who put him back into fighting shape – London orthopaedic specialist Ken Kennedy and West Ham United's "physio" Robert Jenkins.

Harry Carpenter is often accused of having an inbuilt bias against Scottish boxers yet it was this most English of Englishmen whose advice was crucial in helping Watt overcome Doncaster's Harry Hayes. As Jim himself recounts he believed that Hayes had a dangerous right hand punch and made his battle plan accordingly. It was Carpenter who told the Scots fighter during a dressing-room chat that Hayes' left hook was the punch to watch. The advice was vindicated when the Englishman buckled Watt's knees with this very punch. Yet the pale-skinned Glaswegian went on to win on points. Had he failed to do so there would have been no ABA semi-final victory by 35-second kayo over future world welterweight kingpin John H. Stracey.

Had he failed to beat Stracey then the fruitful union with Lawless would have been jeopardised for it was Watt's devastating demolition of Cockney John H. that first alerted Terry Lawless to the Glasgow man's fistic potential.

There are those of course who will argue that without Glasgow and the fervour of his hometown fans Watt would never have held the world lightweight championship for the two years that he did. Certainly in favour of this argument was the first voluntary defence of his title against Mexican-American Roberto Vasquez in November 1979. Vasquez had been nominated on what with the benefit of hindsight can only be described as a lucky punch kayo of the top American contender Andy Ganigan.

Terry Lawless told me: "Vasquez was beaten by the bagpipes before he even entered the ring – he was overawed by the occasion . . ." – a statement justified by Vasquez's tactics during the fight when the Mexican-American played Little Jack Horner in the four corners of the Kelvin Hall ring whilst Watt beat a tattoo of "What a Good Little Boy am I" on the hapless challenger's head and ribs until referee Rudy Ortega stopped the one-sided bout in round nine.

However, even though Watt was fighting in Glasgow it was according to the Lawless-style blueprint. Jim Watt may have been Clyde-built but he functioned best with an English captain at the helm. In his one world title defence outwith Scotland – on Saturday, 20 June 1981 in London's Wembley Stadium – the Possilpark-born southpaw regressed to his old Scottish style, the one that had kept him in the fistic shadows for so long.

I have watched this contest on film several times and I still find it hard to square the passionless figure going through a boring *pas de deux* with Alexis Arguello with the ring tiger who pulverised and demoralised Alfredo Pitalua to stoppage defeat. It is one of the paradoxes of Watt's world championship career that when he fought like an Englishman in Glasgow (the Lawless style) he always won but when he fought in London in the Glasgow style (Jim Murray) he lost.

Terry Lawless explains his performance against Arguello thus: "Jim was fighting with a full belly that night. . . the old hunger was gone. . . I told him then and I still believe now that despite Arguello decking him he could have possibly knocked the South American out. I tried to convince Jim but the motivation was gone."

Watt himself has admitted that earlier in his career he suffered from an inferiority complex and in my view this resurfaced at Wembley that June evening. In this respect Watt was more insular than his arch-domestic rival, Ken Buchanan. He travelled less well than his Edinburgh rival at world level. Buchanan's greatest triumphs were in such distinctly unfriendly places as San Juan, Puerto Rico, and Madison Square Garden.

On the other hand, when the Scottish nation's collective ego was crushed and bleeding from the greatest South American débâcle suffered by the Scots since the ill-fated Darien scheme in the 1690s, it was Watt who gave his countrymen a large measure of restored self-respect. Just ten months before Scotland had crashed spectacularly out of the 1978 Argentina World Cup finals in a particularly inglorious fashion. It was perhaps fitting that Watt should resurrect ailing national pride by battering to defeat another South American, Alfredo Pitalua of Colombia, in the 12th round.

Pitalua was no Roberto Vasquez; whilst Vasquez had behaved and acted like the Aztec Emperor Montezuma alone and defenceless in the bullring of Pamplona, Pitalua defiantly entered the Kelvin Hall ring in a purple sombrero and then proceeded to demonstrate that they breed 'em just as tough in Cartagena as in the Calton. Terry Lawless told me: "Pitalua was without doubt Jim's toughest opponent – people still don't realise how tough Jim was finding the going in the fifth round." (Pitalua hit Watt with the punch he considered the hardest he ever took – a right to the jaw.)

Nevertheless, according to Lawless the Pitalua fight encapsulated one of the major factors in the Glasgow southpaw's success. "Jim's greatest asset," Terry lawless informed me, "was his concentration. You know, I watched him during the Pitalua fight and Jim didn't blink once (between actual blows being landed) throughout the contest – his concentration against opponents was uncanny. Also another huge asset that Jim had was that people consistently underestimated him. I recall when he first arrived at the Royal Oak, Canning Town, gym. Several of the boxers there were licking their lips at the prospect of taking on this guy who didn't even look like a fighter. After a few rounds they didn't want to know him." Lawless continued, "He was a ruthlessly dedicated trainer – a dream to handle."

Someone who agrees with my assessment of Lawless playing Lincoln to Jim Watt's Ulysses Sinclair Grant (although he did not put it as such) is shrewd fight judge Peter Keenan. I had asked Keenan why he, with his international contacts and pull had never considered buying Jim Watt's contract. Keenan's reply could not have been more honest. "Jim Watt was a quiet sensitive guy. He had an inferiority complex before he went with Lawless. I mean, most boxers like a crowded gym so they can show off a bit, but Watt would ask me for the key to my gym and train on his own. Nor do I think I would have been right for him as a manager – I would have been too tough, too abrasive for him. Watt needed someone like Lawless – a father to his fighters who cared for them as well as having the contacts. Besides, Lawless is the greatest fight manager this country has ever produced – his record proves that."

Peter Keenan also made the point that ex-manager Murray's timing was suspect in permitting Watt to step into the same ring as Ken Buchanan at the St Andrew's Sporting Club in January 1973. Buchanan emerged as the winner after 15 rounds on referee George Smith's card. Keenan opined: "Watt took the Buchanan fight too early in his career. At that point he had an inferiority complex about Buchanan who had just lost his world title seven months before to Duran. Watt showed Buchanan far too much respect on this occasion. That's how he lost the fight."

As always Keenan's judgement must command respect. However in August 1970 Murray was telling the trade paper *Boxing News* that Watt would be ready to fight Buchanan, a prime-time Buchanan, in the following year (1971) – this two years before they did meet.

Yet Watt himself has always acknowledged his early debt to James "Careful" Murray. The latter is a Nye Bevan Socialist with a passion for ex-English public school boy, Raymond Chandler's writings, writings which expressed a world-weary cynicism oddly at variance with the crystal-like purity of Bevan's idealism.

One factor that is beyond contradiction is that the choir boy looks still enjoyed by Scotland's last world boxing champion can be directly attributed to Murray's early and often stern refusal to throw Watt to the Wolves for a few pounds of pecuniary gain.

It was becoming fashionable to regard Murray and Lawless as somehow the anthithesis of each other. Lawless supplied Watt as we have previously acknowledged with crucial self-belief and connections but in many respects Murray and Lawless were, in my submission strikingly similar in approach.

Both were father figures to Watt (whose own father died at a ridiculously young age). In concern for Watt's physical welfare, Murray, in no sense, played second fiddle to Lawless.

Again, as the Chuck Gardner fiasco proves the very criticisms of over protectiveness that used to be levelled at Murray have been heaped upon Terry Lawless.

Nevertheless, if Murray was a perfectly adequate pilot navigating the inland waterways of British boxing, without Lawless at the helm in the more treacherous tidal waters of international boxing Watt would have sunk without trace.

In this connection it was Murray's lack of sophistication in international negotiations with the South Africans the ultimately cost him his "navigators" ticket for Jim Watt, a lack that meant Watt having to fight Kokkie Oliver for a sum of money below what Watt himself judged he could obtain.

Nevertheless, on the subject of Watt v. Buchanan I think that whilst the former scored numerically more successful title defences than Buchanan the latter was a more accomplished ring craftsman in nearly every respect. By way of stressing this it is salutary to remember that the highly respected *Ring* magazine placed Buchanan on their front cover with the caption: "Is Buchanan the Name for Boxing?" The same publication (wrongly in my view) named Watt as one of the ten worst world lightweight champs ever. On the other hand the Americans do not like "Limey" fighters who administer the bitter laxative of defeat repeatedly to their fighters as Watt did with Vasquez, Davis and O'Grady.

The blond southpaw-cum-accomplished-media-man is also a much more complex and interesting character than the bland "nice guy" image with which he is perpetually saddled. His accomplishments too are all the more laudable given that he had little inkling that he was capable of them. Amongst these achievements were some notable boxing "firsts": (A) first white fighter to fight a black boxer in a South African ring – v. Tony "Blue Jaguar" Morodi in October 1974; (B) first Scot to register four consecutive world title defences; (C) first Glaswegian winner of a European lightweight title – v. Perico Fernandez; (D) first British boxer to win a European title in Spain.

Watt also has another achievement that makes him uniquely successful in Scottish boxing terms – he ended most emphatically the years of civic indifference and sometimes hostility shown to professional boxing by Glasgow's city fathers (which we have catalogued elsewhere in this book). True, verger-like he was in the right place at the right time in that Lord Provost David Hodge of Glasgow was a boxing fan, but it was Watt's own character that clinched it – as David Hodge made abundantly clear to me in November 1980 when he was a spectator at the County Inn, Cambuslang, where I was refereeing a boxing show.

But what makes Watt's success all the more interesting is that it rests on a profound paradox. Jim Watt MBE was the *Flower of Scotland* who bloomed best transplanted in the flatlands of Essex.